Anonymus

Needlework for Ladies for Pleasure and Profit

Anonymus

Needlework for Ladies for Pleasure and Profit

ISBN/EAN: 9783742833914

Manufactured in Europe, USA, Canada, Australia, Japa

Cover: Foto ©Lupo / pixelio.de

Manufactured and distributed by brebook publishing software (www.brebook.com)

Anonymus

Needlework for Ladies for Pleasure and Profit

NEEDLEWORK FOR LADIES

For Pleasure and Profit,

By "DORINDA,"

CONTAINING SUGGESTIONS HOW TO MAKE
NEEDLEWORK REMUNERATIVE;

INSTRUCTIONS
FOR ALL THE NEWEST AND MOST FASHIONABLE KINDS OF
FANCY WORK;

PRACTICAL DIRECTIONS AND RECIPES
FOR MAKING NUMEROUS USEFUL, PRETTY, AND
SALEABLE ARTICLES,
AND
LIST OF ALL THE ESTABLISHED WORK SOCIETIES.

THIRD EDITION. REVISED AND ENLARGED.

London:
SWAN SONNENSCHEIN, LOWREY & CO.,
PATERNOSTER SQUARE,
1886.

And of all Berlin Wool Warehouses and Fancy Repositories.
ALSO OF THE AUTHOR, RINGROSE, MALVERN LINK.

EXTRACTS FROM THE PRESS.

From "The Queen," November 4th, 1883.

The first edition of Dorinda's "Needlework for Ladies, for Pleasure and Profit" has been so speedily disposed of as to necessitate a second and enlarged edition. No better praise can be given of this book, published by W. Swan Sonnenschein and Co., Paternoster-row, and "sold in all Berlin wool warehouses and fancy repositories." One of the features of the manual is a detailed list of useful books on needlework and of work societies, which will prove a guide to would-be workers, always in quest of some channel for their productions. In a chapter under the heading of "New and Fashionable Fancy Work," the authoress enumerates all the latest styles of work that are most in demand at present, notably for bazaars. All these hints will be found valuable, though some of them are perhaps rather brief on account of the short space at command. . . . Here we pass to the most practical part of the manual, that is, the recipes in knitting and crochet. A few we have worked out, and found them clear and correct. Almost any article which can be made in crochet or knitting is treated of, from a baby's boot to a window curtain. Stockings, however, have been omitted. One point to be noticed in the knitting recipes is that they are all worked on two needles, whether vests, gaiters, sleeping socks, or children's boots, and hence are extremely easy to manage. We always meet with pleasure the familiar patterns of the fan, double rose-leaf, brioche, cobweb, cable, looped crochet, and scalloped shell, &c., most of which, in this case, are adapted by the authoress to some useful article. For crochet, the crazy stitch (that must not be confounded with tricot) is given for a shawl worked from the centre in 1 DC., 2 chain, and 3 trebles, much in the way of the popular grouped trebles. A pretty shoulder cape is executed in Dutch crochet, consisting of elongated clumps set by alternate lines of 1 Ch. and 1 DC. For these little wraps, now much in vogue, we have still two more descriptions, the feathery stitch and the double point neige; the latter, very effective, is chosen besides for a bassinette cover. Watch guards, cheese cloths, respirators, and kettle-holders, are not forgotten; thus the book answers exactly to the wants of every age and taste. In short, it is a most handy compendium, just appearing in time to be a suggestive friend for Christmas gifts, as well as the whiling away of long winter evenings.

From "The Governess," December 1st, 1883.

All those ladies who in this busy world find time for fancy work will do well to possess themselves of this little volume. It is specially suited to those who are desirous of increasing a small income in a quiet and private manner. It gives careful and full directions for working a variety of useful and ornamental articles, with hints as to the most saleable of these, and the best way of disposing of them in a profitable and private manner. A list of Work Societies is appended. Those who are about to start working for a bazaar, invalids, ladies' schools, &c.; will find it equally useful. It is, in its way, as desirable an addition to the home library of every family as "Enquire Within," or "Mrs. Beeton's Cookery Book," giving full details as to the manufacture of numerous little articles that add so greatly to the comfort and beauty of *home*.

From "The Christian Age," February 21st, 1883.

"Needlework for Ladies, for Pleasure and Profit," by "Dorinda," is unique, and will be popular as it becomes known among those for whom it has been so skilfully prepared.

NEEDLEWORK FOR LADIES, FOR PLEASURE AND PROFIT.

From "The Church Times," June 7th, 1884.

There are so many ladies now-a-days who are trying to increase their scanty incomes by doing needlework for sale that we are glad to see anything brought out which will be likely to help them. Of course those ladies are most successful who can produce most novelties, supposing that the quality of their work is up to the recognised level. And, besides this, fashions in needlework vary, and the ladies in question must, of necessity, keep up with the fashions. Hence eighteenpence will, if we mistake not, be found to be very well spent in the purchase of "Needlework for Ladies, for Pleasure and Profit" (W. Swan Sonnenschein and Co., Paternoster-row), which is now in its second edition—a sign in itself, we presume, that such a book was needed, and that it has been found useful. The first chapter contains a number of thoroughly good practical hints to ladies wishing to sell their work, and explains how they should go about it. After this come a number of descriptive recipes and directions as to how this or that article is to be made, and the shops where the best materials of different kinds are to be obtained; the quantity of wool, &c., which will be required for such and such articles, and various other details, which cannot fail to be useful. The little book strikes one as being most complete, for at the end is a list of work societies for the assistance of lady needlewomen in the sale of their productions.

From "The Scotsman," December 4th, 1883.

A second and enlarged edition is issued of "Needlework for Ladies," a little book which contains suggestions and instructions for a great many varieties of needlework, fancy wool work, and so forth; and explains how ladies who may wish to earn money by such work can most easily bring their wares to market.

From "The Christian World," January 6th, 1883.

Ladies will be obliged to us for mentioning a small book, "Needlework for Ladies, for Pleasure and Profit," containing suggestions how to make needlework remunerative; and instructions for all the newest and most fashionable kinds of fancy work, &c., with a list of all the established work societies. It is the production of "Dorinda." It strikes us that there must be a large number of ladies who will be very thankful to meet with so useful a publication.

From "The Christian Commonwealth," April 12th, 1883.

There is no department of woman's work which has recently received such decided emphasis as that of needlework and fancy work. Hence a book like this is almost indispensable as a trustworthy guide to every lady who wishes to understand the mysteries of knitting, crochet, patchwork, church needlework, Berlin wool work, German cross-stitch, &c., &c. The volume is truly a *vade mecum* to every woman of culture in all the land.

From "The Literary World," March 28th, 1884.

A lady friend who has looked through this work (which is already in a second edition) speaks of it in the highest terms. From crewel work to crochet no department of fancy work has been omitted, and the instructions seem ample. There are some useful, practical recipes for knitting. To many, a most important feature will be the list of work societies and depôts where fancy work may be sold, and the names of persons to whom application can be made for information regarding each.

◁ PREFACE. ▷

THE THIRD EDITION of this little volume is brought forward in full confidence that it will be as useful and acceptable to Lady-workers as previous editions. All directions and recipes have been carefully revised; many NEW PATTERNS and IDEAS are presented to notice; due prominence is given to all FASHIONABLE KINDS of ART NEEDLEWORK; and the pages devoted to KNITTING and CROCHET contain instructions for making a vast number of useful and wearable articles.

As far as space will allow, my endeavour has been to render this book a trustworthy guide in all matters appertaining to Ladies' Work.

"DORINDA."

RINGROSE VILLA,
    MALVERN LINK,
        September, 1886.

CONTENTS.

	PAGE
American Over-Shoe	67
Antimacassars, Domino Pattern	134
,, Double Rose-Leaf	82
,, Embroidered	152
,, Narcissus	136
,, Princesse Stripe	135
,, Raised Crosses of Chain	132
,, Sea Anemone	137
,, Tricot Vandyke	133
,, Venetian Lattice Stripe	138
,, Wrinkled Shell	83
Appliqué Work	23
,, Ornaments	30
Aprons	18
Armseue Embroidery	23
Ball, Knitted	87
,, Soft	151
Banners, Sunday-School	152
Bassinette Cover	126
Basket Pattern	59
Bazaar, Articles for	17
Bed-Rest	84
Berceaunette Blanket	74
,, Cover	125
Boots, Baby's Crochet	90, 92
,, ,, Knitted	31, 32

	PAGE
Border and Fringe, Crochet	128, 132
,, ,, Knitted	76
Borders, Crochet	115, 128, 130, 148
,, Knitted	69, 70, 72, 80, 81, 88
Braces	150
Braces and Belts	17
Bread-Tray Cloth	144
Breton Embroidery	25
Brioche Knitting	35, 55
,, Mats	86
Cable Pattern	73
Canadian Cloud	68
Cap, Puffed Knitting	65
Capote, Lady's	118
Cardigan Jacket	51
Carriage Rugs	156
Chair Covers	155
Cheese Cloth	144
Children's Garments	15
Church Needlework	21
Clox	16
Cobweb Pattern	113
Comforter, Gentleman's	50
Couvrepied, Diagonal Squares	74
,, Pine Pattern	124
Cradle Quilt	125
Crazy Pattern	114
Cretonne Work	22

CONTENTS.

	PAGE
Crewel Work	19
Crossed Treble Stitch	117
Cross-Stitch Knitting	70
Cuffs	55
,, with Frill	55
,, Beaded	56
Curtains, Knitted	80
Cushions	155
Darned Embroidery	21
Diagonal Squares	74
Domino Pattern	134
Double Knitting	74
,, Point Neige	108
,, Rose-Leaf Pattern	82
D'oyleys	156
Drawers, Lady's Knitted	59
Drawn Thread Work	26
Dutch Crochet	107
Edgings, Crochet	146, 147
,, Knitted	87, 88, 89
Excelsior Stripe	122
Fanchon	66, 117
Fan Pattern	71
Foxglove Pattern	78
Frock, Baby's	101
,, Child's	46
Gaiters, Child's	40
,, ,, with Knee	42
German Cross-Stitch Work	26
Gloves, Baby's	34
Hat, Baby's Looped Crochet	94
Holbein Work	27
Honeycomb Darning	25
,, Lattice Pattern	123
Hood, Baby's Knitted	35
,, Crochet	99
,, and Shawl Combined	93
Housewives	17, 151
Ivy-Leaf Pattern	80

	PAGE
Jacket, Baby's Crochet	95
,, Child's	101
,, Lady's Bodice	61
,, Puzzle	62
Jersey Suit	48
Kneecaps	56, 57
Kettle Holder	140
Leggings, Baby's	36
Looped Crochet	94
,, Knitting	66
Macrâme Work	28
Mantel Borders	158
Mats, La Belle	141
,, Queen Anne	141
,, Toilet	18, 143
,, Water Lily	142
Mittens, Gentlemen's	52
,, Lady's	53
,, Open work	53
Mont Mellick Work	28
Moss, Knitted	86
Muff, Child's	103
Narcissus, Square	136
Necktie, Child's	72
Nightdress Cases	159
Open Chain Net Work Pattern	114
Oriental Work	24
Outline Embroidery	21
Overalls, Baby's	43
Over-Shoe, Knitted	67
Patchwork	29
Penwiper, Ball	150
Petticoat, for Baby	96
,, Child's	64
,, with Bodice	45, 98
,, Lady's Crochet	104
,, Knitted	63, 64
Pheasant's Eye Pattern	71
Pincushions	18, 160
Pine Pattern	124

	PAGE
Point de Chantilly	116
" Muscovite	103
" Neige	126
Princesse Stripe Pattern	135
Purse, Crochet	145
" Knitted	85
Quilt, Cradle	125
" Crochet Shell for	131
" Crochet Square for	127, 128
" Embroidered	161, 162, 163
" Knitted Square for	75
" Foxglove	78
" Mouse Pattern	77
" Raised Square of Tufts	128
Raised Crosses Pattern	132
Reins, Children's	151
Respirator	68
Rug, Thick Warm	85
Scarf, Boy's Knitted	50
" Chantilly Pattern	116
" Crossed Treble Pattern	117
" Diaper Pattern	116
Scallop, Shell Pattern	111
Scrap Books	17
Sea Anemone Square	137
Sermon Cases	17
Shawl, Arrasene	70
" Cobweb Pattern	113
" Crazy Pattern	114
" Crossover	112
" Cross-Stitch Knitting	70
" Fan Pattern	71
" Half Square	68, 69, 111
" Open Chain Net Work	114
" Pheasant's Eye Pattern	71
" Square	113, 114
" Three-cornered	110
" Tufted Pattern	116
Shoulder Cape	107
" " Feathery Pattern	109
" " Warm	108

	PAGE
Silk Ornaments	30
Sleeping Socks	57, 58
Slippers, Bedroom	107
" Knitted	66
Smoking Cap	121
Smyrna Rug Knitting	28
Sofa Blanket, Cable Pattern	73
" " Honeycomb Lattice	123
" " Stripe	122
Stays, Baby's	37
Stockings, Knitted	16
Sunday-School Banners	152
Tam O'Shanter	119, 120
Tea Cloths	158
" Cosy	140
Teapot Holder	84
Toilet Glass Cloth	143
" Mats	18, 143
" Tidies	18, 143
Travelling Cap	121
Tricot and Crochet Squares	125
" Vandyke	133
Tufted Fringe	150
" Pattern	116
Underlinen	15
Useful Books	164
Vest, Baby's Knitted	37
" " Ribbed	38
" Child's	39, 97
" Lady's	59
Venetian Lattice Stripe	138
Wall Pockets	163
Watchguards	145
Wools	16
Work, Advertising	15
" Cases	17
" Given Out	14
Work Societies, List of	165
" " On sending work to	13
Writing Cases	17

NEEDLEWORK FOR LADIES.

LADIES so frequently have leisure time, which they desire to turn to useful and profitable account, that, although a great deal has already been written on the subject, I think a few plain and practical remarks will be found generally acceptable to those who are desirous of making needlework remunerative.

There is always a market for really good work, but there is no demand for old-fashioned fancy work at the present time, fine art needlework has taken its place; the most elaborate embroideries are everywhere to be seen, and private workers must keep pace with the times and work up to the standard.

In the first place, decide what kind of work you can do best and quickest, and keep to it as much as possible, for by that means you become known, and get repeated orders. Then again, whatever is undertaken must be thoroughly well done; not tumbled, crooked, or puckered, but perfectly clean, fresh, and as tasty as possible; and, if made to order, must be ready punctually at the appointed time. A fair, reasonable price should be named, estimated according to the cost of the materials, and the time the article has taken to complete, sitting steadily at it for five or six hours a day; but in no case should it exceed the ordinary shop price of the article.

The Work Societies (of which a list is appended at the end of this book) were established for the express purpose of enabling ladies to dispose of needlework, both plain and ornamental. Some of the Societies are managed by a Committee, and workers must be presented with a nomination, or produce references from a clergyman, and be prepared to have their circumstances fully inquired into. Other Societies are self-supporting, the expenses being met by an annual subscription from each worker, and a certain percentage on the work sold. All the Societies aim at helping those who are wishful for employment, but who, from some cause or other, do not care to offer their work for sale openly. It is as well to say that the benefit derived from joining a Society depends mainly upon the workers themselves, and the kind of work they send in. Well-made, useful articles—things that are *really* useful for dress or for furniture—particularly large pieces of work, will generally sell readily; but small, easily-soiled nicknacks are useless, and it is but waste of time to make them, to say nothing of the disappointment when a parcel of work is returned marked "unsaleable." The Work Societies are accustomed to receive the very choicest work, therefore anything sent to them should be thoroughly good of its kind. During the winter season there is a demand for woollen articles in knitting and crochet, which always sell if moderately priced and of good shape. Young and good workers might make sets of baby linen, not only very delicate ones, but neat plain sets for the poor; wealthy ladies and district visitors are often glad to purchase bundles for gifts to their *protégés*. All Work Societies gladly take orders from customers, which they entrust to their best working members for satisfactory execution, and this is invariably much more advantageous to the Society and more profitable to the working members, than the uncertainty attending the selling of a miscellaneous collection of ladies' own work.

Many London firms give out a great quantity of work, such as making up trousseau, layettes, and ladies' and children's wearing apparel, stocking embroidery, beading on net for bonnet crowns, and lace flounces, muslin and lace work, etc.; this is generally constant work, and is fairly well paid for; but being undertaken strictly in the way of business, must be sent in punctually on the very day for which it is promised.

Fancy shops are generally willing to purchase really pretty saleable things from lady workers, and one of the best means of disposing of work is to take specimens to all the best fancy repositories in the neighbourhood, and request orders, or offer to supply on commission. Do not be afraid to give your work publicity; it stands to reason that if it be *good* work, the more it is known the more it will be likely to sell and bring in a profit.

Work may also be sold through the medium of an advertisement, and this will generally be found the quickest, most independent, and satisfactory way of all. The " Bazaar " devotes two or three columns to articles made by amateurs, and if the work is of a kind for which there is a demand, there will probably be several replies to any advertisement, so that in a short time a connection may be made, and repeated orders obtained. " Myra's," " Sylvia's," and " Weldon's" Journals, the " Lady," the " Lady's Pictorial," and Mrs. Leach's " Family Dressmaker," too, have a column reserved for the sale of ladies' work. The " Queen " has an exchange column. In all these papers a number can be used instead of an address if privacy be desired. Remember it is essential to answer all business letters by return of post, giving a clear description of the article offered for sale, and fixing a moderate price, according to the cost of materials used, and the time it has taken to complete it.

Those who possess a sewing machine need never be at a loss to know what to do, as frocks, ulsters, pinafores, etc., for little girls, coats, jackets, and suits for boys, are always in demand, and will sell almost more readily than anything. These garments should be cut to measurement, as perfect fit is not a necessity for children. The " Princesse " shape is the most useful for frocks ; and to make them complete they should have a little shoulder cape to wear our of doors, and a sash of the material pleated round above the knees, finishing off with a pouf at the back. Some of the prettiest frocks are taken from Kate Greenaway's illustrations, others are prettily trimmed with frills and flounces, many are embroidered with crewel work, and some are ornamented with gauging : a little " Granny " or " Poke " bonnet should be made of the same material as the dress.

Underlinen, made neatly and strongly by hand, is certain to be bought up ; trim it with ornamental stitching and nice everlasting embroidery, or with a pretty crochet edging. Ladies are often glad to know where to purchase sets of garments made by hand, as they wash and wear so much better than machine-made articles.

Hand-knitted stockings are in considerable demand, and are far more durable and, therefore, more economical than woven ones, and if made of good wool and properly washed, the shrinking is very slight indeed. Stocking knitting is easy work, requires little thought, and can be taken up at any odd moment, and if not disposed of privately, and not wanted for own use, the stockings could probably be sold through a hosier, in fact, many hosiers give orders for these things. Of materials for stocking knitting, Scotch yarn and Wheeling are used for men's common stockings. Scotch fingering is very nice for gentlemen's winter socks, and for shooting and knickerbocker stockings; also for boys' wear, and for the same purposes Penelope knickerbocker yarn and Alloa yarn will be found very satisfactory. Peacock fingering, Strutts' Merino yarn, Balmoral, Alliance, and Rutland yarns, are excellent soft strong wools for ladies' stockings, while for those who desire a still softer make and yet very durable, and for little girls' wear, nothing can be better than either German Fingering, Eider or Beehive yarn, Penelope knitting, or Andalusian wool. Cocoon wool, which is, perhaps, the very nicest and softest of all wools, has the great advantage of being sold ready wound in 1-oz. balls. Any of these last-named wools work in capitally for babies' boots and gaiters, for vests, shawls, and numerous other purposes. Heatherine is an invention of Messrs. Faudel & Phillips for knitting cotton stockings and socks; it is made in all the leading colours and mixtures of colour. For children's white stockings use Strutts' best knitting cotton (that in yellow packets), 3-threads, No. 18 or 20; if wanted very fine indeed, Strutts' crochet cotton or Evans' crochet cotton, No. 14 or 16, will be suitable. Silk stockings are very much worn, and may be knitted with Pearsall's extra quality knitting silk, by those who desire a high-class silk, keeping its colour to the last; the same firm's Imperial knitting silk, or the Penelope silk of Baylis, Gilles, & Co., either of which are beautiful quality, as also is Briggs' new knitting silk. The best and most useful colours for stockings are navy, cardinal, and black. Clox should be embroidered with fine floss silk; the newest clox have a double line extending from the join of the heel about 8 inches up the leg, finished off with a diamond, or a spray, at the top.

Among the wools for fancy purposes, suitable either for knitting or crochet, Berlin wool is by far the most extensively used, double

Berlin for sofa blankets, bassinette covers, thick antimacassars, etc., and single Berlin for finer antimacassars, and many articles of personal wear. Wick wool, or, as it is sometimes called, Leviathan wool, is very thick wool indeed, twisted like a cable. Fleecy wool is strong and durable, and is nice for any purpose for which great warmth is required. Shetland wool is a favourite wool for fine things, especially for shawls. Pyrenees wool is very, very fine, almost like a thread. Lady Betty wool is the very softest of all kinds of wool, but is made in white, black, and scarlet only. Arrasene wool is pretty, and many handsome things can be made with it. Pompadour wool is a mixture of wool and silk, and looks very pretty for cuffs, shawls, and other articles. Baylis, Gilles, & Co.'s Poplin wool is a mixture of silk and wool, of the finest quality, very soft, yet strong, and nice for socks, stockings, cuffs, and shawls. Pearsall's Shawl silk, as the name implies, is specially intended for shawls. The new Crystal wool, or Tinsel wool, is very effective. Ice wool is a kind of mohair, and twists in process of working. Rabbit or Angora wool is soft and furry.

Bone or wood needles should always be used for working with wool, and steel needles for cotton work. The sizes of knitting and crochet needles in this book are regulated by Walker's Bell gauge, excepting the steel Penelope crochet needles which have their number marked on the handle.

Among the various articles likely to meet with sale, or that would be useful to make for bazaars, may be enumerated knitted and crochet petticoats, shawls, scarves, cross-overs, bedroom slippers, sleeping socks, babies' boots, children's pinafores, men's jerseys and travelling and cricketing caps, pretty garden hats, and sun bonnets. Also such trifles as housewives, made of brown holland or American cloth, with pockets to hold pins and needles, cottons, tapes, and buttons; cases for crewel wools, made with straps for keeping each shade in its own compartment; children's holland scrap books, each page bound with coloured braid and filled with pictures; workcases, or sermon cases, of black or coloured velvet, with a design worked on in gold twist, and a cord of twist sewn round; writing cases of silk kid, or soft leather, with a painting in front, the back plain, and two or three leaves of blotting paper inside; cases for carrying letters, photographs, or railway tickets in the pocket; gentlemen's braces and cricketing belts, in cross-stitch on canvas; knitted gloves and mittens to wear when out shooting or riding; lawn tennis aprons and pouches, made of holland bound with braid, or worked with crewels; brown holland work aprons, the bottom turned up so as to form three deep pockets; pretty muslin aprons, and mob caps, ornamented with coloured bows; neckties and bows of soft India muslin and lace; silk chatelaine pockets and bag purses; long purses in knitting or crochet; beaded cuffs; scent sachets for gloves and handkerchiefs; pocket pincushions, made of kid, velvet, or satin, with a wreath or bouquet of flowers and leaves worked in floss silk on one side, or a little picture painted on both sides; pincushions for a toilet table, made over a box covered with glazed lining and muslin, and ornamented with a ruche of satin ribbon and bows; toilet tidies of silver or gold perforated card worked in patterns with coloured silks or wools; small toilet mats, made of darned honeycomb towelling; nightdress cases and comb bags of honeycomb towelling or crewel work, or of cotton crochet over pink or blue cambric; brown holland shoe bags; antimacassars of various kinds; tea, coffee, and egg cosies in wool work or crewels; mats, with a border of wool flowers and tufted fringe; dolls dressed in foreign costumes, or as models for fancy dress.

Notice what is displayed in the shop windows, and copy anything new and pretty. If it be difficult work, get a lesson or two, for when a thing is first brought out, then is the time to make money by it. Art needlework, both as applied to furniture and dress, is at present decidedly the fashion, and the demand great and increasing; table linen, house linen, and even window blinds, are now immensely ornamented. There is work for everyone, and the value and importance of really good needlework cannot be overrated. The lower branches may be mastered by anyone of average ability, while the higher branches afford scope for the most artistic talent and the most refined skill.

NEW AND FASHIONABLE FANCY WORK.

Crewel Work has risen to be quite an Art Work, and is now chiefly undertaken in the form of silk embroidery; there is no end to the uses to which it can be put, both for articles of dress and for the ornamentation of rooms. It is applicable for trimming dresses, for afternoon and tennis aprons, children's pelisses and pinafores, tea cloths, mantel borders, curtains, counterpanes, toilet covers, chair backs, nightdress sachets, comb bags, d'oyleys, etc., etc., and for rapid work and excellent effect there is nothing like it. The materials used for crewel work proper are Bolton sheeting, oatmeal cloth, crash, and brown and white linens, and on these almost anything can be worked; but Roman satin sheeting, diagonal serge, and black and coloured satin are used for the best work. The work is executed with wool crewels, crewel embroidery silks, and filoselles, or Filo-floss. The best crewels are Appleton's, of 34, Hart Street, Bloomsbury, London; they are used at the Royal School of Art Needlework, South Kensington, and similar institutions, and can be obtained at all the principal fancy shops in the kingdom; they are very smooth and fine, and give the work a richer appearance than any other crewels, and, being all dyed in fast colours, they wash well. For silk crewel embroidery, Pearsall's silk and filoselle is highly recommended, also the Penelope, and Briggs'; all these are made in every variety of shade, are guaranteed fast dye, and are obtainable everywhere.

The shading should be in exact imitation of the flower, fruit, bird, butterfly, or whatever it is intended to represent, as the great beauty of the work depends upon the skilful blending of the different shades of colour. All leaves are worked in the direction the fibres take in the natural plant, and it makes a pretty contrast to do one side of the leaf dark, and the other lighter, and put a vein down the centre. Choose bold designs and artistic patterns. There are several methods of transferring patterns :—To take a design from a piece of work, place a sheet of paper on the work, and rub well over with hellebore (a clean black substance to be procured from a shoemaker) until a clear impression is formed, which can then be inked over. Designs on paper may be copied by pricking small holes at intervals along the lines of the pattern; and laying it right side uppermost on the material, dust powdered chalk through, after which trace the outline with Chinese white; or procure some carbonic paper, or transferring cloth, and placing it between the material and the design, go over the latter with a blunt bone needle, and an exact copy will be left, and should be inked over. Briggs' crewel patterns are in very general use; they are good in design, and can easily be transferred to any material by simply pressing with a warm iron, when the design becomes permanent at once; borders of apple-blossom, wild rose, and poppies, table cloth corners, lilium auratum and water lilies, and antimacassars, tiger lilies and water scenes, may be mentioned as most charmingly artistic, and as all the shades necessary for the skilful rendering of each design are designated by number in a little book issued by the firm, and each skein of silk and filoselle is labelled to correspond, there is not the slightest difficulty in tinting the flowers, leaves, and other subjects in harmonious shading. Poirson's patterns are applied by passing a damp sponge over the back of the transfer. The "S. A. N." designs, used by the Royal School of Art Needlework at South Kensington, designed by some of the first artists in the kingdom, excel all others. It is a good plan to have a worked pattern to copy from when the worker has not correct ideas of introducing the various shades required for the pattern, for by this means a true shading is obtained. "Beta," whose advertisement appears at the end of this book, has all kinds of "S. A. N." crewel work, as well as good original designs, with exquisitely worked copies of the same, to lend to be copied, and will, on application, send a printed list giving all particulars. These are really worth writing for, and are very superior.

Outline Embroidery.—This work, as its name implies, consists of a simple outline of any desired pattern, and is very quick and easy of execution, as the design is not filled in closely like crewel work, and no shading is required. There are various patterns arranged on purpose for outline embroidery; little figures and geometrical designs are the most suitable. Bolton sheeting, oatmeal cloth, and linen, are good materials to work upon. The design is worked in one or two shades of colour in the ordinary crewel-work stitch. Double crewels can be used with good effect.

Darned Embroidery is outline work with the ground darned all over in and out in straight lines backwards and forwards, taking up two threads of the material from right to left, and reversely. The outline design should be worked in crewel stitch, with crewels or filoselles of a darker or lighter shade than the ground-work, and should be enclosed all round in a straight line to form a terminating point to the darning. Also two shades of blue or brown filoselle look well for the design, and the ground filled in with darning in gold knitting silk; this is called Cloth of Gold, and has an exceedingly rich appearance. Huckaback and honeycomb towelling are the best materials to work on, as then the darning is easily done by taking up the raised threads.

Church Needlework.—During recent years Ecclesiastical Embroidery has been improved and perfected to an extent hitherto unknown. Nearly every Church is embellished with a handsome altar cloth, pulpit and lectern frontals, communion kneeling mats, embroidered altar linen, almsbags, etc. The very best materials should be used for Church-work—plush, velvet, satin, silk, and fine linen—and the embroidery is worked with pure gold thread and rich coloured silks. The stitches are very simple and few in number—satin stitch, basket stitch, and French knots are all that are really necessary; in fact, satin stitch alone is sufficient, provided the work is well raised and the stitches even and close together. Colours are emblematic, and certain colours are appropriate for the different seasons; thus, gold and blue for Easter; silver and white for Whitsuntide and Christmas; violet for Advent and Lent; black for Good Friday; crimson for Festivals of Martyrs; green, the emblem of eternal spring, is suitable for all seasons. The Cross, being the special symbol of Christianity, should always occupy a prominent position, and be clear and distinct; next in importance comes the holy monogram, I.H.S., which may be either in separate letters or entwined; other ecclesiastical monograms can be employed as required. Passion flowers and lilies are appropriate as floral representations, and may be embroidered as orphreys on each side of the altar cloth, or twined in with the monogram on cushions and almsbags; these flowers should be worked with silks in the ordinary crewel stitch. Vestments, stoles, book-markers, sermon cases, may all be embroidered. For satin-stitch work it is a good plan to purchase a pattern monogram of red untearable flock, to lay on the material and work over, as this gives the raised appearance so much admired. Altar-rail kneelers and chancel carpets are worked in cross-stitch with Berlin wool upon canvas.

Cretonne Work is composed of groups of flowers, leaves, birds, etc., cut out from cretonne, and worked artistically upon the material chosen for the ground, which may be twill, serge, cloth, or satin. A black ground looks well, and serves to heighten the effect of the colours employed in the work. Cut out a sufficient number of scraps, then place them on the material to judge of the effect, and having arranged them in nice position, tack them down securely, and work them all round in button-hole stitch or overcast stitch, with embroidery silk or filoselle the same shade as the cretonne. Work a few effective stitches with bright-coloured filoselles in the centre of the flowers, putting shaded green veinings upon the leaves. The shades of filoselles should match each flower and leaf, and the most important flowers and leaves must be the most worked; the others will only require a few stitches here and there. The very thin stalks and stamens, in places where the cretonne would be apt to fray, must be worked entirely in silk. In this work a great deal depends upon the correct taste of the worker, as no two pieces of cretonne work can be exactly alike. A little practice is necessary to be able to vary the stitches in length, and put in the stalks of silk with good effect. Bundles of cretonne scraps can be had from the Manufacturing Company, Silver Street, Manchester, and remnants from Maple, 145, Tottenham Court Road, and other furnishing warehouses.

Appliqué Work is remarkably effective for cushions, curtains, valances, banner screens, antimacassars, etc. The materials used should form a good contrast, as holland appliquéd upon blue satteen, or red Turkey twill upon oatmeal cloth, or *vice versâ*. The pattern should be large, bold, and continuous; pomegranates, oranges, chestnuts, lilies, and sunflowers look well. On a piece of red Turkey twill trace the pattern that is to be in appliqué the same as you would trace it for crewel work; tack this securely upon the foundation material with long tacking threads going across and across the pattern, as well as only round the margin; then, with coarse red ingrain knitting cotton (Strutt's No. 10), work chain-stitch exactly upon the lines of the tracing; that done, pull out the tacking threads, and cut away the whole of the Turkey twill outside the chain-stitch, and the design will be distinctly visible upon the foundation. Now the stems, stalks, and lower part of all leaves and flowers, are to be button-hole stitched, inserting the needle in the chain-stitch, and bringing it out just beyond the raw edge of the twill, so covering the raw edge; and round the main part of the leaves and flowers, where the button-hole stitch is not, work long crossed spike stitches; decorate the inner part of the design with feather-stitch or coral-stitch, according to pattern; fill in the cut-away centres of flowers with crossed lines of crewel-stitch, and introduce French knots where required. Silks and satins can be used in Appliqué Work if preferred.

Arrasene Embroidery is a most attractive work, and though it may seem difficult at the first commencing, it is really very simple and rapid of execution, and at the same time of peculiarly rich and elegant appearance. It is suitable for chair backs, table borders, curtains, screens, and, in fact, for any purpose for which the highest class of art needlework is required. It may be worked either with or without a frame, but a frame is of great service in keeping the work level. The arrasene very much resembles a fine chenille. The work looks especially handsome upon a ground of plush or velvet, though it is equally effective on Roman sheeting, satin, and serge. A No. 1 chenille needle is used, and short needlefuls should be taken; the stitch is the same as that used in crewel work—a long stitch forward on the surface, and a shorter one backward under the fabric; all flowers, leaves, and the thickest stems can be most successfully imitated with the arrasene, and very fine stems are done with embroidery silk or crewels in a long chain stitch. When the work is finished, for every material except plush or velvet, it should be laid face downwards upon a folded flannel, then a damp cloth placed at the back, and a warm iron passed lightly over the damp cloth, which proceeding sends the steam through the work, and raises the pile of the arrasene. Work on plush or velvet should be treated in the same manner, only nothing should be placed at the right side, as it would injure the material; therefore it can more conveniently be ironed whilst stretched out in the frame. A special make of arrasene is the latest novelty for knitting and crochet; it may be had both in silk and wool, in various shades of colour, and looks well for shawls and clouds, baby's hoods and jackets, antimacassars, and other articles.

Oriental Work may be applied to almost anything capable of needlework decoration; music-stool covers, foot-stool covers, cushions, banner screens, tea cosies, work baskets, reticules, mats, etc., all look lovely in this work, which is easy and full of variety; indeed, its variety makes it difficult to describe. Any old scraps of silk, satin, velvet, plush, cloth, satteen, and even flannel, work up beautifully. Supposing it is decided to make a square mat for a table, first of all take a piece of canvas or any kind of linen, the size it is intended the mat shall be, and using this as a foundation, tack on to it a much smaller square, exactly in the centre; next tack four very small pieces in each corner (calculating for a margin of about an inch round the outside to unravel afterwards for fringe), and four long pieces in the spaces still left, leaving about a third of an inch space between the pieces, which space should be covered with any dark self-coloured silk lapped over by the edges of the square pieces. All these pieces will be raw at the edges, and the next thing will be to make them neat and firm. Take a length of Berlin wool, or, better still, three thicknesses of worsted crewels, hold them with the left hand exactly over the edge of the stuff, and threading a needle with three threads of filoselle of any shade that is liked, proceed to overcast them; this will give a cord-like finish. More pieces of any imaginable shape may be tacked on to those already arranged, always taking care to make them firm in the manner described. Take the tacking threads out of each piece as it is finished. All the pieces, as well as the spaces between them, are to be filled in with various pretty fancy stitches, worked with bright-coloured filoselles, according to taste; no two pieces should be alike; the worker will very soon find no difficulty in inventing new stitches, as one seems to suggest another—feather stitch, coral stitch, button-hole, any long-crossed stitches, darning, or French knots, all look well, and gold cord may be intermingled with them. Of course, excepting for a mat, it is not necessary always to arrange the work in squares, nor in any particular shape; the most irregularly-formed pieces can be used, as uniformity is not to be aimed at.

Breton Embroidery.—This charming variety of Oriental work is done on a cotton background, such as one of the old-fashioned printed gaudy red and yellow pocket handkerchiefs, or an Oriental bold-patterned cretonne; something after the "pine" design, so used in Indian shawls, is very appropriate. First line the handkerchief to strengthen it, and prevent the work becoming puckered, then outline the principal parts of the pattern with chain stitch or crewel stitch, and fill in the rest with feather stitch, coral stitch, or herring bone, using plenty of rich deep blue, red, and yellow silk, and filoselle to give due effect to the pattern, and where little spots or specks are printed employ French knots or beads. When the pattern is complete, the entire background is also to be filled, leaving no great space between the stitches; here a neutral tint of grey or brown may be introduced, as tending to heighten the effect of the brighter shades which form the pattern. A whole handkerchief will be useful for a gipsy table cover, one side of a handkerchief will make a pretty bracket border, mantel borders can be accomplished, also sachets, and other fancy articles.

Honeycomb Darning.—This pretty work is suitable for toilet covers, chair backs for a bedroom, nightdress cases, mats, etc., and is worked with coloured yarns or Berlin wool. It can be most effectively rendered on the honeycomb towelling, which material, as its name implies, is divided into tiny squares like the cells of the honeycomb. The threads that form these squares stand up from the surface, and the wool is passed underneath them instead of through the entire material, and is shown in dots or darning at the bottom of the cells. The Grecian key pattern is a good one for beginners, but almost any geometrical design can be adapted to the work. The material is also to be had in alternate squares, plain and honeycombed, and in this form will make up into cot quilts and summer counterpanes, having a little square pattern darned on the honeycomb, and large stars worked on the plain squares.

Drawn Thread Work is tedious, and requires great patience, but looks exceedingly well for serviettes, d'oyleys, etc., and is also very effective for antimacassars when used in combination with other work. Coarse linen is best to work upon. The threads must be drawn regularly one way of the material at certain intervals, according to the pattern chosen, and those that remain are afterwards caught together here and there and worked over so as to form a continuous design; sometimes a wool is run through the threads, drawing them over and over in crosses, and then stitches are not required.

German Cross-Stitch Work is a fashionable work for sideboard cloths, five o'clock tea cloths, serviettes, and all kinds of table-linen, and also for towel borderings. Many of the old Berlin woolwork patterns will come in useful for this work, and a great variety of new designs has been prepared on purpose for it. Lessing's patterns on cards give many effective borders, figures, and stripes, and Kuehn's series of small German books afford good coloured patterns for working from. Several new kinds of linen and cotton are woven in small canvas-like squares so that the pattern can be followed on linen the same as on canvas; that called respectively Java canvas, Connaught check, and toile Colbert, is woven all over alike, and can be worked in continuous patterns or not as desired; German canvas, or toile Carrée, is woven in diamonds of close and open threads, and it is intended for a small entire design to be worked in each open diamond. Besides these materials, which are sold by the yard, there are various linen and damask cloths woven and fringed complete in certain sizes for special articles, as d'oyleys, tea cloths, tray cloths, antimacassars, mantel bordering, etc. Berlin wool canvas, 9-in., 17-in., and 36-in. wide, in fine art shades, is very nice for best work. It also is made with a pretty heading ready fringed in still narrower width for borders. Ingrain cotton is used for working upon linen; silks and filoselles for working on wool canvas. Of cotton there are several makes, among the best may be mentioned Mieg's "D M C" cotton, which is manufactured in every variety of shade and colour, Ermen and Roby's, and the French "Croix" embroidery cotton. German cross-stitch work is fashionable also for embroidery with silks and filoselles on cloth or velvet for table covers, and on Roman sheeting for chair backs, likewise with wool for ornamenting bath blankets, flannels, etc. To work on these materials it is necessary to have a canvas tacked down to work over, and of course when following the pattern the needle is to be passed through the material as well as through the canvas, and when the work is finished the canvas is drawn away thread by thread, and the pattern remains clear and distinct. This has a remarkably good effect, and the work is very easy and pleasant. A variety of cross-stitch, done upon felt, with perforations in regular holes, is known as Toile Crosse. Briggs' has a new felt perforated in design all over, and a specially prepared silk for working thereon, which stands out well and pearly-looking.

Holbein Work is often combined with German cross-stitch as it gives a delicate finish to the curves. It is also a work by itself, and is much used for table cloths, serviettes, and things in which it is an advantage to have both sides alike, for the design is formed in straight lines, and the stitches taken in rotation, one to the front and one to the back, so that the pattern is produced with equal distinctness on the wrong as on the right side. To effect this, you cover a certain number of threads on one side and leave them on the other, and then, working back, cover the threads that were missed. The cotton is to be fastened off invisibly by running it in and commencing again over the last few stitches; use long needlefuls, so as to have as few joins as possible. Geometrical designs and quaint figures are most suitable for this stitch. If working in squares, go round each square on both sides the material before proceeding to the next. The materials and cotton used for this work are the same as for German Cross-stitch work.

Macramé Work, or Knotting, is a very old work that has lately been revived, and is now a favourite occupation with many ladies; the materials are quite inexpensive; the work is easily and quickly executed, and is so durable that, once done, it lasts almost for ever. It is chiefly used for lace and trimmings of various kinds, for wall pockets, tidies, and workbags, for the hangings of brackets and mantel drapery. Macramé work can be done with silk or with fine or coarse thread: the latter is generally preferred, but the fine thread is certainly lighter and more lacy-looking; these threads are manufactured in all art colours. Macramé work requires to be done very tightly and evenly. Much good work is executed on a cushion. Some like a plain deal board; most useful are the inexpensive patent frames, having ingenious contrivances for stretching the foundation cords and keeping the work in place. The work consists simply in tying knots and making bars of various kinds; every thread is begun upon the first foundation cord, and knotted thence downwards, over and under, according to the pattern selected.

Mont Mellick Embroidery is a strong and durable work, very suitable for bedroom ornamentation, for nightdress cases, comb bags, and toilet sets, as it possesses the great merit of washing over and over again, and remaining good to the last. Satin jean is the best material for working upon. Select any pretty embroidery design, and, having transferred it to the material, carry out the work in satin stitch with Strutts' No. 12, 3-thread, white knitting cotton for the fine parts of the pattern, and No. 8 for stems and the outlining of any scrolls. Red ingrain cotton can be used if preferred, but the real Irish Mellick work is always done with white.

Smyrna Rug Knitting.—This work was greatly admired when exhibited at the Inventions Exhibition in 1885. It ought to be popular as a useful occupation for long winter evenings, as it is simplicity itself, being done in convenient narrow strips; and any number of workers, even children, may combine in the making of one large rug, which, when finished, will be as handsome as any Persian rug, and will last a life-time. The Smyrna wool is a spécialité of Messrs. Schulze, and, though soft, is of a peculiarly springy nature, so that it stands well up. The various shades are beautifully dyed in imitation of true Oriental colouring, and every shade is numbered to correspond with coloured designs, twenty-four in number, issued expressly for the work. Directions for knitting these rugs will be found on page 85. Specimen boxes of material, with knit sample of work, are obtainable at any Berlin repository.

Patchwork, which formerly was only valued as a means of using up odd scraps, or for teaching children to sew, has lately become quite a favourite work, and though it is becoming more elaborate and more difficult, it is at the same time far more satisfactory, and, if well arranged, is particularly effective. It is invaluable for quilts, and is handsome for cushions and window seatings; the patterns that can be contrived are innumerable, and the work may be taken up at any odd moment. The Sexagon, though an old pattern, is always pretty; the shape should first of all be cut out in tin, but a shape of stout cardboard answers the purpose very well; cut a number of papers carefully, true to the pattern, tack the patches on the papers, and sew six sexagons round one centre piece, so as to form a kind of star. If working in cottons, connect these stars together by sexagons covered with red Turkey twill, but if using silk pieces it is well to have black between each star. The Box pattern is easy; in this the black should represent the shadow, and be on the left-hand side of each box. The Twist is a lovely pattern, for three colours only; it represents a black twist running between red octagons and yellow squares. A simple Mosaic pattern of octagons and diamonds can be arranged with only two colours, while a more elaborate Mosaic will require six or eight shapes, and as many colours. American Log patchwork is made of a series of narrow straight pieces, two shades of every colour, set round a small square centre piece, the light shades on two sides and the dark on two sides, and when the squares are joined together the light side of one square joins to the light side of another, and the dark comes against dark. In all the best designs certain colours are kept to for each shaped piece;

and silk with a pattern on is used for the centre pieces; or a tiny design may be embroidered according to fancy. The papers must all be taken out when the work is finished. Crazy patchwork is a novelty: in this all kinds of odd bits of silks, satins, and velvets are sewn on to a linen foundation, and the joins covered with gold braid, tinsel thread, or various fancy stitches; the more irregular the shape of the pieces the better the effect of the work when finished; stars, sprays, baskets, bellows, and all kinds of little designs may be embroidered in the centre of the larger patches, some may be decorated with beads and spangles, so the work is very amusing, and affords plenty of scope for the imagination. Odd scraps of prints, silk, satin, and bits of ribbons, may often be obtained from dressmakers, and many shopkeepers will sell remnants cheaply by weight.

Silk Ornaments.—These are in the form of transfers, which by a simple process of damping and ironing, produce an instantaneous and beautiful painting upon silk, satin, cardboard, wood, or any smooth-surface material, exactly resembling hand-painting, the colours are artistically blended, and the designs exquisite. Several designs may be grouped together in combination, thus: for a piano-back, several groups of bulrushes, water fowl and pheasants, birds and butterflies, surrounded by a gold Greek pattern border; for a cushion, clusters of Marguerites, forget-me-nots, and primroses, or sprays of autumn leaves, and begonia. Brackets, banner screens, white wood boxes, and all kinds of fancy articles may be handsomely decorated by means of these useful transfers, made by the Patent Silk Ornament Company, which, though not strictly coming under the designation of "work," are here mentioned as an *aid* to work.

Crewel Appliqué Ornaments are another invention of the same firm. These are embroidered in coloured silks in detached subjects, and when appliquéd on a ground of cloth, satin, or velvet, give precisely the effect of the most exquisitely-finished crewel work at a minimum of trouble. All sorts of flowers are represented, birds in gay plumage, butterflies, and animals; and these can be arranged in groups according to fancy. They also would be useful to an amateur crewel worker as a guide to artistic shading. Some beautiful crosses, I.H.S., and other monograms, in raised gold, will be acceptable to church workers.

PRACTICAL RECIPES

FOR

MAKING USEFUL AND ORNAMENTAL ARTICLES.

KNITTING.

Infant's Polish Boots.—1 oz. of crimson, 1 oz. of white single Berlin wool. Knitting pins No. 16. Cast on 28 stitches with the crimson wool, and knit 1 plain row. 2nd row—knit 2, increase 1 by picking up the thread which lies directly below the third stitch and knitting it, knit 24, increase 1, knit 2. 3rd row—plain. 4th row—knit 2, increase 1, knit 26, increase 1, knit 2. 5th row—plain. 6th row—knit 2, increase 1, knit 28, increase 1, knit 2. 7th row—plain. 8th row—knit 2, increase 1, knit 30, increase 1, knit 2. 9th row—plain. 10th row—knit 2, increase 1, knit 34. 11th row—plain. 12th row—knit 2, increase 1, knit 35. 13th row—plain. 14th row—knit 2, increase 1, knit 36. 15th row—plain. 16th row—knit 2, increase 1, knit 37. There will now be 40 stitches on the needle. Knit 5 plain rows. 22nd row—knit 15, then, keeping the other stitches still on the needle, knit these 15 stitches backwards and forwards for 25 more rows. 48th row—knit 15, and cast on 25 stitches. Knit 5 plain rows. 54th row—knit 2, knit 2 together, knit 36. 55th row—plain. 56th row—knit 2, knit 2 together, knit 35. 57th row—plain. 58th row—knit 2, knit 2 together, knit 34. 59th row—plain. 60th row—knit 2, knit 2 together, knit 33. 61st row—plain. 62nd row—knit 2, knit 2 together, knit 28, knit 2 together, knit 2. 63rd row—plain. 64th row—knit 2, knit 2 together, knit 26 knit 2 together, knit 2. 65th row—plain. 66th row—knit 2, knit 2 together, knit 24, knit 2 together, knit 2. 67th row—plain. 68th row—knit 2, knit 2 together, knit 22, knit 2 together, knit 2. 69th row—plain. Cast off. Then with the same needle on which you still have 25 stitches, pick up 13 stitches across the instep, and 25 stitches along the other side, knitting each stitch as you pick it up, knit 1 plain row, and cast off all. This completes the boot. For the sock, take the white wool, and pick up 15 stitches across the instep. (In all the picking up now take the back threads only.) 1st row—purl. 2nd row—knit 2, make 1, knit 4, slip one, knit 2 together, pass the slip stitch over, knit 4, make 1, knit 2. 3rd row—purl. Repeat the second and third rows three times more. 10th row—knit 2, make 1, knit 4, slip 1, knit 2 together, pass the slip stitch over, knit 4, make 1, knit 2, pick up 18 stitches along the side, that is, missing the first 6 stitches and picking up thence to the end. 11th row—purl 33, and then pick up 18 stitches along the other side, purling each stitch as you pick it up. 12th row—knit 2, make 1, knit 2 together, knit 2, make 1, knit 4, slip 1, knit 2 together, pass the slip stitch over, knit 4, make 1, knit 3, make 1, knit 4, slip 1, knit 2 together, pass the slip stitch over, knit 4, make 1, knit 3, make 1, knit 4, slip 1, knit 2 together, pass the slip stitch over, knit 4, make 1, knit 2, knit 2 together, make 1, knit 2. 13th row—purl. Repeat the twelfth and thirteenth rows sixteen times, or until you have the leg as high as is desired. Then knit 7 plain rows, and cast off. Sew the boot up. Run a crimson ribbon in the holes round the ankle, and tie with a bow in front.

Baby's Boots with Open Work Shell Pattern Sock. —1 oz. of blue, 1 oz. of white single Berlin wool. Knitting pins No. 16. Cast on 43 stitches with the blue wool, and knit 1 plain row. 2nd row—slip 1, knit 2 together, knit 37, knit 2 together, knit 1. 3rd row—plain. 4th row—slip 1, knit 2 together, knit 35, knit 2 together, knit 1. 5th row—plain. 6th row—slip 1, knit 2 together, knit 33, knit 2 together, knit 1. 7th row—plain. 8th row—slip 1, knit 2 together, knit 31, knit 2 together, knit 1. 9th row—plain. 10th row—slip 1, knit 2 together, knit 29, knit 2 together, knit 1. 11th row—plain. 12th row—slip 1, knit 2 together, knit 27, knit 2 together, knit 1. 13th row—plain. 14th row—slip 1, knit 2 together, knit 25, knit 2 together, knit 1. Cast on 7. 15th row—plain. 16th row—slip 1, increase 1 by picking up the thread which lies directly under the second stitch and knitting it, knit plain to the end. 17th row—plain. Repeat the last 2 rows six more times. 30th row—knit 17, and leaving the other 26 stitches on the pin, turn, and knit these 17 stitches backwards and forwards for 21 more rows. 52nd row—knit 17, and cast on 26 stitches. 53rd row—plain. 54th row—slip 1, knit 2 together, knit plain to the end. 55th row—plain. Repeat the last two rows five more times. 66th row, slip 1, knit 2 together, knit 33. 67th row—cast off 7, knit 28. 68th row—slip 1, increase 1, knit 27, increase 1, knit 1. 69th row—plain. 70th row—slip 1, increase 1, knit 29, increase 1, knit 1. 71st row—plain. 72nd row—slip 1, increase 1, knit 31, increase 1, knit 1. 73rd row—plain. 74th row—slip 1, increase 1, knit 33, increase 1, knit 1. 75th row—plain. 76th row—slip 1, increase 1, knit 35, increase 1, knit 1. 77th row—plain. 78th row—slip 1, increase 1, knit 37, increase 1, knit 1. 79th row—plain. 80th row—slip 1, increase 1, knit 39, increase 1, knit 1. 81st row—plain. Cast off. Then, with the same needle, on which you still have 26 stitches, pick up 11 stitches across the instep, and 26 stitches along the other side, knitting each stitch as you pick it up. There will be 63 stitches on the pin. Cast off all. For the sock, take the white wool, and pick up 11 stitches across the instep. (In all the picking up now, take the threads which lie behind the row of casting off.) 1st row—purl. 2nd row—purl 2 together, purl 2 together, make 1 and knit 1 three times (it is not necessary to turn the wool round the needle when making 1 after the purled stitch, as it is already in the right position), make 2, purl 2 together, purl 2 together. 3rd row—purl. 4th row—plain. 5th row—purl. 6th row—the same as the second row. 7th row—purl. 8th row—plain, and pick up 22 stitches along the side, that is, missing the first 4 stitches and picking up thence to the end. 9th row—purl 33, and pick up 22 stitches along the other side, purling each stitch as you pick it up. 10th row—purl 2 together, purl 2 together, make 1 and knit 1 three times, make 2, purl 2 together, purl 2 together, and repeat. 11th row—purl. 12th row—plain. 13th row—purl. Repeat from the tenth row ten times. Then, next row, for ribbing round the top of the leg, purl 2, * knit 3, purl 3, repeat from *, purl 2 at the end of the row. Next row—knit 2 * purl 3, knit 3, repeat from *, knit 2 at the end of the row. Repeat the last 2 rows alternately ten times. Then cast off. Sew the boot up neatly, commencing with the little gussets, and rounding the toe off to shape, make the purl stitches at the back of the sock meet each other, and finish off with a white ribbon rosette in front, and a white ribbon to tie round the ankle.

Baby's Gloves.—Knitting pins, No. 16. 1 oz. of white merino wool. Cast on 26 stitches, and knit 2 plain rows. 3rd row—plain, and increase 1 stitch at the end of the needle. 4th row—plain. Repeat these last two rows three times more, and then, having 30 stitches on the needle, knit 16 rows of plain knitting. 27th row—plain, and knit 2 stitches together at the end of the needle, this will decrease at the same end of the work at which you before increased. 28th row—plain. Repeat these last two rows three times more, and there will again be 26 stitches on the needle. 35th row—plain. 36th row—cast off 8 stitches, knit the remaining 17 stitches plain. 37th row—plain. 38th row—cast off 4 stitches, knit 13. 39th row—knit the 14 stitches, and cast on eight more for the thumb. 40th row—plain. 41st row—plain, and increase 1 stitch at the end of the needle. Repeat the last two rows, and then, having 24 stitches on the needle, knit 12 plain rows. 56th row—plain, and knit 2 stitches together at the end of the needle. 57th row—plain. Repeat the last 2 rows. 60th row—cast off 8 stitches, knit the remaining 13 stitches plain. 61st row—knit 14 stitches, and cast on 4 stitches. 62nd row—plain. 63rd row—knit 18, and cast on 8 more stitches. 64th row—plain. You now again have 26 stitches on the needle. Repeat from the third row to the end of the thirty-fifth row for the other half of the hand, and having done that, cast off all. Now for the wrist :—Pick up 54 stitches along the straight edge of the glove, knitting each stitch as you pick it up. 1st row—purl. 2nd row—plain. 3rd row—purl. 4th row—slip 1,* knit 2 together, make 2, knit 2 together, repeat from *, and knit 1 at the end of the row. 5th row—purl 3, knit 1, and repeat, there will be 2 to purl at the end of the row. 6th row—plain. 7th row—purl. Then knit in a rib of three plain and three purl alternately for 36 rows. 44th row—purl. 45th row—plain. Repeat the last two rows twice more, and then cast off in this way, * knit 2 together, put the loop on the right-hand needle back on the left-hand needle, and repeat from * till all the stitches are knitted off. The other glove is to be knitted in exactly the same manner. Run a piece of narrow white ribbon through the holes at the wrist to tie in a bow.

Baby's Hood in Brioche Knitting.—Knitting pins No. 14. Three balls of white cocoon wool. Cast on 74 stitches. 1st row—make 1, slip 1, putting the needle in as if about to purl, knit 1, and repeat to the end. 2nd row—make 1, slip 1, knit the next stitch and the thread that lies over it together; repeat. Continue knitting as the second row until you have done a piece of seven inches. Next row, for the crown: Commence in the same way, and knit till you come to within 26 stitches, or 13 ribs, of the end; leave these 26 stitches on the left-hand pin: turn, knit 22 stitches, or 11 ribs, when you will come to within 26 stitches, or 13 ribs, of the other side; turn, knit on as far as the place where you turned in former row, and when knitting the last stitch (which will need to be turned so as to keep the work flat, as it must lie above the stitch that was taken from the side) knit in with it the first of the stitches that were left on the left-hand pin; turn, knit on to the place where you turned in former row, and there knit the last stitch in the same way, together with the first of those on the left-hand pin; turn, and continue in this manner, taking one of the side stitches in at the end of each row to form the crown, until you have taken in all the side stitches, and then cast off. For the curtain—cast on 120 stitches. Commence as for the hood, knit a piece 4½ inches long, and cast off. Sew the curtain to the hood by the end at which it is begun. Turn the front of the hood over about 2 inches deep, tack it down in place, and on the edge of this and round the bottom of the curtain put a narrow white swansdown trimming; or instead, knit a feather trimming, which, however, will necessitate another ball of cocoon wool. To make feather trimming, proceed as follows: Cast on 8 stitches, knit 1 plain row. 2nd row—slip 1, insert the right-hand needle in the stitch in the usual way, wind the wool three times round the needle and the two first fingers of the left-hand, wool over the needle, and draw all four threads of wool through the stitch, and repeat, and knit one at the end of the row. 3rd row—plain, knitting all four threads as one stitch, and rather tightly. Repeat from the second row for the length required. Run a white ribbon in just above the sewing on of the curtain, making a little bow at the back. Add ribbon strings to tie under the chin, and a little cap in front then completes the hood.

Baby's Leggings.—2 ounces of white single Berlin wool. Knitting pins No. 10. Cast on 48 stitches, and knit, in ribbed knitting, 2 stitches plain and 2 stitches purl, for 21 rows. Then commence the pattern. 1st row—plain. 2nd row—plain. 3rd row—purl. 4th row—plain. Continue this pattern to the ankle, but when you have done the seventh raised row make a decrease in the next row by knitting 2 stitches together at the beginning and at the end of the row; decrease again after the ninth raised row, and again after the eleventh. There will now be 42 stitches on the needle. When you have completed 19 raised rows commence the heel. Knit 10 stitches only, turn, and continue the pattern on the 10 stitches until 2 more raised rows are done; next row decrease by knitting the second and third stitches, and the fourth and fifth stitches together; purl the next row, and decrease the same again in the next row; there will now be 6 stitches on the needle, knit 2 plain rows, and cast off. Pass 22 stitches on to the right-hand pin without knitting them, then knit the 10 stitches which remain in the same way to form the other half of the heel; of course, making the decreasings at the ending of the rows instead of at the beginning. Slip the 22 stitches back on to the left-hand pin, and continue the pattern until you have done 11 raised rows, but after the eighth raised row knit 2 together at the beginning and end of every alternate row, so that when you have done the eleventh raised row there will only be 10 stitches remaining. Next row—knit 1, knit 2 together four times, knit 1, then cast off. Sew the two parts of the heel together where it was cast off, and pick up 22 stitches along the side for the sole of the foot, knitting each stitch as you pick it up. Knit the next row plain to form a raised row, and then continue the pattern, knitting a similar piece to that already done for the upper part of the foot. Sew neatly round the foot and up the leg, making the raised rows meet one another.

Baby's Stays.—1½ oz. of white double Berlin wool. Knitting pins No. 9. For the front, cast on 34 stitches, and knit 2 plain rows. 3rd row—knit 4, purl 2 and knit 2 seven times, knit 2. Fourth row—knit 2, purl 2 all along. Repeat the third and fourth rows alternately until 38 rows of the ribbing are done, then knit four plain rows. Next row—knit 7, cast off until you come to the last 6 stitches, which knit plain. Knit the 7 stitches backwards and forwards in plain knitting for 24 rows, then cast off; this forms one shoulder strap. Knit the other 7 stitches in the same way for the other shoulder strap. For the right back, cast on 20 stitches, and knit 2 plain rows. 3rd row—knit 4, purl 2, knit 2, purl 2, knit 10. 4th row—knit 8, purl 2, and knit 2 three times. 5th row—knit 4, purl 2, knit 2, purl 2, knit 4, make 1, knit 2 together, knit 2; a button hole is formed by the stitch made in this row. 6th row—the same as the fourth. 7th row—the same as the third. 8th row—the same as the fourth. 9th row—the same as the third. 10th row—the same as the fourth. Repeat from the third row four times more, the fourth time working only as far as the eighth row, after which knit 4 plain rows, and cast off. For the left back, cast on 20 stitches, and knit 2 plain rows. 3rd row—knit 10, purl 2, knit 2, purl 2, knit 4. 4th row—knit 2 and purl 2 three times, knit 8. Repeat the third and fourth rows alternately, until you have done 38 rows of the ribbing, then knit 4 plain rows, and cast off. Sew five small buttons on this side. Sew up the side seams, leaving a space for the armholes, and sew the shoulder straps across to the backs.

Baby's Vest.—4 balls of white cocoon wool. Knitting pins No. 16. Cast on 80 stitches, and knit in ribbed knitting, 2 stitches plain and 2 stitches purl, for 90 rows. 91st row—knit 4, purl 3, * knit 3, purl 3, and repeat from *; there will be 4 stitches to purl at the end of the row. Knit 2 more rows the same as this. 94th row—purl 4, knit 3, * purl 3, knit 3, and repeat from *; there will be four stitches to knit plain at the end of the row. Knit 2 more rows the same as this. Then repeat from the ninety-first row twice more, and these 18 rows will form a dice pattern across the chest. Knit 11 more rows of the ribbing, 2 stitches plain and 2 stitches purl. Next row—knit 1 and purl 1 alternately six times, and slip these 12 stitches on to a spare needle; cast off 56 stitches; then knit 1 and purl 1 alternately six times, and work upon these 12 stitches to form a shoulder strap; always knitting a plain stitch over a purl, and a purl stitch over a plain, for 48 rows, when cast off. Knit the other shoulder strap in the same way. This piece will form the front of the vest. Cast on 80 stitches again, and knit a similar piece for the back, only casting off all the stitches after you have completed the 11 rows of ribbing. Sew the two pieces together up the sides as far as to where the dice knitting commences, and sew the shoulder straps across. Then, for an edging round the neck of the vest and round the armholes, work 1 double crotchet,* 1 chain, miss 1 stitch of the knitting, 1 double crochet in the next; repeat from *. Next row—1 double crochet under a chain stitch, * 2 chain, 1 double crochet in the first chain stitch just done, and 1 double crochet under the next chain stitch of previous row; and repeat from *.

Child's Vest in Ribbed Knitting.—Knitting needles No. 11. 4 oz. of white Peacock fingering wool, or Penelope knitting yarn. Cast on 85 stitches for the length of the vest from shoulder to waist. 1st row—plain. 2nd row—purl. 3rd row—purl. 4th row—plain. Repeat these four rows five times, when you will have 24 rows knitted, and will be able to count six raised ribs on each side of the work. The shoulder is now wide enough, so cast off 14 stitches, and for the front continue the pattern upon 71 stitches for 48 rows (or 56 rows if for a stout child). Cast on 14 stitches for the other shoulder, and now again knit 24 rows upon 85 stitches as at first; and cast off all. Knit another piece similar to this for the back of the vest. Sew the shoulder pieces neatly together, and sew up the sides of the vest, leaving sufficient space for the armholes. Work a crochet edging round the neck and armholes, thus:—1 double crochet in a stitch of the knitting, 2 chain, 2 treble in the same place as the double crochet is worked into, miss 2 stitches of the knitting, and repeat. Run a narrow ribbon below the treble stitches in the crochet edging to tie round the neck and arms.

Vest for Child Knitted in Check Pattern.

—Knitting needles No. 10. 3 oz. of white merino wool. Cast on 70 stitches. 1st row—knit 2, purl 2, and repeat, ending with knit 2. 2nd row—purl 2, knit 2, and repeat, ending with purl 2. Repeat these 2 rows three times. 9th row—plain. 10th row—purl. 11th row—knit 2 together, knit 2, * purl 2, knit 2; repeat from *, and end by knitting 2 together. 12th row—slip 1, purl 2, * knit 2, purl 2, repeat from *, end with knit 1. 13th row—slip 1, knit 2, * purl 2, knit 2; repeat from *, end with purl 1. 14th row—slip 1, purl 2, * knit 2, purl 2; repeat from *, end with knit 1. 15th row—slip 1, knit 2 together, * purl 2, knit 2, repeat from *, and end with purl 2, knit 2 together, knit 1. 16th row—purl 2, * knit 2, purl 2, and repeat from *. 17th row—plain. 18th row—purl. Repeat from the 11th row. 27th row—purl 2, knit 2, and repeat, end with purl 2. 28th row—knit 2, purl 2, and repeat, end with knit 2. Repeat these two rows twice. 33rd row—plain. 34th row—purl. 35th row—knit 2, purl 2, and repeat, end with knit 2. 36th row—purl 2, knit 2, and repeat, end with purl 2. Repeat these two rows twice. 41st row—plain. 42nd row—purl. Repeat the check pattern from the 27th row twice. Then begin again at the 27th row and go on to the end of the 32nd row, making 10 checks in all. Next row—knit 2, increase 1, by picking up the thread that lies under the next stitch and knitting it, knit plain to within 2 stitches of the end, increase 1, knit 2. Next row—purl. Repeat these 2 rows three times more. Next row—knit 22, * purl 2, knit 2, repeat from * six times, purl 2, knit 22. Next row—purl 22, * knit 2, purl 2, repeat from * 6 times, knit 2, purl 22. Repeat these 2 rows twice. For the Shoulder: 1st row—knit 26 stitches, turn. 2nd row—purl 26. 3rd row—knit 23, knit 2 together, knit 1. 4th row—purl. 5th row—knit 22, knit 2 together, knit 1. 6th row—purl. Decrease thus every alternate row at the neck end till you have 20 stitches on the needle; then knit 6 rows alternately a plain row and a purl row, and cast off. The wool being at the neck end, pick up and knit 11 stitches down the slope of the shoulder, knit plain along to the end of the row. Knit another shoulder to correspond with the shoulder already done, making the decreasings at the beginning of the plain rows at the neck end. When the same number of rows are knitted as in the other shoulder, cast off towards the neck end, pick up and knit 11 stitches down the slope of the shoulder, and knit plain to the end of the pin. Knit 1 plain row all along, and cast off all. Knit a similar piece for the back of the vest. Sew the shoulder pieces together, and sew up the sides as far as the armholes. Work a crochet edge round the neck, armholes, and bottom of the vest. 1 double crochet in a stitch of the knitting, 2 chain, 2 treble in the same place as the double crochet stitch, miss 2 stitches of the knitting, and repeat.

Child's Gaiters.—These pretty gaiters measure 9 inches in length. They will require 2 ounces of maroon Scotch fingering, 2 bone knitting needles, No. 11. Cast on 47 stitches. 1st row—knit 2, purl 1, and repeat, and the row will end with knit 2 as it began. 2nd row—purl 2, knit 1, and repeat, and the row will end with purl 2. Repeat these two rows seven times. 17th row Purl 2, knit 1, and repeat. 18th row—purl. 19th row—plain. 20th row—purl. Repeat from the 17th row seven times. 49th row—purl 2, knit 1, and repeat. 50th row—purl, taking 2 stitches together at the beginning of the needle and 2 stitches together at the end. 51st row—plain. 52nd row—purl. 53rd row—purl 1, knit 1, * purl 2, knit 1, repeat from *, and the row will end with purl 1. 54th row—purl, taking 2 stitches together at the beginning of the needle and 2 stitches together at the end. 55th row—plain. 56th row—purl. 57th row—knit 1, * purl 2, knit 1, repeat from *. 58th row—purl, taking 2 stitches together at the beginning of the needle and 2 stitches together at the end. 59th row—plain. 60th row—purl. 61st row—purl 2, knit 1, and repeat. 62nd row, purl. 63rd row—knit 2 together, knit the remainder. 64th row—purl. 65th row—purl, this is a raised row, and has 40 stitches on the needle. 66th row—purl. 67th row, plain. 68th row—knit 2, purl 2, and repeat. 69th row—knit 2, purl 2, and repeat. 70th row—purl. 71st row—plain. 72nd row—purl 2, knit 2, and repeat. 73rd row—purl 2, knit 2, and repeat. 74th row—purl. 75th row—plain. 76th row—knit 2, purl 2, and repeat. 77th row—knit 2, purl 2, and repeat. 78th row—purl. 79th row—plain. 80th row—purl 2, knit 2, purl 2, knit 2, purl 2, knit 1, increase 1 (by picking up the thread that lies directly under the next stitch and knitting it), knit 1, purl 2, knit 2, purl 2, knit 2, purl 2, knit 2, purl 2, knit 2, purl 1, increase 1, purl 1, knit 2, purl 2, knit 2, purl 2, knit 2. 81st row—Purl where you knitted and knit where you purled in last row. 82nd row—purl 11, increase 1, purl 20, increase 1, purl 11. 83rd row—plain. 84th row—knit 2, purl 2, knit 2, purl 2, knit 2, purl 1, increase 1, purl 3, knit 2, purl 2, knit 2, purl 2, knit 2, purl 2, knit 2, purl 2, knit 3, increase 1, knit 1, purl 2, knit 2, purl 2, knit 2, purl 2. 85th row—purl where you knitted and knit where you purled in last row. 86th row—purl 11, increase 1, purl 24, increase 1, purl 11. 87th row—plain. 88th row—purl 2, knit 2, purl 2, knit 2, purl 2, knit 1, increase 1, knit 1, purl 2, and knit 2 six times, purl 1, increase 1, purl 1, knit 2, purl 2, knit 2, purl 2, knit 2. 89th row—purl where you knitted and knit where you purled in last row. 90th row—purl 11, increase 1, purl 28, increase 1, purl 11. 91st row—plain. 92nd row—knit 2, purl 2, knit 2, purl 2, knit 2, purl 1, increase 1, purl 3, knit 2 and purl 2 six times, knit 2, purl 1, increase 1, knit 1, purl 2, knit 2, purl 2, knit 2, purl 2. 93rd row—purl where you knitted and knit where you purled in last row. 94th row—cast off 13, purl the remaining 39 stitches. 95th row—cast off 13, knit the remaining 26 stitches. Now for the Foot. 1st row—purl 2 together, purl 1, * knit 2, purl 2, and repeat from *. 2nd row—knit 2 together, purl 2, and knit 2 alternately to the end of the row. 3rd row—purl 2 together, purl 23. 4th row—knit 2 together, knit 22. 5th row—purl 2 together, purl 1, *, knit 2, purl 2, and repeat from *. 6th row—knit 2 together, purl 2 and knit 2 alternately to the end of the row. 7th row—purl 2 together, purl 19. 8th row—knit 2 together, knit 18. 9th row—purl 2 together, purl 1, * knit 2, purl 2, and repeat from *. 10th row—knit 2 together, purl 2 and knit 2 alternately to the end of the row. 11th row—purl 2 together, purl 15. 12th row—knit 2 together, knit 14. 13th row—purl 3, * knit 2, purl 2, and repeat from *. 14th row—knit 2, purl 2, and repeat, and there will be 1 stitch to purl at the end of the row. 15th row—purl. 16th row—plain. 17th row—knit 3, * purl 2, knit 2, and repeat from *. 18th row—purl 2, knit 2, and repeat, and there will be 1 stitch to knit at the end of the row. 19th row—purl. 20th row—plain. Cast off. Now along the bottom of the gaiter pick up stitches, taking up into the back of the work and knitting each stitch as you pick it up, 13 stitches at the bottom of the heel, 15 stitches along the side, 15 stitches across the front, 15 stitches along the other side, and 13 stitches again at the bottom of the heel—71 stitches in all; and knit 1 and purl 1 alternately for 2 rows, and cast off. Sew up the leg of the gaiter. For the little band where the buttons are sewn on, cast on 20 stitches, purl 1 row. 2nd row—knit 2 together, increase 1, knit 1, increase 1, knit 2 together, and repeat to the end of the row. 3rd row—purl. Cast off. Sew this little band to the outer side of the gaiter and over the place where the increasings are made, the cast-off stitches being placed towards the front of the gaiter. Sew four white pearl buttons along the centre of the band. Procure a strip of leather 1 inch wide and $3\frac{1}{2}$ inches long, and sew under the foot. The other gaiter is to be knitted in exactly the same manner.

Child's Gaiters, with Knee.—3 ounces of single Berlin wool. Needles No. 11. Cast on 50 stitches. Knit 6 plain rows. 7th row—make 1, slip 1, putting the needle in as if about to purl, knit 1; repeat. 8th row—make 1, slip 1, knit the next stitch and the thread that lies over it together; repeat. Knit 10 more rows the same as the eighth row. 19th row—purl 1, knit 1, and repeat. 20th row—plain. 21st row—knit plain to within 1 stitch of the end of the row, turn the work, and knit plain to within 1 stitch of the other side; turn again, and knit to within 2 stitches of the end, turn, and again knit to within 2 stitches of the end; and so on till you have 18 unknitted stitches waiting on either end of the needle; then knit straight along to the end of the pin, turn, and again knit straight to the end of the pin, 50 stitches. Knit 6 plain rows. Now knit the same as the 7th row, then the 8th row, and then knit 68 rows the same as the 8th row. Next row—purl 1, knit 1, and repeat. Next row—plain. Knit 4 plain rows. 5th row—slip 1, knit 2 together, knit plain to within 3 stitches of the end, knit 2 together, knit 1. Knit 5 plain rows. Repeat from the 5th row twice, 23 rows of plain knitting done, and 44 stitches on the needle. Knit 30 plain rows. Then knit 34, turn, knit 24; turn, knit 23, turn, knit 22, and so on, knitting 1 stitch less each time till you knit only 6 stitches, turn, knit the 6 stitches back again, knit the next 10 stitches, picking up with each a thread of the gaiter, to prevent a hole being formed, knit 9 at end of pin; turn, knit 25, knit the next 10 stitches, picking up with each a thread of the gaiter, knit 9 at end of pin; 44 stitches now on; purl 20, increase 1, purl 4, increase 1, purl 20. Next row—knit 20, increase 1, knit 6, increase 1, knit 20. Next row, purl. Cast off all. Knit the other gaiter in the same way and sew them up. Round the top of each, work a little crochet edge, 1 double crochet in a stitch of the knitting, 4 chain, miss 2 stitches of the knitting, 1 double crochet in the next, and repeat.

Child's Overalls.—5 ounces of best white Alliance yarn and a pair of long bone knitting needles, No. 10. Begin by casting on 58 stitches for the foot. 1st row—plain. 2nd row—slip 1, increase 1, by picking up the thread that lies directly under the next stitch and knitting it, knit 27, increase 1, knit 2, increase 1, knit 27, increase 1, knit 1. 3rd row—plain, but slip the first stitch in this and *every* row. 4th row—slip 1, increase 1, knit 29, increase 1, knit 2, increase 1, knit 29, increase 1, knit 1. 5th row—plain. 6th row—slip 1, increase 1, knit 31, increase 1, knit 2, increase 1, knit 31, increase 1, knit 1. 7th row—plain. 8th row—knit 34, increase 1, knit 2, increase 1, knit 34. 9th row—plain. 10th row—knit 35, increase 1, knit 2, increase 1, knit 35. 11th row—plain. 12th row—knit 36, increase 1, knit 2, increase 1, knit 36. There are now 76 stitches on the needle. Knit 10 plain rows. 23rd row—beginning at the end where the tag of wool is. Knit 31, knit 2 together, purl 2, knit 2, purl 2, knit 2, purl 2, purl 2 together, slip the last stitch on to the left-hand needle, pass the first stitch of the left-hand needle over it, and replace it on the right-hand pin, turn, leaving 30 stitches on the left-hand needle. 24th row—slip the first stitch, knit 11, slip the last stitch on to the left-hand needle, pass the first stitch of the left-hand needle over it, and replace it on the right-hand pin. 25th row—turn the work, slip the first stitch, purl 2, knit 2, purl 2, knit 2, purl 3, slip the last stitch on to the left-hand needle, pass the first stitch of the left-hand needle over it, and replace it on the right-hand pin, turn the work. Repeat these last 2 rows alternately, till, ending with the plain row, there are only 17 stitches left on each side the foot, then knit the 17 stitches plain to the tag end of the needle. There should now be 46 stitches on the needle. For the Leg. 1st row—knit 17, purl 3, knit 2, purl 2, knit 2, purl 3, knit 17. 2nd row—plain. 3rd row—knit 2, * make 1, knit 2 together, knit 1, and repeat from * to the end of the row. 4th row—plain.

5th row—knit 2, purl 2, and repeat, end with knit 2. 6th row—plain; 46 stitches on the needle. Repeat the last 2 rows seven times. 21st row—knit 2, purl 2, and repeat, knit 2 at the end. 22nd row—knit 1, increase 1, knit to within one stitch of the end, increase 1, knit 1. 23rd row—knit 3, * purl 2, knit 2, repeat from *, and knit 3 at the end of the row. 24th row—plain. 25th row—same as the 23rd row. 26th row—increase same as the 22nd row. 27th row—purl 2, knit 2, and repeat, purl 2 at the end. 28th row—plain. 29th row—same as the 27th row. 30th row increase same as the 22nd row. 31st row—slip 1, purl 2, * knit 2, purl 2, repeat from *, and knit one at the end of the row. 32nd row—plain. 33rd row—same as the 31st row. 34th row—increase same as the 22nd row. 35th row—knit 2, purl 2, and repeat, end with knit 2. 36th row—plain. 37th row—same as the 35th row. 38th row increase same as the 22nd row. Repeat from the 23rd row, till in the 66th row of the knitting you have 70 stitches on the needle. Then increase in every plain row, and keep the pattern straight accordingly, till you have done 82 rows and have 86 stitches on the needle. 83rd row—knit 2, purl 2, and repeat, end with knit 2, cast on 3. 84th row—plain, and cast on 3 at the end. 85th row—knit 5, * purl 2, knit 2, repeat from *, end with purl 2, knit 1, cast on 2. There should be 94 stitches on the needle. Now break off the wool and leave this leg, the stitches being slipped on to a spare pin. Knit another leg exactly the same, but end with casting on 3 stitches instead of 2. 86th row of the 2nd leg—knit plain, cast on 2 at the end; take the first leg, and beginning where the wool is broken off, knit plain along, and cast on 3 at the end. You now have both legs on one needle, 194 stitches. 1st row of body—knit 8, * purl 2, knit 2, repeat from *, knit 8 at the end. 2nd row—plain. Repeat these 2 rows three times. 9th row—same as the first, 194 stitches on the needle. 10th row—knit 92, knit 2 together, knit 6, knit 2 together, knit 92. 11th row—same as the first, but purling only one stitch over the decrease. 12th row—knit 91, knit 2 together, knit 6, knit 2 together, knit 91. 13th row—same as the eleventh. 14th row—knit 91, knit 2 together, knit 4, knit 2 together, knit 91. 15th row—same as the first, but knitting 3 stitches over the decrease. 16th row—knit 90, knit 2 together, knit 4, knit 2 together, knit 90. 17th row—same as the fifteenth.

18th row—knit 90, knit 2 together, knit 2, slip 1, knit 1, pass the slipped stitch over, knit 90. 19th row—same as the first, but knitting only 1 stitch over the decrease. 20th row—knit 90, knit 2 together, slip 1, knit 1, pass the slipped stitch over, knit 90. 21st row—knit 8, * purl 2, knit 2, repeat from *, knit 8 at the end. 22nd row—plain; 182 stitches on the needle. Repeat the last two rows 29 times. There should be 80 rows knitted from the first row of the body. 81st row—knit 8, knit 2 together, and repeat; there will be 10 stitches to knit at the end of the row. Knit 5 plain rows. 87th row—knit 8, * make 1, knit 2 together, knit 2, repeat from *, knit 8 at the end. Knit 7 plain rows. Cast off. Sew up the feet and legs. Crochet a cord with double wool to run in through the holes at the waist and ankles, and finish off the ends with tassels. These overalls are intended to draw over a child's shoes and socks for extra warmth when taken out. The directions as far as the 66th row up the leg, and there cast off, will produce a pretty bootikin; and if commenced with 46 stitches on the needle for the leg, and knitted thence to the end, the result will be a nice-fitting pair of drawers.

Child's Petticoat, with Bodice.—Knitting needles No. 10. 2 oz. of ruby, 4 oz. of grey petticoat yarn.

With ruby wool cast on 131 stitches for the front breadth. 1st row—purl. 2nd row—plain. 3rd row—purl. 4th row—purl. 5th row—slip 1, * make 1, knit 3, knit 3 together, knit 3, make 1, knit 1, and repeat from *. 6th row—purl. 7th row—same as the fifth row. 8th row—purl. 9th row—same as the fifth row. 10th row—purl. 11th row—same as the fifth row. 12th row—purl with grey wool, and repeat from the first row with grey. At the 24th row join on ruby, and knit 12 pattern rows; then 12 rows with grey, and 12 again with ruby. Take grey to purl the 60th row, and knit all the remainder of the petticoat with grey, doing ribbing of 1 stitch plain and 1 stitch purl for about 34 rows (these rows may vary in number according to the length required for the skirt). 35th row —knit 1 and purl 1 seven times, * knit 3 together, rib 17, and repeat from * ; 14 to rib at end of the row, and 119 stitches now on. Continue ribbing for 13 rows. 49th row—knit 1 and purl 1 twice, * knit 3 together, rib 9, and repeat from * ; 4 to rib at end of the row, and 99 stitches now on. Knit ribbing for 13 rows.

63rd row—knit 1, purl 1, knit 3 together, and purl 1 four times, knit 3 together, and rib 3 ten times, knit 3 together, and purl 1 five times, knit 1 ; 61 stitches on, and this brings the petticoat to the waist. 64th row—knit 1, purl 1, and repeat. 65th row—work holes thus : knit 2, * make 1, knit 2 together, and repeat from *, knit 1 at end. Now for the front of the body. Knit on in ribbing as before for 63 rows. Now rib same way, but cast off 3 at beginning of every row for 10 rows. Next row—knit 2, * make 1, knit 2 together, repeat from *. Knit a purl row and a plain row, and cast off all. Commence again with 131 stitches for the back, and knit same as for the front till in the 35th row of the ribbing you are to knit only so far as the middle stitch of the row, and turn, and rib back, thus dividing the work into 2 portions; proceed with the right side of back knitting just the same as the corresponding half of the front, and shape shoulder the same, and cast off. Before going on with the left side cast on 6 stitches, which knit plain in every row to lie underneath the opening, and knit this side to correspond with half of front, and cast off. Sew up the side seams of the petticoat, leaving sufficient space for the armholes, sew up the shoulders. With ruby wool work a crochet edging round the neck and armholes. 1st row—double crochet. 2nd round—1 double crochet, * miss one, 5 treble in the next, miss one and repeat. Run a piece of ruby ribbon in the holes round the neck and waist.

Knitted Frock for Child of Three.—This stylish little frock is knitted with a deep kilted flounce, a fancy pattern for the skirt, and another pattern for the body. Procure ½ lb. of Alliance fingering ; bone knitting needles No. 8, No. 10, No. 12, a pair of each, and a bone crochet needle No. 10. Commence for the Flounce with No. 8 needles, by casting on 30 stitches. 1st row—plain. 2nd row—purl 28, and turn, leaving two stitches unknitted on the left-hand needle. 3rd row—knit 28. 4th row—purl 28, knit 2. 5th row—plain. 6th row—plain. 7th row—purl. 8th row—plain. 9th row—purl. 10th row—plain. Repeat these ten rows till you have done 50 raised and 50 depressed kilts, when cast off. The raised kilts which have the small hole near the upper edge are the right side of the work. Now with needles No. 10, and holding the right side of the flounce towards you, pick up 200 stitches along the top of the flounce, knitting each stitch as you pick it up. Knit 1 plain row. 1st row of the pattern—knit 2, purl 3, and repeat. 2nd row—knit 3, purl 2, and repeat. 3rd row—purl 2, knit 2, * purl 3, knit 2, repeat from *, and purl 1 at the end of the row. 4th row—knit 1, * purl 2, knit 3, repeat from *, and knit 2 at the end of the row. Repeat these four rows five times more; and at the end of the 24th row cast on 6 stitches for the under side of the placket hole; these 6 stitches are now always to be knitted plain in every row, and so also are 6 stitches to be knitted plain on the other side of the work. Knit 20 more rows of the pattern. 45th row—knit 6, * knit 2 together, knit 4, and repeat from *, working 6 plain stitches at the end of the row. 46th row—plain. 47th row—knit 6, knit 2 together, * knit 2 together, knit 4, repeat from * till within eight stitches of the end of the row, when knit 2 together, knit 6. 48th row—plain. 49th row—knit 6 edge stitches, * knit 2, make 1, knit 2 together, repeat from * till within eight stitches of the end of the row, then cast off 3 stitches (for a button-hole), knit 4. 50th row—knit 4, cast on 3, knit plain to the end. There are now 129 stitches on the needle with which to knit the body. 1st row—knit 6, * knit 3, purl 3, repeat from * till you have 45 stitches knitted, turn the work, and continue upon these 45 stitches for the left side of the back. 2nd row—purl 3 and knit 3 alternately six times, purl 3, knit 6. Repeat these two rows twice. 7th row—knit 6, purl 39. Knit 6 more rows of ribbing, keeping the work in stripes perpendicularly. 14th row—plain. Repeat these 14 rows four times more, and cast off. Continuing from the place where you divided for the back, slip the next 39 stitches on to a spare pin for the present, and knit the remaining 45 stitches in pattern (knit 3 and purl 3), to correspond with the half-back you have just done; but in the plain knitted edge make two button holes, the first when knitting the 23rd and 24th rows, and the second when knitting the 47th and 48th rows; and cast off when 70 rows are done. Now slip back the stitches from the spare pin, and for the front of the body work the same pattern ribbing, knit 3, purl 3, and no edge stitches, for 70 rows. 71st row—knit 15 stitches in ribbing, turn, and knit 18 little rows on these 15 stitches for the shoulder, and cast off. Cast off the stitches across the front, excepting only 15, which knit in the same way for the other shoulder. Sew these shoulder straps to the back pieces. Sew up the sides of the body for 36 rows from the waist. Sew up the skirt to where the placket hole begins, fastening the extra 6 stitches down on the inside. For the sleeves—With No. 10 needles cast on 69 stitches, and work 14 rows in the body pattern, knitting 2 stitches together at the beginning of every row. Take No. 12 needles, and knit 7 more rows without decrease, and cast off. For Crochet Edging round the Flounce.—Holding the flounce the right side towards you, work 6 treble stitches in the centre of the first raised kilt, 1 double crochet in the centre of the depressed kilt, and repeat the same all round. For Crochet Edging round the neck.—1st round—1 double crochet in a stitch of the knitting, 2 chain, miss two stitches, and repeat. 2nd round—6 treble under the first two chain of last round, 1 double crochet, under each of the next two chain, and repeat. Work a crochet chain with double wool to run in round the neck and waist to tie, and finish the ends with tassels. Sew three buttons on the back of the frock.

Jersey Suit for Boy of Four.—This suit consists of knickerbocker trousers and a jacket fitting high in the neck, and with long sleeves. The trousers measure 21 inches round the waist and 16 inches from the waist downwards, and the jacket is 14 inches in length. Materials required, 12 oz. of navy blue Alloa wool; a pair of bone knitting needles, No. 12, and four knitting needles, No. 13; and one yard of inch wide navy blue ribbon. The finer needles are only used in knitting the collar. For the trousers, with No. 12 needles, commence at the bottom of the leg by casting on 54 stitches, and knit, in ribbed knitting, 2 stitches plain and 2 stitches purl, for 16 rows, always slip the first stitch in every row. Knit 4 plain rows. 21st row—knit 1, increase 1, by picking up the thread that lies directly under the next stitch and knitting it, knit 52, increase 1, knit 1. Knit 3 plain rows. 25th row—knit 1, increase 1, knit 54, increase 1, knit 1. Knit 3 plain rows. 29th row—Knit 1, increase 1, knit 56, increase 1, knit 1. Knit 3 plain rows, and continue in this manner, increasing every fourth row, till you have 80 stitches on the needle. Then knit 5 plain rows between each row of increasings till there are 86 stitches on the needle. Knit 7 plain rows. Break off the wool, slip the stitches on to a spare needle, and re-commence with 54 stitches for the other leg, which knit exactly the same.

Having done this, knit 1 row plain all along, getting all the stitches of the two legs on to one pin. Knit 2 more rows all along and then on the left side cast on 6 extra stitches to fold under the front of the trousers. Knit 7 plain rows. You now have ten rows knitted of the body. 11th row—beginning on the right-hand side, knit 3, cast off 3 for a buttonhole, knit 75, knit 2 together, knit 6, knit 2 together, knit 87. 12th row—knit plain, and cast on 3 stitches above the 3 cast off. Knit 6 plain rows. 19th row—knit 80, knit 2 together, knit 6, knit 2 together, knit 86. Knit 5 plain rows. 25th row—knit 3, cast off 3, knit 73, knit 2 together, knit 6, knit 2 together, knit 85. 26th row—knit plain, and cast on 3 stitches above the 3 cast off. Knit 12 plain rows. 37th row—knit 3, cast off 3, knit plain to the end of the row. 38th row—knit plain, and cast on three stitches above the 3 cast off. Repeat from the 37th row till you have worked 5 buttonholes. Then knit 2 plain rows. Next row—knit 83, which brings you to the middle of the row, turn, and knit 44, turn and knit back to the middle, knit 38, turn, and knit back to the middle. Knit 32, turn, and knit back to the middle. Knit 26, turn, and knit back to the middle. Knit 20, turn, and knit back to the middle. Knit on the other leg in rows to correspond. The space thus left is for a buttonhole to keep the trousers up at the back. Knit 1 plain row all along both legs. Then knit 12 rows of ribbing for a waistband, making a buttonhole in the 7th row of ribbing on the same side as the five buttonholes already worked. Cast off. Sew up the legs of the trousers, and sew the 6 cast-on stitches neatly on the opposite leg. For the Jacket. With No. 12 needles cast on for the front 64 stitches, and knit, in ribbed knitting of 2 stitches plain and 2 stitches purl, for 16 rows. Then knit entirely in plain knitting forwards and backwards till you have a piece measuring 11 inches or 12 inches in length. Next row—knit 13 stitches only, and continue on these 13 stitches for 47 rows for the shoulder, leaving off at the neck end. Slip the next 38 stitches on to a spare pin, and knit the remaining 13 stitches for 48 rows, cast on 38 stitches for the back of the neck, and knit the 13 stitches belonging to the other shoulder; you now again have 64 stitches on the needle, and those on the spare pin remain there, while you knit in plain knitting the same length as already done on the front of the jacket, and finish with 16 rows of ribbing, and cast off. For the neck—hold the front of the jacket towards you, and knit 2 and purl 2 alternately along the 38 front stitches, pick up and knit, still in ribbing, 24 stitches on the first shoulder, 38 stitches along the back, and 24 stitches on the other shoulder, using for this three No. 13 needles, and continue with the fourth needle in ribbing for 22 rounds, then a round of holes, make 1, knit 2 together, knit 2, then 3 more rounds of ribbing, and cast off. Sew up 9 inches from the bottom of both sides of the jacket. For the sleeves—with No. 12 needles cast on 40 stitches, and knit 16 rows of ribbing. Then knit 6 inches of plain knitting, cast on 14 more stitches for a gusset, knit 24 more plain rows, and cast off. Knit the other sleeve the same. Sew up the sleeves, folding the gussets reversely right and left. Sew the sleeves in the armholes, placing the seam of the gusset to the back of the jacket. Run the ribbon in through the holes at the neck to tie in front.

Boy's Scarf.—Required 3 oz. of white single Berlin wool, and a pair of No. 10 bone knitting needles. The pattern is simple and, at the same time, very pretty, and nearly alike on both sides. Cast on 54 stitches. 1st row—knit 2, purl 2, and repeat, ending the row with knit 2. 2nd row—purl 2, knit 2, and repeat, ending the row with purl 2. Repeat these 2 rows four times. 11th row—plain. 12th row—purl. 13th row—purl 2, knit 2, and repeat. 14th row—knit 2, purl 2, and repeat. Repeat these 2 rows four times. 23rd row—plain. 24th row—purl. Repeat from the first row for the length required, and cast off after knitting the tenth row of the pattern. Cut some wool into lengths of six inches, and fringe the ends of the scarf by knotting two strands of wool into every alternate stitch of the knitting.

Gentleman's Comforter.—Decidedly the best stitch for comforters is the Brioche stitch, as it is thick and elastic, and yet is alike on both sides. With single Berlin wool of any colour, and No. 9 needles, cast on any even number of stitches, according to the width required; then work as follows—make 1, slip 1, putting the needle in front as if about to purl it, knit 1 all along. Every succeeding row is the same, excepting that when knitting 1 you will knit the stitch that was slipped in the preceding row, and the thread that lies over it together. A comforter should be about 2 yards long, to go twice round the neck, and with ends to wrap over and cover the chest. Add a fringe at each end.

Gentleman's Cardigan Jacket.

—Required: 1-lb. of best brown Scotch fingering wool; a pair of long bone knitting needles, No. 12; also a pair of No. 16; and a few brown bone buttons. With No. 12 needles cast on 200 stitches for the whole width of the bottom of the jacket, and knit in ribbed knitting, 1 stitch plain and 1 stitch purl, for 5 inches. Here make the pocket holes; first knit 20 stitches in ribs as usual, then cast off 30 stitches, knit on in ribbing till within 50 stitches of the end of the needle, cast off 30, knit 20 in ribbing. Next row, knit in ribbing, and cast on 30 stitches each side to replace those cast off. Continue the ribbed knitting upon the 200 stitches till you have done a length sufficient to reach to the armhole, about 15 inches. Next row, knit 50 stitches, turn, and knit backwards and forwards upon these 50 stitches for 6 inches, then every sixth row decrease one stitch at the front, and every fourth row increase one stitch at the shoulder, till the work measures 8 inches from the sleeve opening. Ending on the left-hand side of the work, leave this piece and re-commence where you divided for the armhole, cast off 8 stitches, knit 84 stitches for the back, straight on in ribbing for 7 inches. Re-commence again at the bottom of the 84 stitches, cast off 8, knit 15, cast off 15 for the breast pocket, knit 20. Next row, knit 20, cast on 15, knit 15, and proceed with the shaping of this half-front to correspond with the half-front already knitted. This done, knit a row from end to end, taking care to keep the ribs perfectly straight. Knit 4 more rows all along. Then mark the 3 centre stitches over each shoulder, as they are to be kept unbroken up to the neck, and on either side of these 3 stitches you are to knit 2 stitches together in every alternate row, keeping the ribbed knitting straight all the time. At the beginning and at the end of the rows decreasings are to be made to carry on the shaping of the neck. When the shoulder is the right height, cast off the remaining stitches. For the Sleeves—With No. 12 needles cast on 80 stitches, and knit straight on in ribbing of 1 plain, 1 purl, for 60 rows. Then increase one stitch at the beginning and one stitch at the end of the row, and do the same every sixth row, always working in ribs, till you have 96 stitches on the needle, when knit 20 more rows (or till the sleeve is long enough) without any more increase. Next row knit 80 stitches; turn, knit 64; turn, knit 54; turn, knit 44; turn, knit 34; turn, knit 24; turn, knit all the stitches to the end of the needle. Knit 2 more rows on all the 96 stitches, and cast off loosely. Knit the other sleeve in exactly the same manner, and sew them in. For the Pockets.—Pick up the cast-on stitches, knitting each stitch as you pick it up, and knit in stocking stitch, 1 row plain and 1 row purl (having the smooth side of the knitting for the inside of the pocket), till you have a piece long enough for the depth of the pocket, and to fold up to sew to the cast-off stitches of the pocket hole, sew up the sides. For the Border round the Jacket and Sleeves.—Take No. 16 needles and cast on 16 stitches, and knit entirely in plain knitting till you have a length sufficient for the bottom of the jacket. Knit a similar piece to go up the fronts and round the neck, and in this in the 16th row and at regular intervals up the left front make button-holes by casting off 4 stitches in the middle of the row, and in the next row casting on 4 other stitches in place of them. The border for the sleeves is also done in plain knitting, and is 24 stitches wide. Sew these borders neatly on to the jacket. Sew the buttons on the right front, and the jacket is complete.

Gentleman's Mittens.—Knitting pins No. 14. 1 oz. of deep crimson, and ¼ oz. of black single Berlin wool. Cast on 60 stitches with the crimson wool, and knit 2 rows plain and 2 rows purl alternately for 88 rows, when there will be 22 raised ribs. The ribs go up and down the hand from wrist to knuckle, and the end where you began, and where the tag of wool is, is the wrist end. Having done the 88 rows, knit along to knuckle end again, and at the commencement of the next row, cast off 9 stitches. Then cast on 6 stitches for the beginning of the thumb. Purl down to the wrist, which is now wide enough. Next row—cast off 20 stitches and knit the remainder. Continue the knitting in ribs, and to shape the thumb take 2 stitches together both at the end and at the beginning of every row at the end where the 20 stitches were cast off, until 8 raised ribs are done, and there are only 8 stitches left. Cast these off. With black wool, pick up the stitches along the top of the thumb (there should be 18), knitting each one as you pick it up, and knit 5 plain rows, and cast off. Pick up 46 stitches along the top of the hand, knit 5 plain rows, and cast off. These rows of black form an edge, and this will be the left-hand mitten. Knit the other mitten in the same way; the only difference is in picking up the stitches with the black wool, when you will hold the mitten for the right hand the reverse way towards you, so as to begin at the opposite end, and do the thumb last. Sew up the mittens, and work 3 rows of feather stitch with black wool on the ribs which come in the middle of the back of the hand.

Lady's Mittens.—Knitting pins No. 14. 1 oz. of brown, and ¼ oz. of blue single Berlin wool. With the brown wool cast on 48 stitches, and knit in ribbed knitting 1 stitch plain and 1 stitch purl for 40 rows. The side where the tag of wool is, is the side to increase for the thumb. Having done the 40 rows, make 1 extra stitch in every row which begins on the thumb side of the mitten, by picking up the thread that lies directly under the second stitch and knitting it, keeping the work in regular ribs as before. When you have done 40 more rows there will be 68 stitches on the needle. Next row—beginning at the thumb end without any increase, knit 20 stitches still in ribs, and leaving the other stitches on the pin, knit these 20 stitches backwards and forwards for 8 rows, then join on the blue wool, knit 5 more rows, and cast off. With brown wool commence again where you divided for the thumb, and knit 12 rows, then join on the blue wool and knit 5 more rows, and cast off. The other mitten is to be knitted exactly the same. Sew them up, one for the right and the other for the left hand, and work 3 rows of herring-bone stitch with the blue wool on the ribs which come in the middle of the back.

Open Work Mittens.—2 oz. of black Penelope knitting yarn, or Andalusian wool. Knitting pins No. 16 and No. 18. Commence with No. 16 pins, cast on 60 stitches, and knit in ribbed knitting, 2 stitches plain and 2 stitches purl, for 40 rows. Then take No. 18 pins, and knit 1 plain row and 1 purl row alternately four times. 49th row—knit 12, slip 1, knit 1, pass the slipped stitch over the knitted one, * make 1, knit 1, make 1, knit

1, slip 1, knit 2 together, pass the slipped stitch over, knit 1, repeat from *, then make 1, knit 1, make 1, knit 2 together, knit 31. 50th row—purl. Repeat these last 2 rows three times more. 57th row—to increase for the thumb, slip the first stitch, increase 1 by picking up the thread that lies directly under the second stitch and knitting it, knit 11, slip 1, knit 1, pass the slipped stitch over, * make 1, knit 1, make 1, knit 1, slip 1, knit 2 together, pass the slipped stitch over, knit 1, repeat from * ; then make 1, knit 1, make 1, knit 2 together, knit 31. 58th row—purl. Continue knitting these 2 rows alternately, only in the fancy rows knitting one additional stitch each time before commencing the pattern, until you can count 26 holes straight up the back of the hand, when there should be 82 stitches on the needle. Next row—for the thumb, knit 24 stitches, and leaving 58 stitches on the pin, turn, and purl the 24 stitches ; knit a plain row and a purl row alternately till you have 10 of these little rows done ; then next row - knit 2 stitches and purl 2 stitches alternately ; repeat this ribbing till you have done 9 rows, and then cast off. Commence again where you divided for the thumb and repeat the 49th and 50th rows four times ; then knit a plain row and a purl row alternately for 10 rows, and finish with 9 rows of ribbing like the thumb, and cast off. This will be the right-hand mitten. For the left-hand mitten, cast on 60 stitches, and work as directed above as far as the 48th row. 49th row—knit 31, slip 1, knit 1, pass the slipped stitch over the knitted one,* make 1. knit 1, make 1, knit 1, slip 1, knit 2 together, pass the slipped stitch over, knit 1, repeat from *, then make 1, knit 1, make 1, knit 2 together, knit 12. 50th row—purl. Repeat the last 2 rows three times more. 57th row—in which the thumb is commenced, knit the same as the 49th row till you come to the last stitch, and there increase 1 by picking up the thread that lies directly under the last stitch and knitting it, then knit the last stitch. 58th row—purl. Repeat these 2 rows, increasing a stitch for the thumb at the end of every fancy row, until you have 82 stitches on the needle and can count 26 holes up the back of the hand. Next row—the same as the 49th row, and leaving the 24 thumb stitches unknitted on the pin, turn, and purl the 58 stitches. Repeat these 2 rows three times more, then knit a plain row and a purl row alternately ten times, work 9 rows of ribbed knitting, like the other mitten, and cast off. Commence again with the 24 stitches that remain on the left-hand needle, knit a row and purl a row alternately till you have 10 of these little rows done, then 9 rows of ribbed knitting, and cast off. Sew the mittens up.

Cuffs. Brioche Knitting.—1½ oz. of red, ½ oz. of white double Berlin wool. Knitting pins No. 10. Cast on 28 stitches with the red wool. 1st row—make 1, slip 1, putting the needle in as if about to purl, knit 1 ; repeat. 2nd row—make 1, slip 1, knit the next stitch and the thread that lies over it together ; repeat. The whole of the cuff is worked as the second row. Knit four rows with the red wool, 4 with white, 2 with red, 4 with white, 12 with red, 4 with white, 2 with red, 6 with white, 2 with red, 4 with white, 12 with red, 4 with white, 2 with red, 4 with white, 4 with red, and cast off. Sew the cuff up neatly, bringing the stripes together colour to colour.

Cuffs with Frill.—These are alike on both sides, and the frill may be worn falling over the hand or turned back. Knitting needles No. 18. 2 oz. of Andalusian wool. Cast on 80 stitches. Knit in ribbed knitting, 2 stitches plain and 2 stitches purl, for 60 rows. 1st row of frill—knit 1, make 1, knit 1, purl 2, and repeat. 2nd row—knit 2, purl 3. 3rd row—knit 3, purl 2. 4th row—knit 2, purl 3. 5th row—knit 3, purl 1, make 1, purl 1, and repeat. 6th, 7th, and 8th rows—knit 3, purl 3. 9th row—knit 1, make 1, knit 2, purl 3, and repeat. 10th row—knit 3, purl 4. 11th row—knit 4, purl 3. 12th row—knit 3, purl 4. 13th row—knit 4, purl 1, make 1, purl 2, and repeat. 14th, 15th, and 16th rows—knit 4, purl 4. 17th row—knit 1, make 1, knit 2, make 1, knit 1, purl 4, and repeat. 18th row—knit 4, purl 6. 19th row—knit 6, purl 4. 20th row—knit 4, purl 6. 21st row—knit 6, purl 1, make 1, purl 2, make 1, purl 1, and repeat. 22nd, 23rd, and 24th rows—knit 6, purl 6. 25th row—knit 2, make 1, knit 2, make 1, knit 2, purl 6, and repeat. 26th row—knit 6, purl 8. 27th row—knit 8, purl 6. 28th row—knit 6, purl 8. 29th row—knit 8, purl 2, make 1, purl 2, make 1, purl 2, and repeat. 30th, 31st, and 32nd rows—knit 8, purl 8. Cast off all. Knit the other cuff in the same way, and sew up.

Beaded Cuffs. Vandyke Pattern.—1 oz. of Pearsall's Imperial knitting silk or Penelope knitting silk. 1 bunch of beads. Knitting needles No. 18. The prettiest cuffs are made with black silk and gold or silver cut beads, the smaller the beads the better they look. Andalusian wool and coloured beads of good contrast may be used if preferred. The beads must first of all be threaded on the silk or wool, and passed down a considerable distance; you then bring each bead up as required, and push it close to the needle before knitting the stitch. Cast on 32 stitches. 1st row—plain. 2nd row—slip 1, knit 2 stitches plain, 5 with beads, 3 plain, 5 beads, 3 plain, 5 beads, 8 plain. 3rd row—plain. 4th row—slip 1, 3 plain, 5 beads, 3 plain, 5 beads, 3 plain, 5 beads, 7 plain. 5th row—plain. 6th row—slip 1, 4 plain, 5 beads, 3 plain, 5 beads, 3 plain, 5 beads, 6 plain. 7th row—plain. 8th row—slip 1, 5 plain, 5 beads, 3 plain, 5 beads, 3 plain, 5 beads, 5 plain. 9th row—plain. 10th row—slip 1, 6 plain, 5 beads, 3 plain, 5 beads, 3 plain, 5 beads, 4 plain. 11th row—plain. 12th row—slip 1, 5 plain, 5 beads, 3 plain, 5 beads, 3 plain, 5 beads, 5 plain. 13th row—plain. 14th row—slip 1, 4 plain, 5 beads, 3 plain, 5 beads, 3 plain, 5 beads, 6 plain. 15th row—plain. 16th row—slip 1, 3 plain, 5 beads, 3 plain, 5 beads, 3 plain, 5 beads, 7 plain. 17th row—plain. Repeat from the 2nd row seven times more. Cast off. Pick up 68 stitches along the widest edge from the beads, and knit in ribbed knitting, 2 stitches plain and 2 stitches purl, for 32 rows. Cast off loosely. Work the other cuff in exactly the same manner, and sew them up. If a beaded edge is desired, take a long needleful of silk, upon which beads have previously been threaded, and sew over from the slipped stitch at the commencement of the rows to two stitches lower down in a slanting direction, making 3 beads sit upon the right side of the cuff in every stitch.

Plain Knitted Kneecaps.—Knitting pins No. 11, 3 oz. of white Scotch fingering. Cast on 47 stitches. 1st row—plain. 2nd row—purl 6, knit 35, purl 6. 3rd row—plain. 4th row—plain. 5th row—purl 6, knit 35, purl 6. 6th row—plain. Repeat these six rows three times. 25th row—knit 23, increase 1 by picking up the thread that lies directly under the next stitch and knitting it, knit 24. 26th row—purl 6, knit 17, increase 1, knit

19, purl 6. 27th row—knit 23, increase 1, knit 26. And continue thus, always increasing after the 23rd stitch, and keeping the edge in notches, till there are 19 notches done; then knit 6 rows without any increase; and henceforward in every row knit 2 together after knitting the 23rd stitch, so as to decrease in the same ratio as was before increased, and when 47 stitches are attained knit 24 rows thereon to match the beginning, and cast off. Sew the cast-off to the cast-on stitches, and the kneecap is complete. Knit the other in the same manner.

Kneecaps.—Knitting pins No. 14. 4 oz. of Scotch fingering wool. Cast on 7 stitches. Knit 10 plain rows. Knit 34 rows, increasing 1 at the beginning of each row, by picking up the thread that lies directly under the second stitch and knitting it, until there are 41 stitches on the pin. Knit 50 plain rows. Knit 34 plain rows, in which decrease by knitting two together before the end stitch in each row. Knit 10 plain rows. Cast off. This forms the centre piece. For the top of the kneecap, pick up 76 stitches and knit 3 plain rows. Then do 40 rows of ribbed knitting; that is, 2 stitches plain, and 2 stitches purl, all along. Knit 4 plain rows. Next row—knit 2, make 1, knit 2 together, throughout. Knit 4 more plain rows, and cast off. For the bottom of the kneecap pick up 76 stitches on the opposite side of the work, and knit the same as for the top, casting off after the first 4 plain rows. Sew the sides together, and run an elastic through the row of holes.

Sleeping Socks. Double Knitting.—Knitting needles No. 9 for the ribbing, No. 4 for the double knitting. 4 oz. of white white 4-thread superfine fleecy wool. Cast on 56 stitches with the smaller pins. Work 26 rows of ribbed knitting, 2 stitches plain, 2 stitches purl. Then with the larger pins begin the double knitting: * knit the first stitch, putting the needle in the middle of the stitch instead of in the usual way, bring the wool to the front, slip 1, pass the wool to the back; repeat from *. Every row is the same, and the stitches that are slipped in one row will be knitted in the next. Work the double knitting for 56 rows. Next row, for the heel, knit 14 stitches in double knitting, backwards and forwards for 16 rows. In the 17th row, take the 5th and the 6th stitches together, and the 7th and the 8th together, and the same in the 19th row. In the 21st row, take the 3rd and the 4th stitches together, and the 5th and the 6th together. In the 23rd row, take the 3rd and the 4th stitches together. Knit the next row (which will only consist of 7 stitches) plain. Cast off 6. Pick up 13 stitches to meet the stitches that have been resting on the needle, knit across in double knitting, and then work 14 stitches on that side the same as above for the other half of the heel. Then proceed with the double knitting for the foot. Knit 56 rows straight on; in the 57th, 59th, 61st, 63rd, and 65th rows, knit the 9th and 10th stitches, and the 11th and 12th stitches together, counting from each end, to decrease for the toe. 67th row—knit 2, knit 2 together, all along. Cast off. Sew the sock up on the wrong side, and finish off with 2 or 3 rows of crochet frilling round the top of the leg.

Sleeping Socks. Plain Knitting.—6 oz. of 3-thread superfine fleecy wool. Knitting needles No. 10. Cast on 56 stitches, and knit in ribbed knitting, 2 stitches plain and 2 stitches purl, for 30 rows. Then knit 30 rows of all plain knitting. 61st row—slip 1, knit 2 together, knit all along till within 3 stitches of the end of the row, then knit 2 together, knit 1. Knit 7 rows of plain knitting. Repeat from the 61st row four times more. Next row—for the heel, knit 12 stitches, turn, and knit these 12 stitches backwards and forwards for 20 rows. 21st row—slip 1, knit 2 together, knit the remainder. 22nd row—plain. Repeat the last 2 rows four times more. 31st row—cast off 6; pick up 12 stitches along the side of the heel (knitting each stitch as you pick it up). Knit all the stitches upon the other needle, and then work 12 stitches on that side, the same as above, to form the other half of the heel. Then having 46 stitches on the needle, continue for the foot, working all plain knitting for 44 rows. 45th row—slip 1, knit 2 together, knit all along till within 3 stitches of the end of the row, then knit 2 together, knit 1. 46th row—plain. Repeat the last 2 rows nine times more. Next row—slip 1, * knit 2 together, knit 2, repeat from * ; there will be 1 stitch to knit at the end of the row. Next row—plain. Next row—slip 1, * knit 2 together, knit 1, repeat from *. Cast off. Sew the sock up neatly.

Lady's Knitted Drawers.—Peacock fingering wool. Knitting pins No. 10. Each leg is knitted separately, and commenced at the bottom. Cast on 108 stitches, and knit in ribbed knitting, 3 stitches plain and 3 stitches purl, for 26 rows. Then knit 12 plain rows. 39th row—knit 2, increase 1 by picking up the thread that lies immediately below the third stitch and knitting it, then knit plain to within 2 stitches of the end of the row, increase 1 again, and knit the 2 last stitches. Then knit 3 plain rows. Repeat these 4 rows until you have done about 14 inches in all. In the next row commence to decrease by knitting 2 together at the beginning and end of the row, and do the same in every fourth row, until you have 12 inches of decreasings. Next row—knit 60 stitches, turn, and knit back; then knit 55 stitches, turn, and knit back, and repeat in this way for 12 rows in all, leaving 5 more stitches unknitted each time; this produces the extra length required for the back. Knit 2 plain rows the whole length, and then knit 20 rows of ribbing the same as at the bottom of the leg. Cast off. Knit the other leg exactly as this. Sew them up from the bottom to where the increasings end, and join the two fronts together from the waist to about 6 inches down. For the crochet border round the leg, work 1 double crochet into a stitch of the commencing row, 2 chain, miss 2, and repeat. 2nd round—2 treble under each 2 chain, with 2 chain between the 4 trebles. 3rd round—1 double crochet between the 2 trebles, 3 chain, 1 treble under the 2 chain of last round; 5 chain, 1 double crochet five times, each time working the double crochet into the treble just done, 3 chain, and repeat. A linen band can be sewn on at the top of the drawers, or a string run through the ribbing to tie at the waist.

Lady's Vest. Basket Pattern.—6 balls of white Cocoon wool. Knitting pins No. 10. Commence at the bottom with a scallop border, for which cast on 119 stitches. 1st row—plain. 2nd row—purl. 3rd row—plain. 4th row—slip 1, * knit 2 together, knit 4, make 1, knit 1, make 1, knit 4, slip 1, knit 1, pass the slipped stitch over; repeat from * 8 times, and knit the last stitch plain. 5th row—purl. 6th row—same as the 4th row. 7th row—plain. 8th row—purl. 9th row—plain. Repeat from the 4th row to the 9th row; then knit another plain row, and this completes the border. Now work for the basket pattern. 1st row—knit 7, purl 3, and repeat to the end of the row; there will be 1 stitch short, so increase 1 stitch in the last. 2nd row—knit 3, purl 7, and repeat. 3rd row—knit 7, purl 3, and repeat. 4th row—plain. 5th row—knit 2, * purl 3, knit 7; repeat from *, and knit only 5 at the end of the row. 6th row—purl 5, * knit 3, purl 7; repeat from *, and purl only 2 at the end of the row. 7th row —knit 2, * purl 3, knit 7; repeat from *, and knit only 5 at the end of the row. 8th row—plain. Repeat from the first row of the basket pattern; and to gore the sides of the vest, knit 2 together at the beginning and end of this row, and at the beginning and end of every sixth row, always keeping the pattern straight, till you have reduced to 100 stitches. Then knit straight on in the basket pattern until the work measures about eighteen inches from the commencement. For the shoulder piece—knit 7, purl 3, repeat twice, knit 3, knit 2 together; turn the work, and knit back, purling the first 4 stitches, and then basket pattern as before; knit on in basket pattern, taking two stitches together at the end of every alternate row to shape for the neck, till the shoulder piece is reduced to 20 stitches, when cast off. Re-commence where you divided for the shoulder, and cast off 31 stitches, and then knit upon the remaining 34 stitches, shaping the same as the other shoulder, by taking 2 together at the neck end of every alternate row. For the back—again cast on 119 stitches, and knit another piece exactly similar to this piece. Join the shoulder pieces together, and sew up the sides, leaving space for the sleeves. For the sleeve—cast on 71 stitches, and knit the border the same as the bottom of the vest, only working 3 plain stitches at the beginning and end of each row, instead of only 1 plain stitch. Knit 21 rows of the border, then 1 more plain row, and cast off. For the gusset—pick up 10 stitches along the side of the sleeve where you finished casting off, and knit 18 rows of plain knitting, and cast off. Sew this in the sleeve cornerways, like a gusset. Knit the other sleeve in the same manner, but pick up the gusset stitches on the opposite side. Sew the sleeves in the vest. For a crochet edge round the neck, work: 1st row—4 treble in 1 stitch of the knitting, miss 3 stitches of the knitting, and repeat. 2nd row—one double crochet, two treble, one double crochet, under each space between the groups of 4 trebles. Finish the vest with a ribbon run through the holes to tie in front.

Lady's Jacket Bodice.—This will take 7 oz. of best speckled fingering yarn. Long bone knitting needles, No. 10. Commence for the right side of the front—cast on 52 stitches, and knit in ribbed knitting, 4 stitches plain and 4 stitches purl, for 8 rows. Then work 1 plain row and 1 purl row alternately, decreasing 1 stitch at the end of the first plain row, and at the end of every fourth row afterwards, and knitting 4 stitches plain for an edge at the end of every purl row. Make a button-hole in every eighth row of the front plain edge by beginning in those rows, slip 1, knit 1, make 1, knit 2 together. Continue decreasing at the left-hand side of the knitting, until you have decreased to 39 stitches, which brings you to the waist, and this being one-quarter of the waist should here measure about 6¼ inches. Now begin to widen by increasing a stitch, picking up a stitch and knitting it before knitting the last one, every fourth row on the same side as you decreased, until you have 49 stitches on the pin, and 101 rows worked. For the armhole—at the beginning of the 102nd row cast off 4 stitches, then continue knitting without either increasing or decreasing for 19 rows. Then increase 1 stitch at the end of the 20th row, and 1 stitch every fourth row for seven times—making eight increasings in all. When you have made twenty button-holes, cast off for the neck, at the beginning of the row, 4 stitches, and cast off 1 stitch at the beginning of every row on this side twelve times; and at the same time, in beginning the rows at the shoulder end, cast off 3 stitches there for thirteen times; all the stitches should now be worked off. For the left side of the front, knit the same as the right side, but reversing the increasings and omitting the button-holes. For the back, cast on 100 stitches and knit in ribbed knitting, 4 stitches plain and 4 stitches purl, for 8 rows. Then work 1 plain row and 1 purl row alternately, decreasing 1 stitch at the beginning and at the end of the first plain row, and in every fourth row afterwards, until you have decreased 13 stitches each side; then increase at both ends of the row every fourth row, until you have 101 rows worked, which brings you to the armhole. Here cast off two stitches at each end, and knit on for 19 rows, without either increasing or decreasing. Increase 1 stitch at each end of the 20th row, and 1 stitch every fourth row for six times; then cast off 3 stitches at beginning of every row for the shoulders to correspond with the fronts. In the

165th row, knit to within 3 stitches of the centre, and there cast off 6 stitches for the neck; cast off 1 stitch in each row, at the neck side, and the same as before at the shoulder end, till all the stitches are cast off. Then, in the same way, finish knitting the stitches that remain on the opposite shoulder. Sew the parts neatly together, and sew 20 buttons down the front to meet the button-holes. Pick up 74 stitches round the neck, knitting each stitch as you pick it up, and knit 2 stitches plain and 2 stitches purl alternately for 7 rows, and cast off. For the sleeves—cast on 66 stitches, and knit in ribbed knitting, 2 stitches plain and 2 stitches purl, for 28 rows. 29th row—increase 1 stitch at the beginning and another at the end of the row, and knit the rest plain. Knit next row purl, and alternately plain and purl for 4 more rows. 35th row increase again at each end of the row. Knit 3 rows without increase. And now proceed in this way: 3 rows between each row of increasings, till there are 80 stitches on the needle. Cast off 13 stitches at the beginning of the two next rows, then 2 at the beginning of each row till you have 24 stitches left. Cast off all. Knit the other sleeve the same, and sew them neatly and firmly into the armholes.

Puzzle Jacket.—Fitting like a Zouave. Knitting pins No. 11. 5 oz. of single Berlin wool. Cast on 56 stitches, and knit 109 plain rows. At the end of the 109th row, cast on 56 more stitches, and now knit 86 rows. At the beginning of the 87th row, cast off 56 stitches, and knit 109 rows on the 56 stitches that remain. Cast off. You thus get a straight piece of knitting as wide again in the middle as at the ends. Fold the wide piece down flat upon the other part of the work, take the cast-on end, fold it to meet the other cast-on stitches, and sew both rows of cast-on stitches together; the opening you will see at the side is for an armhole. Fold the cast-off end in the same way and sew up. Now open the work: the seams come at the back; the centre of the top of the straight piece of knitting is for the back of the neck, turn it down a little in circular fashion, and tack it to simulate a collar; put four or five buttons to the left-hand side, and four or five loops on the right-hand side. Now if the jacket is intended to wear out of doors, under a cloak, work a row or two of simple crochet edging all round; if for a house jacket, a strip of looped knitting, as directed for the trimming of the baby's hood, makes a pretty finish.

Lady's Petticoat. Arrow Pattern.—Knitted in alternate stripes of cardinal and grey, six stripes of each colour, gored and shaped to the figure. 4-thread fleecy wool, 14 oz. of each colour; knitting needles No. 7. With cardinal wool cast on 31 stitches, and knit 1 plain row. 2nd row—wool over the needle so as to make a stitch, knit 15, knit 2 together, knit 14. 3rd row—the same, and continue this till 32 rows are done. 33rd row—make 1, knit 7, knit 2 together, knit 6, knit 2 together, knit 6, knit 2 together, knit 6. 34th row—make 1, knit 14, knit 2 together, knit 13. Knit 20 more rows the same as the last. 55th row—make 1, knit 6, knit 2 together, knit 6, knit 2 together, knit 6, knit 2 together, knit 5. 56th row—make 1, knit 13, knit 2 together, knit 12. Knit 14 more rows the same as the last. 71st row—make 1, knit 6, knit 2 together, knit 5, knit 2 together, knit 5, knit 2 together, knit 5. 72nd row—make 1, knit 12, knit 2 together, knit 11. Knit 14 more rows the same as the last. 87th row—make 1, knit 5, knit 2 together, knit 5, knit 2 together, knit 5, knit 2 together, knit 4. 88th row—make 1, knit 11, knit 2 together, knit 10. Knit 10 more rows the same as the last. 99th row—make 1, knit 5, knit 2 together, knit 4, knit 2 together, knit 4, knit 2 together, knit 4. 100th row—make 1, knit 10, knit 2 together, knit 9. Knit 10 more rows the same as the last. 111th row—make 1, knit 4, knit 2 together, knit 4, knit 2 together, knit 4, knit 2 together, knit 3. 112th row—make 1, knit 9, knit 2 together, knit 8. Knit 6 more rows the same as the last. 119th row—make 1, knit 4, knit 2 together, knit 3, knit 2 together, knit 3, knit 2 together, knit 3. 120th row—make 1, knit 8, knit 2 together, knit 7. Knit 6 more rows the same as the last. 127th row—make 1, knit 3, knit 2 together, knit 3, knit 2 together, knit 3, knit 2 together, knit 2. 128th row—make 1, knit 7, knit 2 together, knit 6. Knit 4 more rows the same as the last. 133rd row—make 1, knit 3, knit 2 together, knit 2, knit 2 together, knit 2, knit 2 together, knit 2. 134th row—make 1, knit 6, knit 2 together, knit 5. Knit 2 more rows the same as the last. 137th row—make 1, knit 2, knit 2 together, knit 2, knit 2 together, knit 2, knit 2 together, knit 1. 138th row—make 1, knit 5, knit 2 together, knit 4. Knit 2 more rows the same as the last. 141st row—make 1, knit 2, knit 2 together, knit 1, knit 2 together, knit 1, knit 2 together, knit 1. 142nd row—make 1, knit 4, knit 2 together, knit 3. Knit 1 more row the same as the last, and cast off. This completes 1 stripe. Knit 5 more stripes with cardinal and 6 with grey. When all are finished sew them together. A place must be left in one join for a placket hole, work double crochet in every stitch round here to strengthen it. Sew the petticoat into a band. For an edging round the bottom, work, commencing at the joining of each stripe, 1 double crochet, * 3 chain, 1 treble in the lower part of the double crochet stitch, 1 double crochet in the third stitch of the knitting, repeat from *, and get 11 of these little scallops round each stripe, cardinal on the cardinal and grey on the grey. A petticoat for a child can be made in the same manner, commencing at about the 55th row, or according to the length required.

Petticoat.—This petticoat is knitted in 2 breadths, the flounce being first of all knitted separately in two pieces, and the upper part worked on thereto. It is a nice comfortable shape, and though chiefly suitable for winter, is not too heavy for ordinary wear. Procure 1½ lb. of the best 4-thread cardinal fleecy wool, and a pair of long wooden knitting needles No. 10. For the flounce—cast on 50 stitches. 1st row—plain knitting, and at the end of the row knit 2 together, knit 1. 2nd row—knit 2, purl the remainder, and knit the 2 last stitches. Repeat these two rows twice. 7th row—knit 3, purl the remainder, and at the end of the row knit the 2 last stitches, turning the wool *over* the needle instead of passing it under, so as to make a stitch. 8th row—plain knitting. Repeat these two rows twice. Now repeat from the first row and knit a piece as long as is required for half the width of the petticoat; the flounce falls like a number of box plaitings, and about 40 plaits, 20 raised and 20 depressed, will bring it a nice width. Cast off, and knit another piece the same as the first. For the upper part of the petticoat—pick up the stitches at the top of the first piece of flouncing, knitting each stitch as you pick it up, get 3 stitches on each plait, which will make 120 stitches. Knit 1 plain row, and then begin for the dice pattern. 1st row—knit 2, purl 2, and repeat. 2nd row—the same. 3rd row—purl 2, knit 2, and repeat. 4th row—the same. Repeat these 4 rows 14 times, making 60 rows of the dice knitting. Then finish to the length required for the petticoat with a ribbing of 3 plain, 3 purl alternately, and cast off. Take the second piece of flouncing, pick up 120 stitches, and knit the dice knitting the same as above. Then in the 1st row of the ribbing begin forming a placket hole. Commencing on the right-hand side of the work, knit only half the breadth, viz., 60 stitches in ribbing, 3 plain, 3 purl, and 3 stitches besides for the selvage of the placket, which 3 stitches are to be knitted plain at the placket end in every row. When you have the same number of rows knitted as in the 1st breadth of the petticoat, cast off, taking two stitches together so as to bring the fulness more to the back. Cast on 5 stitches before beginning to knit the left half of the back breadth, knit in ribs of 3 plain and 3 purl as before, and knit the 5 cast-on stitches plain in every row to wrap under the right-hand side. Cast off 2 stitches together. Sew the breadths together, and sew the petticoat into a band, and it is finished.

Lady's Cap in Puffed Knitting.—½ oz. of white single Berlin wool, 1 oz. of blue double Berlin wool. Knitting pins No. 11. With the white wool cast on 66 stitches, and knit 4 rows as follows: 1st row—plain. 2nd row—purl. 3rd row—plain. 4th row—purl. Then commence knitting with the blue wool. 1st row—knit 3, * wool over the needle, knit 1, wool over the needle, knit 1, wool twice over the needle, knit 1, wool twice over the needle, knit 1, wool once over the needle, knit 1, wool over the needle, knit 4; repeat from *. 2nd row—the same as the preceding row, letting the wool that was passed round the needle slip off without being knitted, and this will form a series of graduated puffs. 3rd row—the same, but purled instead of knitted. 4th row—same as the second row. The work is continued in alternate colours, 4 rows of white and 4 of blue; do not break off the wool, but carry it on from stripe to stripe. The blue is to be knitted in puffs (as above) throughout the cap, but when you have completed 3 stripes of each colour, the remaining white stripes are to be knitted with decreasings as follows, to bring the cap to shape (it slopes off from the ears, and forms a point at the back of the head): 1st row—knit 5, knit 2 together, continue knitting until you get to the middle of the row, then knit 2 together, and when 7 stitches from the end, knit 2 together, knit 5. 2nd row—purl 5, purl 2 together, purl along to within 7 stitches from the end, then purl 2 together, purl 5. 3rd row—knit 5, knit 2 together, knit to within 7 stitches of the end, then knit 2 together, knit 5 4th row—the same as the second row. When you have knitted 9 stripes of each colour, there will be only 12 stitches left, finish these off with white wool, so as to form a point. 1st row—knit 3, knit 2 together three times, knit 3. 2nd row—purl. 3rd row—knit 2, knit 2 together, knit 1, knit 2 together, knit 2. 4th row—purl. 5th row—knit 1, knit 2 together, knit 1, knit 2 together, knit 1. 6th row—purl. 7th row—knit 2 together, knit 1, pass the first stitch over the second, knit 2 together, pass the first stitch over the last, and fasten off. Add blue-ribbon strings to tie under the chin, and a small bow on the point.

Fanchon.—Pink and white Shetland wool. Knitting pins No. 16 and No. 10. This fanchon is knitted throughout in plain knitting; it covers the head, and has long ends to wind round the neck. Use No. 16 pins for the pink wool, and No. 10 pins for the white wool. Cast on 20 stitches with the pink wool, and knit 6 plain rows. Join on the white wool, and knit 18 plain rows, increasing 1 stitch at the end of every alternate row by picking up the wool that lies under the second stitch from the end and knitting it. All the increasings are to come at the same side of the fanchon, and the two colours are to be repeated in this manner alternately, until there are 9 pink stripes done. Then decreasings are to be made by knitting 2 stitches together at the end of every alternate white row, until there are 20 stitches again as at the commencement. Knit 6 rows with the pink wool and cast off. Make four tassels, and sew two on each end of the fanchon.

Slippers.—These comfortable warm slippers are knitted in looped knitting, having the loops in the inside. To make them, procure 6 oz. of maroon double Berlin wool, a pair of bone knitting needles, No. 9, and a pair of cork soles. Commence across the instep by casting on 27 stitches. Knit the first row plain. 2nd row—insert the needle in the first stitch as if about to knit, put the wool *over* the point of the needle and round the first finger of the left hand *twice*, then wool again over the needle, and knit the stitch in the usual manner, drawing all three threads of wool through, knit the other stitches in the same way. 3rd row—plain knitting. 4th row—looped knitting, the same as directed for the second row, but decrease in the middle of the row by knitting two stitches together. 5th row—plain. Repeat the last two rows till you have only 11 stitches on the needle, and cast off. This is the front of the slipper. Now holding the looped side of the knitting towards you, pick up 12 of the cast-on stitches, knitting each stitch as you pick it up. Knit one row of looped knitting and 1 row of plain knitting alternately, till you have a piece long enough to reach round the heel and to join on to the other side of the front. Next make the frill round the ankle by casting on 4 stitches, and knitting in the same manner a piece sufficient to go round the top of the slipper, sew it on so that the loops come on the outside. Now neatly bind the sole with a piece of narrow ribbon, and sew the work on to it. Finish with a nice bow of satin ribbon on the instep.

American Over-Shoe.—2 oz. of black, 1 oz. of crimson double Berlin wool. Knitting pins No. 8. Cast on 44 stitches with the black wool, and knit in ribbed knitting, 2 stitches plain and 2 stitches purl, for 6 rows. Break off the black wool, and join on crimson, and knit another 6 rows in the same way. Then black again for 40 rows, followed by 6 rows with crimson, and 6 rows with black wool. Cast off. Fold the knitting in half, across the ribs, and sew the seams up as if making a bag. Work as follows with crimson wool for an edging round the top: 1st round—1 double crochet in the centre of a raised rib, * 3 chain, 1 double crochet in the lower part of the double crochet just done, 1 double crochet in the next raised rib; repeat from *. 2nd round—1 double crochet in the indented rib that was missed in the previous round, * 5 chain, 1 double crochet in the 4th from the needle, 1 double crochet in the next indented rib, repeat from *. Run an elastic in the ribbed knitting below the crochet edge. Make a tuft of crimson wool to place upon one of the seams just below the crimson stripe. This is to be the front of the shoe. It will fit over any-sized boot, and is most comfortable to wear when driving or travelling, or may be used as a bedroom slipper.

Respirator.—¼ oz. of dove-grey single Berlin wool. Knitting pins No. 16. Cast on 6 stitches. 1st row—slip 1, knit 1, bring the wool in front of the needle, slip 1, pass the wool back again, knit the next stitch with the wool turned twice round the needle, knit 1 and purl 1 in each of the two remaining stitches. 2nd row —slip 1, knit 1, * bring the wool in front of the needle, slip 1, pass the wool back, knit the next stitch with the wool turned twice round the needle, repeat from *, and knit 1 and purl 1 in each of the 2 remaining stitches. Continue working as for the second row, making additional repeats each time in the middle of the row, until you have 28 stitches on the needle. Then knit straight on for two inches without any increase, and afterwards decrease by knitting 2 together twice at the end of every row until only 6 stitches remain. Cast off. Take two pieces of narrow elastic, each piece eight inches long, and sew on double to each end of the respirator.

Canadian Cloud.—Knitting pins No. 4. ½ lb. of white double Berlin wool, 4 oz. of blue Andalusian. This cloud is worked throughout in plain knitting. With blue wool cast on 66 stitches, and knit 2 rows. Join on white and knit 2 rows. Then 2 rows with blue, 2 rows with white, and so on alternately. Do not break off the wool at every change of colour, but carry it on. When a sufficient length is knitted, cast off after doing 2 blue rows. A cloud should be about 2 yards long, to go twice round the neck and once over the head. One end is to be drawn together and finished off with a large tassel, the other end may be fringed.

Half-square Shawl in plain knitting.—This shawl is easy to make, and is very warm and pretty. Procure ½ lb. of grey and 2 oz. of coloured Scotch fingering. Bone or wooden knitting needles No. 9. Cast on 180 stitches, knit 1 plain row. Afterwards continue all plain knitting, and knit 2 stitches together at the end of every row. Knit 24 rows with grey wool; then 20 rows with coloured; then take the grey again and work on in plain knitting, taking 2 stitches together at the end of every row till all the stitches are worked off. Cast on 180 stitches again, and knit a second half-square the same as above. Join the two pieces together at the back, making the rows of colour meet nicely. Now with coloured wool, work a little crochet edge along the two outer sides of the shawl. 1st row—1 double crochet in the 1st stitch of the knitting, * 2 chain, miss 1 stitch of the knitting, double crochet in the next stitch, and repeat from *. 2nd row—1 double crochet under the 2 chain of last row, 2 chain, and repeat. Cut a quantity of grey wool into 6-inch lengths, and tie in a nice thick fringe round the two sides of the shawl, 5 strands of wool knotted into each loop of 2 chain.

Half-square Shawl in Spotted Knitting.—Andalusian wool or soft German fingering. Pins No. 4. Cast on stitches sufficient for the length of one side of the shawl, any number divisible by 4, and 2 stitches over for the edge. 202 stitches will make a nice medium-sized shawl, and with border will take about 6 oz. of wool. 1st row—knit 2, purl all the rest. 2nd row—purl all but the last 2 stitches, which knit plain. 3rd row—slip 1, knit 1, * make 3 stitches out of the next stitch by first knitting 1, then purling 1, and then knitting 1 (all three of these stitches to be knitted before taking the stitch of the last row off the left-hand needle), next purl 3 stitches together, and repeat from * to the end of the row. No edge stitches at the end. 4th row—purl all but the last 2 stitches, which knit plain. 5th row—is worked in the same manner as the 3rd row, only commence with slip 1, knit 1, * purl 3 together, and then make 3 stitches out of 1 by knitting 1, purling 1 and knitting 1 in the next, and repeat from *, thus reversing the position of the little spots. There will be 4 stitches to purl together at the end of this row, and at the end of *every* fancy row after this, which makes a decrease in the number of stitches, and will presently bring the shawl into a perfect half-square shape. 6th row—purl all but the last 2 stitches, which must be knitted plain. Repeat the 5th and 6th rows until all the stitches are gradually worked off.

Border for Half-square Shawl.—Pins No. 9. Cast on 9 stitches and knit 1 plain row. 1st row—slip 1, knit 1, make 1, knit 2 together, knit 1, make 2, knit 4. 2nd row—slip 1, knit 4, purl 1, knit 5. 3rd row—slip 1, knit 1, make 1, knit 2 together, knit 4, make 1, knit 3. 4th row—slip 1, knit 11. 5th row—slip

1, knit 1, make 1, knit 2 together, knit 1, make 2, knit 7. 6th row, cast off 3, knit 4, purl 1, knit 5. Repeat from the third row. Apportion the border so as to get the same number of scallops on each side the shawl, and it may be continued along the top if desired, but is not necessary.

Cross-Stitch Knitting for a Shawl or Cloud.—White

Cocoon wool. Knitting pins No. 7. Cast on any number of stitches divisible by 6, and 4 extra for edge stitches. 1st row—plain. 2nd row—plain. 3rd row—knit 3, twist the wool 3 times round the pin before knitting each succeeding stitch, and end the row by knitting the last stitch plain without making a twist. 4th row—knit 2, * let the twist slip off the left-hand needle, insert the right-hand needle in the knitted stitch as if about to purl it, and slip it on to the right-hand needle in 1 long loop, slip the next 5 stitches in the same way, and then, with the left-hand needle, lift the 3 first loops over the 3 last loops, and having all 6 in regular order on the left-hand pin, knit them plain one after the other; this forms a cross; repeat from *, and knit 2 at the end of the row. 5th row—plain. 6th row—plain. 7th row—knit 6, twist the wool 3 times round the pin before knitting each succeeding stitch, and end the row by knitting the last 4 stitches plain without making a twist. 8th row—knit 5, proceed as in the 4th row, and knit the last 5 stitches plain. Repeat from the first row for the length required. When the shawl is large enough cast off after doing the 6th row.

Border for Shawl.—Cast on 16 stitches, and knit 1 plain

row. 1st row—slip 1, knit 3, twist the wool 3 times round the pin before knitting each of the six next stitches, knit 1, make 2, knit 2 together, make 2, knit 2 together, knit 1. 2nd row—knit 3, purl 1, knit 2, purl 1, knit 2, let the twist slip off the pin, and knit the 6 stitches as directed in the 4th row of the shawl, knit 2. 3rd row—slip 1, knit 17. 4th row—cast off 2, knit 15. Repeat from the 1st row, and when a sufficient length is done, sew it to the shawl, fulling it in round the corners.

Shawl Knitted with Arrasene. Diamond Pattern.

—The Arrasene wool may be had in white or any colour desired.

Use knitting needles No. 6. Cast on as many stitches as are required for the width of the shawl, allowing 6 stitches for each pattern, and 7 over for edge stitches. Knit 4 plain rows. 5th row—knit 3, * knit 1, knit 2 together, make 1, knit 1, make 1, knit 2 together; repeat from *, and end the row with knit 4. 6th row—plain. 7th row—knit 3, knit 2 together, make 1, knit 3, make 1, slip 1, knit 2 together, pass the slip stitch over; repeat from *, and end the row with make 1, knit 2 together, knit 3. 8th row—plain. 9th row—knit 4, * make 1, knit 2 together, knit 1, knit 2 together, make 1, knit 1 ; repeat from *, and knit the last 3 stitches plain. 10th row—plain. 11th row—knit 5, * make 1, slip 1, knit 2 together, pass the slip stitch over, make 1, knit 3 ; repeat from *, and knit the last 2 stitches plain. 12th row—plain. Repeat from the 5th row until the shawl forms a perfect square. Then knit 4 plain rows. Cast off. Cut some arrasene into lengths of 7 inches for fringe, and knot one piece into every row of the knitting.

Shawl or Scarf. Fan Pattern.—Shetland wool.

Knitting needles No. 9. Cast on stitches sufficient for the width of the shawl, allowing 14 stitches for each pattern, with 1 extra stitch for the beginning. 1st row—purl. 2nd row—plain. 3rd row—purl. 4th row—purl. 5th row—knit 1, * slip 1, knit 1, pass the slip stitch over, knit 4, make 1, knit 1, make 1, knit 4, knit 2 together, knit 1, repeat from *. 6th row—slip 1, * purl 2 together, purl 3, make 1, purl 3, make 1, purl 3, purl 2 together, purl 1, repeat from *. 7th row—knit 1, * slip 1, knit 1, pass the slip stitch over, knit 2, make 1, knit 5, make 1, knit 2, knit 2 together, knit 1 ; repeat from *. 8th row—slip 1, * purl 2 together, purl 1, make 1, purl 7, make 1, purl 1, purl 2 together, purl 1, repeat from * Repeat from the 1st row for the length required, and cast off after doing the 3rd row. The pattern forms in scallops at either end, and if for a scarf the ends may be drawn in and finished off with tassels ; if for a shawl, fringe all round, knotting two threads of wool into every alternate stitch of the knitting.

Shawl or Scarf. Pheasant's Eye Pattern.—Shetland

wool. Knitting needles No. 9. Cast on as many stitches as are required for the width of the shawl, allowing 10 stitches for each pattern, and 10 extra for edge stitches. Knit 10 plain rows. 1st pattern row—knit 5, * knit 1, make 1, knit 2, slip 1, knit 1, pass the slipped stitch over, knit 1. knit 2 together, knit 2, make 1, repeat from *, knit 5 at the end of the row. 2nd row—knit 5, * make 1, purl 2, purl 2 together, purl 1, purl 2 together, purl 2, make 1, purl 1, repeat from *, knit 5 at the end of the row. 3rd row—same as the 1st row. 4th row—same as the 2nd row. 5th row—knit 5, * knit 1, make 1, knit 2, slip 1, knit 1, pass the slipped stitch over, knit 5, repeat from *, knit 5 at the end of the row. 6th row—knit 5, purl to within 5 stitches of the end, and knit those. 7th row—knit 5, * knit 1, knit 2 together, knit 2, make 1, knit 1, make 1, knit 2, slip 1, knit 1, pass the slipped stitch over, repeat from *, knit 5 at the end of the row. 8th row—knit 5, * purl 2 together, purl 2, make 1, purl 1, make 1, purl 2, purl 2 together, purl 1, repeat from *, knit 5 at the end of the row. 9th row—same as the 7th row. 10th row—same as the 8th row. 11th row—knit 5, * knit 5, make 1, knit 3, slip 1, knit 1, pass the slipped stitch over, repeat from *, knit 5 at the end of the row. 12th row—knit 5, purl to within 5 stitches of the end, and knit those. Repeat from the first row till the shawl is long enough, then knit 10 plain rows, and cast off.

Border for Shawl.—Cast on 16 stitches. 1st row—slip 1, knit 2, make 1, knit 2 together, knit 2 together, make 1, knit 1, knit 2 together, make 1, knit 2 together, knit 1, make 1, knit 1, make 2, knit 2 together. The second half of the make 2 is to be dropped in the next row, as it is turned twice simply to make the edge sit easy. 2nd row—make 1, knit 13, make 1, knit 2 together, knit 1. 3rd row—slip 1, knit 2, make 1, knit 2 together, knit 2, knit 2 together, make 1, knit 1, knit 2 together, make 1, knit 1, make 1, knit 2 together, make 2, knit 2 together. 4th row—make 1, knit 14, make 1, knit 2 together, knit 1. 5th row—slip 1, knit 2, make 1, knit 2 together, knit 1, knit 2 together, make 1, knit 1, knit 2 together, make 1, knit 1, make 1, knit 2 together, make 1, knit 2 together, make 2, knit 2 together. 6th row—make 1, knit 15, make 1, knit 2 together, knit 1. 7th row—slip 1, knit 2, make 1, knit 2 together, knit 2 together, make 1, knit 1, knit 2 together, make 1, knit 3, make 1, knit 2 together, make 1, knit 2 together, make 2, knit 2 together. 8th row—knit

16, make 1, knit 2 together, knit 1. 9th row—slip 1, knit 2, make 1, knit 2 together, knit 2, make 1, knit 2 together, knit 1, make 1, slip 1, knit 2 together, pass the slipped stitch over, make 1, knit 2 together, make 1, knit 2 together, make 2, knit 2 together. 10th row—knit 15, make 1, knit 2 together, knit 1. 11th row—slip 1, knit 2, make 1, knit 2 together, knit 3, make 1, knit 2 together, knit 1, make 1, slip 1, knit 2 together, pass the slipped stitch over, make 1, knit 2 together, make 2, knit 2 together. 12th row—knit 14, make 1, knit 2 together, knit 1. 13th row—slip 1, knit 2, make 1, knit 2 together, knit 1, make 1, knit 2 together, knit 1, make 1, knit 2 together, knit 1, make 1, slip 1, knit 2 together, pass the slipped stitch over, make 2, knit 2 together. 14th row—knit 13, make 1, knit 2 together, knit 1. 15th row—slip 1, knit 2, make 1, knit 2 together, knit 2, make 1, knit 2 together, knit 1, make 1, knit 2 together, knit 1, make 2, knit 1, knit 2 together. 16th row—knit 13, make 1, knit 2 together, knit 1. Repeat from the 1st row for the length required, and sew on to the shawl loosely and fulled in at the corners.

Sofa Blanket. Cable Pattern.—Single Berlin wool of any colour preferred. The stripes may be knitted entirely in one colour, or in shades of different colours; if the latter, work 3 rows with each shade. Knitting pins No. 9. Cast on 20 stitches. 1st row—slip 1, make 1, knit 2 together, make 1, knit 2 together, purl 11, make 1, knit 2 together, make 1, knit 2 together. 2nd row—slip 1, make 1, knit 2 together, make 1, knit 2 together, knit 11, make 1, knit 2 together, make 1, knit 2 together. 3rd row—slip 1, make 1, knit 2 together, make 1, knit 2 together, purl 4, turn, and now knit for the cable as follows, on the 4 purled stitches only : * slip 1, knit 3, turn ; slip 1, purl 3, turn ; repeat from * until you have done 10 of these little rows ; then draw the needle out of the 4 stitches, and leaving the cable on the right side of the knitting (the side away from you), take 4 stitches from the left-hand needle on to the right-hand needle, pick up 4 stitches of the cable on the right-hand needle again, and knit off the remaining stitches from the left-hand needle by purling 3, make 1, knit 2 together, make 1, knit 2 together. 4th row—same as the second row. 5th row—same as the first row. 6th row—slip 1, make 1, knit 2 together, make 1, knit 2 together, knit 4, turn, and knit for another cable on the 4 plain stitches only : * slip 1, purl 3, turn ; slip 1, knit 3, turn ; repeat from * until you have done 10 little rows ; then draw the needle out of the 4 stitches, and, leaving the cable again on the right side of the knitting (this time the side next you), take 4 stitches from the left-hand needle on to the right-hand needle, pick up the 4 stitches of the cable, and knit off the remaining stitches from the left-hand needle by knitting 3, make 1, knit 2 together, make 1, knit 2 together. Repeat from the first row for the length required. The stripes may be sewn together, or joined by a row of double crochet.

Couvrepied in Diagonal Squares.—White and blue single Berlin wool. Knitting pins No. 12. With white wool cast on 1 stitch, and knit 2 stitches in it. 2nd row—slip the first stitch, and knit 2 stitches in the second stitch. 3rd row—slip 1, pick up the thread that lies immediately below the second stitch and knit it, and knit the remainder. Continue knitting as directed for the third row, every row the same, until there are 27 stitches on the needle. Then break off the white wool, leaving a long end, and begin with the blue wool, also leaving an end ; these will be used afterwards for sewing up, and will save making a knot. Knit 1 plain row with the blue wool. Next row—slip 1, knit 2 together, knit all the rest plain. Then work on, decreasing in every row by knitting 2 together after the slipped stitch, until there is but 1 stitch left, and fasten off. When a number of squares are ready commence joining them together: take four, and sew all the white sides to meet in a point in the centre ; then four more, with a blue point to meet in the centre ; other squares will be wanted to go at right angles with these, always remembering to join white to white, and blue to blue, so that when finished the work presents the appearance of a stripe of blue and a stripe of white alternating with each small self-coloured square.

Berceaunette Blanket. Double Knitting.—White 4-thread fleecy wool. Knitting pins No. 4. Cast on as many stitches as you require for the width of the blanket, and knit 16 plain rows. Next row—knit 8, knit double knitting, thus : * knit a stitch, putting the needle in the middle of the stitch instead of in the usual way, bring the wool to the front, slip 1, pass the wool to the back ; repeat from * until 8 stitches of the end of the row ; turn, and work double knitting until 8 stitches of the other end ; turn, knit along in double knitting, and knit 8 plain stitches at the end of the row ; then knit 8, knit along in double knitting, and knit 8 plain stitches at the other end. Thus 2 rows are done with 8 stitches left unknitted on each side of the work, and 2 rows are done with all the stitches knitted. Proceed in this manner, remembering always that the stitch that is slipped in one row is to be knitted in the next; and when long enough, finish with 16 rows of plain knitting to match those at the beginning, and cast off. If knitted rightly, the two sides of the double knitting will be quite separate, which makes it very thick and warm.

Square for Quilt. Raised Rib Pattern with Open Work between.—Strutts' 3-thread knitting cotton No. 6. Knitting pins No. 14. Commence with a long end, which will be used afterwards for sewing up. Cast on 1 stitch and knit 1, purl 1, knit 1 in it. 2nd row—slip 1, make 1, knit 1, make 1, knit 1. 3rd row—plain. 4th row—slip 1, make 1, knit 3, make 1, knit 1. 5th row—plain. Continue knitting in this way, making a stitch after the first stitch and before the last stitch in each alternate row, and the remainder plain, until there are 21 stitches on the needle. 22nd row—slip 1, make 1, knit 1, make 1 and knit 2 together nine times, make 1, knit 1. 23rd row—plain. 24th row—slip 1, make 1, knit 1, make 1 and knit 2 together ten times, make 1, knit 1. 25th row—plain. 26th row—slip 1, make 1, purl 23, make 1, knit 1. 27th row—plain. 28th row—slip 1, make 1, knit 25, make 1, knit 1. 29th row—purl. 30th row—slip 1, make 1, knit 27, make 1, knit 1. 31st row—plain. 32nd row—slip 1, make 1, purl 29, make 1, knit 1. 33rd row—plain. 34th row—slip 1, make 1, knit 31, make 1, knit 1. 35th row—purl. There will now be 35 stitches on the needle, and this forms half the square. 36th row—slip 1, knit 2 together, knit 29, knit 2 together, knit 1. 37th row—plain. 38th row—slip 1, purl 2 together, purl 27, purl 2 together, purl 1. 39th row—plain. 40th row—slip 1, knit 2 together, knit 25, knit 2 together, knit 1, 41st row—purl. 42nd row—slip 1, knit 2 together, knit 23, knit 2 together, knit 1.   43rd row—plain.   44th row—slip 1, purl 2 together, purl 21, purl 2 together, purl 1.   45th row—plain.   46th row— slip 1, knit 2 together, make 1 and knit 2 together ten times, knit 2 together.   47th row—plain.   48th row—slip 1, knit 2 together, make 1 and knit 2 together nine times, knit 2 together.   49th row—plain.   50th row—slip 1, knit 2 together, knit 15, knit 2 together, knit 1.   51st row—plain.   Continue knitting as the 2 last rows (only there will be fewer stitches in each row) until you have only 5 stitches left.   Then knit 2 together, knit 1, knit 2 together.   Next row—plain.   Next row—knit the 3 stitches together, and draw the cotton through.   The squares are to be sewn four together, so that the holes along the sides may meet each other, the plain edges being outside, which are to be joined afterwards to the plain edges of other squares. Half squares must be knitted to fit in round the edges of the quilt.

Border and Fringe for Quilt.—To be worked with the same sized cotton and needles as used for the squares. Cast on 7 stitches.   1st row—slip 1, knit 2, make 1, knit 2 together, make 2, knit 2 together.   2nd row—knit 2, purl 1, knit 2, make 1, knit 2 together, knit 1.   3rd row—slip 1, knit 2, make 1, knit 2 together, knit 3.   4th row—knit 5, make 1, knit 2 together, knit 1.   5th row—slip 1, knit 2, make 1, knit 2 together, knit 1, make 2, knit 2 together.   6th row—knit 2, purl 1, knit 3, make 1, knit 2 together, knit 1.   7th row—slip 1, knit 2, make 1, knit 2 together, knit 4.   8th row—knit 6, make 1, knit 2 together, knit 1.   9th row—slip 1, knit 2, make 1, knit 2 together, make 2, knit 2 together, make 2, knit 2 together.   10th row—knit 2, purl 1, knit 2 together, purl 1, make 1, knit 2 together, knit 1.   11th row—slip 1, knit 2, make 1, knit 2 together, knit 5.   12th row— knit 3, knit 2 together, knit 2, make 1, knit 2 together, knit 1. 13th row—slip 1, knit 2, make 1, knit 2 together, knit 2 together make 2, knit 2 together.   14th row—knit 2, purl 1, knit 2 together, knit 1, make 1, knit 2 together, knit 1.   15th row— slip 1, knit 2, make 1, knit 2 together, knit 3.   16th row—knit 2 knit 2 together, knit 1, make 1, knit 2 together, knit 1.   Repeat from the first row for the length required.   For fringe—cut a skein of cotton into lengths of seven inches, and knot 4 strands into every hole along the scalloped edge of the knitting.

Square for Quilt. Mouse Pattern.—Strutts' 3-thread knitting cotton No. 6. Knitting pins No. 14. Commence with a long end, casting on 1 stitch. 1st row—make 1, knit 1. 2nd row—make 1, knit 2. 3rd row—make 1, knit 1, make 1, knit 1, make 1, knit 1. 4th row—make 1, knit 1, purl 3, knit 2. 5th row—make 1, knit 2, make 1, knit 3, make 1, knit 2. 6th row—make 1, knit 2, purl 5, knit 3. 7th row—make 1, knit 3, make 1, knit 5, make 1, knit 3. 8th row—make 1, knit 3, purl 7, knit 4. 9th row—make 1, knit 4, make 1, knit 7, make 1, knit 4. 10th row—make 1, knit 4, purl 9, knit 5. 11th row—make 1, knit 5, make 1, knit 9, make 1, knit 5. 12th row—make 1, knit 5, purl 11, knit 6. 13th row—make 1, knit 6, make 1, knit 11, make 1, knit 6. 14th row—make 1, knit 6, purl 13, knit 7. 15th row—make 1, knit 7, make 1, knit 13, make 1, knit 7. 16th row—make 1, knit 7, purl 15, knit 8. 17th row—make 1, knit plain to the end. 18th row—make 1, knit 8, purl 15, knit 9. 19th row—make 1, knit 9, slip 1, knit 1, pass the slip stitch over, knit 11, knit 2 together, knit 9. 20th row—make 1, knit 9, purl 13, knit 10. 21st row—make 1, knit 10, slip 1, knit 1, pass the slip stitch over, knit 9, knit 2 together, knit 10. 22nd row—make 1, knit 10, purl 11, knit 11. 23rd row—make 1, knit 11, slip 1, knit 1, pass the slip stitch over, knit 7, knit 2 together, knit 11. 24th row—make 1, knit 11, purl 9, knit 12. 25th row—make 1, knit 12, slip 1, knit 1, pass the slip stitch over, knit 5, knit 2 together, knit 12. 26th row—make 1, knit 12, purl 7, knit 13. 27th row—make 1, knit 13, slip 1, knit 1, pass the slip stitch over, knit 3, knit 2 together, knit 13. 28th row—make 1, knit 13, purl 5, knit 14. 29th row—make 1, knit 14, slip 1, knit 1, pass the slip stitch over, knit 1, knit 2 together, knit 14. 30th row—make 1, knit 14, purl 3, knit 15. 31st row—make 1, knit 15, slip 1, knit 2 together, pass the slip stitch over, knit 15. 32nd row—make 1, knit plain to the end. 33rd row—purl. 34th row—plain. 35th row—knit 2 together, knit plain to the end. 36th row—purl 2 together, purl to the end. 37th row—knit 2 together, knit plain to the end. Repeat from the 35th row till the work is reduced to 3 stitches, then slip 1, knit 2 together, pass the slip stitch over, and draw the cotton through, breaking off with a long end. The squares are to be sewn four together, making the raised pieces meet in the centre, and joining by the made stitches so as to give an appearance of two rows of holes.

Square for Quilt. Foxglove Pattern.—Knitting pins No. 14. Strutts' 3-thread knitting cotton No 6. Or, if wool be preferred, use two colours and knit to the end of the 30th row with one colour, then commence the 31st row and knit to the end of the pattern with the other colour. Cast on 1 stitch, and knit 1, purl 1, knit 1, in it. 1st row—make 1, knit 1, make 1, knit 1, make 1, knit 1. 2nd row—make 1, knit 1, purl 3, knit 2. 3rd row—make 1, knit 3, make 1, knit 1, make 1, knit 3. 4th row—make 1, knit 2, purl 5, knit 3. 5th row—make 1, knit 5, make 1, knit 1, make 1, knit 5. 6th row—make 1, knit 3, purl 7, knit 4. 7th row—make 1, knit 7, make 1, knit 1, make 1, knit 7. 8th row—make 1, knit 4, purl 9, knit 5. 9th row—make 1, knit 9, make 1, knit 1, make 1, knit 9. 10th row—make 1, knit 5, purl 11, knit 6. 11th row—make 1, knit 11, make 1, knit 1, make 1, knit 11. 12th row—make 1, knit 6, purl 13, knit 7. 13th row—make 1, knit 13, make 1, knit 1, make 1, knit 13. 14th row—make 1, knit 7, purl 15, knit 8. 15th row—make 1, knit 8, knit 2 together, knit 11, slip 1, knit 1, pass the slipped stitch over, knit 8. 16th row—make 1, knit 8, purl 13, knit 9. 17th row—make 1, knit 9, knit 2 together, knit 9, slip 1, knit 1, pass the slipped stitch over, knit 9. 18th row—make 1, knit 9, purl 11, knit 10. 19th row—make 1, knit 10, knit 2 together, knit 7, slip 1, knit 1, pass the slipped stitch over, knit 10. 20th row—make 1, knit 10, purl 9, knit 11. 21st row—make 1, knit 11, knit 2 together, knit 5, slip 1, knit 1, pass the slipped stitch over, knit 11. 22nd row—make 1, knit 11, purl 7, knit 12. 23rd row—make 1, knit 12, knit 2 together, knit 3, slip 1, knit 1, pass the slipped stitch over, knit 12. 24th row—make 1, knit 12, purl 5, knit 13. 25th row—make 1, knit 13, knit 2 together, knit 1, slip 1, knit 1, pass the slipped stitch over, knit 13. 26th row—make 1, knit 13, purl 3, knit 14. 27th row—make 1, knit 14, slip 1, knit 2 together, pass the slipped stitch over, knit 14. 28th row—make 1, knit 14, purl 1, knit 15. 29th row—make 1, knit 31. 30th row—make 1, knit 1, purl 31. 31st row—make 1, knit 2, make 1, and knit 2 together fifteen times, knit 1. 32nd row—make 1, knit 1, purl 33. 33rd row—make 1, knit 35. 34th row—make 1, knit 1, purl 35. 35th row—make 1, knit 1, purl 1, purl 2 together, * cast on 6 for a foxglove, purl 4, purl 2 together, repeat from * four times, cast on 6, purl 3. 36th row—make 1, knit 3, * purl 6, knit 5, repeat from * four times, purl 6, knit 4. 37th

Practical Recipes.—Knitting.

row—make 1, knit 1, purl 3, * knit 2 together, knit 2, slip 1, knit 1, pass the slipped stitch over, purl 5, repeat from * four times, knit 2 together, knit 2, slip 1, knit 1, pass the slipped stitch over, purl 4. 38th row—make 1, knit 4 * purl 4, knit 5, repeat from * 5 times. 39th row—make 1, knit 1, purl 4 * knit 2 together, slip 1, knit 1, pass the slipped stitch over, purl 5, repeat from * five times. 40th row—make 1, knit 5, * purl 2, knit 5, repeat from * four times, purl 2, knit 6. 41st row—make 1, knit 1, purl 5 * knit 2 together, purl 5, repeat from * four times, knit 2 together, purl 6. 42nd row—make 1, knit 6, * purl 1, knit 5, repeat from * four times, purl 1, knit 7. 43rd row—make 1, knit 1, purl 2, purl 2 together, * cast on 6 for a foxglove, purl 4, purl 2 together, repeat from * five times, cast on 6, purl 4. 44th row—make 1, knit 4, * purl 6, knit 5, repeat from * six times. 45th row—make 1, knit 1, purl 4, * knit 2 together, knit 2, slip 1, knit 1, pass the slipped stitch over, purl 5, repeat from * six times. 46th row—make 1, knit 5, * purl 4, knit 5, repeat from * five times, purl 4, knit 6. 47th row—make 1, knit 1, purl 5, * knit 2 together, slip 1, knit 1, pass the slipped stitch over, purl 5, repeat from * five times, knit 2 together, slip 1, knit 1, pass the slipped stitch over, purl 6. 48th row—make 1, knit 6, * purl 2, knit 5, repeat from * five times, purl 2, knit 7. 49th row—make 1, knit 1, purl 6, * knit 2 together, purl 5, repeat from * five times, knit 2 together, purl 7. 50th row—make 1, knit 7, * purl 1, knit 5, repeat from * five times, purl 1, knit 8. 51st row—make 1, knit 1, purl 3, purl 2 together, * cast on 6 for a foxglove, purl 4, purl 2 together, repeat from * six times, cast on 6, purl 5. 52nd row—make 1, knit 5, * purl 6, knit 5, repeat from * six times, purl 6, knit 6. 53rd row—make 1, knit 1, purl 5, * knit 2 together, knit 2, slip 1, knit 1, pass the slipped stitch over, purl 5, repeat from * six times, knit 2 together, knit 2, slip 1, knit 1, pass the slipped stitch over, purl 6. 54th row—make 1, knit 6, * purl 4, knit 5, repeat from * six times, purl 4, knit 7. 55th row—make 1, knit 1, purl 6, * knit 2 together, slip 1, knit 1, pass the slipped stitch over, purl 5, repeat from * six times, knit 2 together, slip 1, knit 1, pass the slipped stitch over, purl 7. 56th row—make 1, knit 7, * purl 2, knit 5, repeat from * six times, purl 2, knit 8. 57th row—make 1, knit 1, purl 7, * knit 2 together, purl 5, repeat from * six times, knit 2 together, purl 8. 58th row—make 1, knit 8, * purl 1, knit 5, repeat from * six times, purl 1, knit 9. 59th row— Cast off. When you have four of these sections knitted, sew them together, making the four raised leaves meet in the centre, and joining by the made stitches so as to give the appearance of two rows of holes between the sections.

Fluted Border for Quilt.—To be worked with the same-sized cotton and needles as used for the squares. Cast on 40 stitches. 1st row—slip 1, knit 3, make 1, knit 2 together, knit 2, make 1, knit 2 together, knit 2, make 1, knit 2 together, knit 25, knit 1, taking the stitch from the back. 2nd row—slip 1, purl 22, and turn, leaving 17 stitches unknitted on the pin. 3rd row—slip 1, knit 21, knit 1, taking the stitch from the back. 4th row—slip 1, purl 22, knit 4, make 2, purl 2 together, purl 2, pass the cotton over the needle, knit 2 together, knit 2, make 2, purl 2 together, purl 3. Repeat these 4 rows twice. 13th row—slip 1, knit 3, make 1, knit 2 together, knit 2, make 1, knit 2 together, knit 2, make 1, knit 2 together, knit 3, purl 23. 14th row—slip 1, knit 22, and turn, leaving 17 stitches unknitted on the pin. 15th row—slip 1, purl 22. 16th row—slip 1, knit 26, make 2, purl 2 together, purl 2, pass the cotton over the needle, knit 2 together, knit 2, make 2, purl 2 together, purl 3. Repeat these 4 rows twice. Commence again at the first row, and work for the length required.

Window Curtains. Ivy-leaf Pattern.—Strutts' 3-thread knitting cotton No. 10. Long wooden knitting needles No. 6. Cast on sufficient stitches for the width of the curtain, 30 stitches being required for each pattern, 210 stitches make a nice width, allowing 9 extra for edge stitches. Knit 10 plain rows. 1st pattern row—knit 5, * make 1, knit 2 together, make 1, knit 1, make 1, knit 2 together, knit 1, make 1, slip 1, knit 2 together, pass the slip stitch over, make 1, knit 2, knit 2 together, make 1, slip 1, knit 2 together, pass the slip stitch over, make 1, knit 2 together, knit 2, make 1, slip 1, knit 2 together, pass the slip stitch over, make 1, knit 1, knit 2 together, make 1, knit 1, make 1, knit 2 together, make 1, knit 1, repeat from *, knit 4 at the end of the row. 2nd row—plain. 3rd row—knit 5, * make 1, knit 2 together, make 1, knit 3, make 1, knit 2 together, knit 4, knit 2 together, make 1, slip 1, knit 2 together, pass the slip stitch over, make 1, knit 2 together, knit 4, knit 2 together, make 1, knit 3, make 1, knit 2 together, make 1, knit 1, repeat from *, knit 4 at the end of the row. 4th row—plain. 5th row—knit 5, * make 1, knit 2 together, make 1, knit 5, make 1, knit 2 together, knit 2, knit 2 together, make 1, slip 1, knit 2 together, pass the slip stitch over, make 1, knit 2 together, knit 2, knit 2 together, make 1, knit 5, make 1, knit 2 together, make 1, knit 1, repeat from *, knit 4 at the end of the row. 6th row—plain. 7th row—knit 5, * make 1, knit 2 together, make 1, knit 1, make 1, knit 1, slip 1, knit 2 together, pass the slip stitch over, knit 1, make 1, knit 1, make 1, knit 2 together, knit 2 together, make 1, slip 1, knit 2 together, pass the slip stitch over, make 1, knit 2 together, knit 2 together, make 1, knit 1, make 1, knit 1, slip 1, knit 2 together, pass the slip stitch over, knit 1, make 1, knit 1, make 1, knit 2 together, make 1, knit 1, repeat from *, knit 4 at the end of the row. 8th row—plain. 9th row—knit 5,* make 1, knit 2 together, make 1, knit 3, make 1, slip 1, knit 2 together, pass the slip stitch over, make 1, knit 3, make 1, knit 2 together, slip 1, knit 2 together, pass the slip stitch over, knit 2 together, make 1, knit 3, make 1, slip 1, knit 2 together, pass the slip stitch over, make 1, knit 3, make 1, knit 2 together, make 1, knit 1, repeat from *, knit 4 at the end of the row. 10th row—plain. Repeat from the first row for the length required. Finish by knitting 10 plain rows, and cast off. These curtains are both sides alike; if it is desired to make a right and a wrong side, purl each alternate row, only knitting plain stitches at the beginning and at the end.

Lace Border for Curtains.—This should be knitted row by row with the curtain, making allowance for it by casting 18 additional stitches on each side, and commencing the border at the end of the first pattern row, of course knitting the previous rows plain the same as the curtain; or it may be knitted separately and sewn on. Having 18 stitches on the needle, work as follows : 1st row—knit 3, make 1, knit 2 together, knit 1, make 1, knit 2 together, make 1, knit 2 together, knit 1, make 1, knit 2 together, make 1, knit 2 together, make 2, knit 2 together, knit 1. 2nd row—knit 3, purl 1, knit 9, make 1, knit 2 together, knit 1, make 1, knit 2 together, knit 1. 3rd row—knit 3, make 1, knit 2 together, knit 1, make 1, knit 2 together, make 1, knit 2 together, knit 2, make 1, knit 2 together, make 1, knit 2 together, make 2, knit 2 together, knit 1. 4th row—knit 3, purl 1, knit 10, make 1, knit 2 together, knit 1, make 1, knit 2 together, knit 1. 5th row—knit 3, make 1, knit 2 together, knit 1, make 1, knit 2 together, make 1, knit 2 together, knit 3, make 1, knit 2 together, make 1, knit 2 together, make 2, knit 2 together, knit 1. 6th row—knit 3, purl 1, knit 11, make 1, knit 2 together, knit 1, make 1, knit 2 together, knit 1. 7th row—knit 3, make 1, knit 2 together, knit 1, make 1, knit 2 together, make 1, knit 2 together, knit 4, make 1, knit 2 together, make 1, knit 2 together, make 2, knit 2 together, knit 1. 8th row—knit 3, purl 1, knit 12, make 1, knit 2 together, knit 1, make 1, knit 2 together, knit 1. 9th row—knit 3, make 1, knit 2 together, knit 1, make 1, knit 2 together, make 1, knit 2 together, knit 5, make 1, knit 2 together, make 1, knit 2 together, make 2, knit 2 together, knit 1. 10th row—knit 3, purl 1, knit 13, make 1, knit 2 together, knit 1, make 1, knit 2 together, knit 1. 11th row—knit 3, make 1, knit 2 together, knit 1, make 1, knit 2 together, make 1, knit 2 together, knit 6, make 1, knit 2 together, make 1, knit 2 together, make 2, knit 2 together, knit 1. 12th row—knit 3, purl 1, knit 14, make 1, knit 2 together, knit 1, make 1, knit 2 together, knit 1. 13th row—knit 3, make 1, knit 2 together, knit 1, make 1, knit 2 together, make 1, knit 2 together, make 1, knit 2 together, knit 7, make 1, knit 2 together, make 1, knit 2 together, make 2, knit 2 together, knit 1. 14th row—knit 3, purl 1, knit 15, make 1, knit 2 together, knit 1, make 1, knit 2 together, knit 1. 15th row—knit 3, make 1, knit 2 together, knit 1, make 1, knit 2 together, make 1, knit 2 together, knit 15. 16th row—cast off 7, knit 11, make 1, knit 2 together, knit 1, make 1, knit 2 together, knit 1. Repeat from the first row.

Antimacassar. Double Rose-leaf Pattern.—To be knitted in stripes of two colours. Single Berlin wool, maroon and blue, and a small quantity of black and white for joining the stripes together. Knitting needles No. 10. With maroon wool, cast on 25 stitches, and knit 1 plain row. 1st pattern row—knit 4, make 1, knit 2 together, make 1, knit 1, make 1, knit 2 together, purl 1, knit 2 together, purl 1, slip 1, knit 1, pass the slip stitch over, purl 1, slip 1, knit 1, pass the slip stitch over, make 1, knit 1, make 1, slip 1, knit 1, pass the slip stitch over, make 1, knit 4. 2nd row—knit 3, purl 7, knit 1, purl 1, knit 1, purl 1, knit 1, purl 7, knit 3. 3rd row—knit 4, make 1, knit 2 together, make 1, knit 3, make 1, knit 3 together, purl 1, slip 1, knit 2 together, pass the slip stitch over, make 1, knit 3, make 1, slip 1, knit 1, pass the slip stitch over, make 1, knit 4. 4th row—knit 3, purl 9, knit 1, purl 9, knit 3. 5th row—knit 4, make 1, knit 2 together, make 1, knit 5, make 1, slip 1, knit 2 together, pass the slip stitch over, make 1, knit 5, make 1, slip 1, knit 1, pass the slip stitch over, make 1, knit 4. 6th row—knit 3, purl 21, knit 3. 7th row—knit 4, make 1, knit 2 together, make 1, knit 1, knit 2 together, purl 1, knit 2 together, knit 3, knit 2 together, purl 1, slip 1, knit 1, pass the slip stitch over, knit 1, make 1, slip 1, knit 1, pass the slip stitch over, make 1, knit 4. 8th row—knit 3, purl 6, knit 1, purl 5, knit 1, purl 6, knit 3. Repeat from the first pattern row for the length required for the antimacassar, then knit 1 plain row, and cast off. Knit 3 stripes with maroon wool and 2 stripes with blue. With black wool work a row of double crochet along each side of the stripes, doing one stitch on the edge of the work and the next stitch deeper down, so that the deep stitch is twice as long as the other, which gives a pretty finish to the stripe. Join the stripes together with a row of double crochet with white wool. Finish off the top and the bottom of the antimacassar with a fringe of wool, knotting 2 threads into every alternate stitch of the knitting.

Antimacassar. Wrinkled Shell Pattern.—To be knitted in stripes. Single Berlin wool, crimson and fawn colour, and black and white for joining the stripes together. Knitting needles No. 10. With crimson wool cast on 25 stitches, and knit 3 plain rows and 1 purl row. 1st pattern row—slip 1, knit 1, knit 2 together, make 1, slip 1, knit 2, pass the slip stitch over the two knitted ones, make 1, knit 3, make 1 and knit 1 six times, knit 2, make 1, slip 1, knit 2, pass the slip stitch over the two knitted ones, make 1, knit 2 together, knit 2. 2nd row—slip 1, knit 2, purl 4, knit 2, purl 13, knit 2, purl 4, knit 3. 3rd row—slip 1, knit 1, knit 2 together, make 1, slip 1, knit 2, pass the slip stitch over, make 1, knit 2, slip 1, knit 1, pass the slip stitch over, knit 9, knit 2 together, knit 2, make 1, slip 1, knit 2, pass the slip stitch over, make 1, knit 2 together, knit 2, make 1, slip 1, knit 2, pass the slip stitch over, make 1, knit 2 together, knit 2. 4th row—slip 1, knit

2, purl 4, knit 2, purl 2 together, purl 7, purl 2 together backwards, knit 2, purl 4, knit 3. 5th row—slip 1, knit 1, knit 2 together, make 1, slip 1, knit 2, pass the slip stitch over, make 1, knit 2, slip 1, knit 1, pass the slip stitch over, knit 5, knit 2 together, knit 2, make 1, slip 1, knit 2, pass the slip stitch over, make 1, knit 2 together, knit 2. 6th row—slip 1, knit 2, purl 4, knit 2, purl 1, knit 5, purl 1, knit 2, purl 4, knit 3. Repeat from the first pattern row for the length required, knit 3 plain rows, and cast off. Knit 2 more stripes with crimson wool and 2 stripes with fawn colour. Along each side of the stripes, with black wool, * work 1 double crochet into a stitch at the edge of the knitting, and 3 half-treble stitches, taken lower down, into the next stitch of the knitting, the half-treble stitches being caught together at the top, repeat from *. Join the stripes with a row of double crochet with white wool. Finish off the antimacassar with a fringe at the top and bottom, knotting 2 threads of wool into every alternate stitch of the knitting.

Bed Rest for an Invalid.—Strutts' 3-thread knitting cotton No. 4. Knitting Needles No. 8. Cast on 36 stitches, and knit 80 rows all in plain knitting; then increase by picking up and knitting the thread that lies directly under the third stitch at the beginning of each row, until you have 120 stitches on the pin; knit 160 rows straight on without any more increasings; and then decrease by knitting 2 stitches together one stitch before the end one in each row until 36 stitches remain; knit 80 rows and cast off. Sew the cast-off end to the commencement.

Teapot Holder.—Single Berlin wool of two colours, blue and black. Knitting pins No. 16. Cast on 76 stitches with the black wool, and knit 1 plain row. The pattern consists of plain knitting only, having 10 stitches in black on each side to form a border, and the centre is in alternate squares of blue and black. The wool is not to be broken off when changing the colour, but is drawn in rather tightly on the wrong side; and when the holder is finished it looks like a series of square puffs set in a black band. 1st row—knit 10 stitches with the black wool, 8 with blue, 8 black, 8 blue, 8 black, 8 blue, 8 black, 8 blue, and end with 10 black. Knit 7 more rows the same as this. 9th row—

knit 18 stitches with the black wool, 8 with blue, 8 black, 8 blue, 8 black, 8 blue, and 18 at the end with black. Knit 7 more rows the same as this. Then repeat from the first row. When you have done 80 rows, or 10 squares, knit 1 plain row with black, and cast off. Fold the holder in the middle, and sew up the ends as far as the black band (which should be left open), drawing them in as tightly as they will go, and place a little blue bow at each side over the join. The holder can be knitted in other colours if preferred, as scarlet and white, or blue and white, but remember to make the border of the darker shade of colour, not white.

A warm thick Rug.—Schulze's Oriental wool and cotton. Knitting needles No. 13. Cut the various colours of Oriental wool required for the pattern in short pieces about two inches in length. Then with cotton cast on 21 or more stitches, and knit as follows:— 1st row—plain. 2nd row—slip 1, * put a piece of wool between the two needles and knit a stitch, turn one end of the wool back, so that both ends come on the same side (away from you), knit 1, repeat from *. Repeat these two rows for the required length; make as many stripes as are required, and afterwards sew them together. Set patterns for this knitting are procurable at any fancy repository; if these seem too intricate, it looks well to use all black wool for the outside bordering of the rug, next to that a narrow stripe of red, and the centre part of mixed colours. By using string instead of cotton, and pieces of cloth instead of wool, a very strong useful hearthrug can be made.

Long Purse.—Crimson purse silk and gold beads. Knitting pins No. 18. Thread the beads on the silk before commencing. Cast on 72 stitches. 1st row—pass down 2 beads, * make 1, knit 2 together, make 1, knit 2 together, pass down 2 beads, and repeat from *. 2nd row—plain knitting, and keep the beads all on the same side of the work. 3rd row—make 1, knit 2 together, pass down 2 beads, * make 1, knit 2 together, pass down 2 beads, repeat from *, and end the row with make 1, knit 2 together. 4th row—same as the second row. Repeat from the first row until you have done nearly three inches, then knit a similar length without beads, then again with beads the same as at the beginning. Sew up the edges together, leaving a third part open in the centre, draw up both ends, and add gilt tassels, and slip on gilt rings. The Vandyke pattern given for beaded cuffs is very pretty for a purse, casting on about 110 stitches, and knitting lengthways, doing the middle of the purse all in plain knitting, and working the end of each beaded row to correspond with the beginning.

Brioche Mats.—These are usually made of two colours, the circumference being divided into twelve divisions of colour. The first 4 stitches make the fringed border, which is done by passing the wool three times round the two first fingers of the left hand and knitting it in. Next to the border you always knit 1 stitch plain, the remainder is in brioche. Pink and white double Berlin wool, or arrasene, 1 oz. of each colour. Knitting pins No. 9. With pink wool cast on 17 stitches. 1st row—knit 4 border stitches with the wool wound three times round the fingers, knit 1, make 1, slip 1, inserting the needle as if about to purl, knit 2 together four times. 2nd row—make 1, slip 1, knit 2 together four times, knit 5. 3rd row—knit 4 border stitches, knit 1, make 1, slip 1, knit 2 together three times, leaving 3 on the left-hand pin unknitted. 4th row—make 1, slip 1, knit 2 together three times, knit 5. 5th row—knit 4 border stitches, knit 1, make 1, slip 1, knit 2 together twice, leaving 6 on the left-hand pin unknitted. 6th row—make 1, slip 1, knit 2 together twice, knit 5. 7th row—knit 4 border stitches, knit 1, make 1, slip 1, knit 2 together, leaving 9 on the left-hand pin unknitted. 8th row—make 1, slip 1, knit 2 together, knit 5. Break off the blue wool and join on the white, and repeat these 8 rows. Then continue the work until you have 6 sections of blue and 6 of white. Cast off, and sew the casting off to the commencement, drawing the centre in closely.

Moss for Mats.—Single Berlin wool in shades of green. Knitting pins No. 10. Cast on 40 stitches, and do a piece of plain knitting, 10 or 12 rows of each shade from dark to light and to dark again. Having knitted the required length cast it off. Wet it in warm water in which a little sugar has been melted, bake it and iron it; then cut through the middle, and unravel all but the three edge stitches. Four or six pieces of this moss knitting round a wool-worked centre will make a very pretty drawing-room mat, particularly if a few wool flowers are introduced in it.

Knitted Ball.—1 oz. of black, 1 oz. of amber single Berlin wool. Knitting pins No. 14. The ball is composed of 12 sections of Brioche knitting. Cast on 16 stitches with the black wool. 1st row—make 1, slip 1, putting the needle in as if about to purl, knit 1, and repeat to the end. 2nd row—make 1, slip 1, knit the next stitch and the thread that lies over it together; repeat six times, and leave 3 stitches unknitted. 3rd row—the same, leaving 3 stitches unworked at the other end of the knitting. Turn and work as before, until you have only 2 ribs left to knit upon in the centre, knit these 2 ribs, turn, and knit all the stitches off, and then knit two whole rows of all the stitches. Join on the amber wool, knit 2 whole rows with it, and then repeat from the second row. When you have worked the twelve sections, cast off the stitches, and sew together along the ribs, drawing in at one end, and for the present leaving the other end open. Find a ball that will fit into the knitting, or stuff it with wadding, then draw it up securely, and work a few fancy stitches on each end to imitate the little brown tufts of an orange.

Lace Edging for Underlinen.—Evans' crochet cotton No. 20. Knitting needles No. 20. Cast on 13 stitches. 1st row—slip 1, knit 2, make 1, knit 2 together, knit 1, knit 2 together, make 1, knit 5. 2nd row—knit 6, make 1, knit 2 together, knit 2, make 1, knit 2 together, knit 1. 3rd row—slip 1, knit 2, make 1, slip 1, knit 2 together, pass the slip stitch over, make 1, knit 5, make 2, knit 2 together. 4th row—make 1, knit 2, purl 1, knit 3, knit 2 together, make 1, knit 3, make 1, knit 2 together, knit 1. 5th row—slip 1, knit 2, make 1, knit 2 together, knit 2, make 1, knit 2 together, knit 2, make 2, knit 2 together, make 2, knit 2 together. 6th row—knit 2, purl 1, knit 2, purl 1, knit 1, knit 2 together, make 1, knit 5, make 1, knit 2 together, knit 1. 7th row—slip 1, knit 2, make 1, knit 2 together, knit 4, make 1, knit 2 together, knit 6. 8th row—cast off 4, knit 3, make 1, knit 2 together, knit 4, make 1, knit 2 together, knit 1. Repeat from the first row.

Narrow Lace Edging.—Evans' crochet cotton No. 24. Knitting needles No. 22. Cast on 16 stitches. 1st row—slip 1 knit 2, make 1, knit 2 together, knit 1, make 2, knit 2 together, make 1, and knit 2 together four times. 2nd row—make 1, knit 10, purl 1, knit 3, make 1, knit 2 together, knit 1. 3rd row—slip 1, knit 2, make 1, knit 2 together, knit 1, make 2, knit 2 together, make 1 and knit 2 together, five times. 4th row—cast off 3, knit 8, purl 1, knit 3, make 1, knit 2 together, knit 1. Repeat from the first row.

Lace Border.—Cast on 19 stitches. 1st row—slip 1, knit 2, make 1, knit 2 together, knit 1, make 2, and knit 2 together six times, knit 1. 2nd row—slip 1, knit 2, purl 1, and knit 2 five times, purl 1, knit 3, make 1, knit 2 together, knit 1. 3rd row—slip 1, knit 2, make 1, knit 2 together, knit 20. 4th row—cast off 6, knit 15, make 1, knit 2 together, knit 1. Repeat from the first row.

Lace Border.—Cast on 16 stitches. 1st row—slip 1, knit 3, make 1, knit 2 together, knit 1, make 2, knit 2 together, make 2, knit 2 together, knit 5. 2nd row—knit 7, purl 1, knit 2, purl 1, knit 3, make 1, knit 2 together, knit 2. 3rd row—slip 1, knit 3, make 1, knit 2 together, knit 12. 4th row—knit 14, make 1, knit 2 together, knit 2. 5th row—slip 1, knit 3, make 1, knit 2 together, knit 1, make 2, knit 2 together, make 2, knit 2 together, make 2, knit 2 together, knit 5. 6th row—knit 7, purl 1, knit 2, purl 1, knit 2, purl 1, knit 3, make 1, knit 2 together, knit 2. 7th row—slip 1, knit 3, make 1, knit 2 together, knit 15. 8th row—cast off 5, knit 11, make 1, knit 2 together, knit 2. Repeat from the first row.

Fuchsia Edging.—Cast on 17 stitches. 1st row—slip 1, knit 2, make 1, knit 2 together, knit 1, make 1, knit 1, make 1, knit 1, make 1, knit 4, make 2, knit 2 together, make 2, knit 2 together, knit 1. 2nd row—knit 3, purl 1, knit 2, purl 1, knit 12, make 1, knit 2 together, knit 1. 3rd row—slip 1, knit 2, make 1, knit 2 together, knit 2 together, make 1, knit 2, make 1, knit 1, make 1, slip 1, knit 2 together, pass the slipped stitch over, knit 9. 4th row—knit 19, make 1, knit 2 together, knit 1. 5th row—slip

1, knit 2, make 1, knit 2 together, knit 2 together, make 1, knit 3, make 1, knit 1, make 1, slip 1, knit 2 together, pass the slipped stitch over, knit 3, make 2, knit 2 together, make 2, knit 2 together, knit 1. 6th row—knit 3, purl 1, knit 2, purl 1, knit 14, make 1, knit 2 together, knit 1. 7th row—slip 1, knit 2, make 1, knit 2 together, knit 2 together, make 1, knit 4, make 1, knit 1, make 1, slip 1, knit 2 together, pass the slipped stitch over, knit 9. 8th row—cast off 7, knit 13, make 1, knit 2 together, knit 1. Repeat from the first row.

Lilac Edging.—Cast on 15 stitches. 1st row—slip 1, knit 1, make 1, knit 2 together, make 1, knit 2 together, make 1, knit 2 together, knit 1, make 1, knit 1, make 1, knit 1, knit 2 together, make 2, knit 2 together. 2nd row—knit 2, purl to the end. 3rd row—slip 1, knit 1, make 1, knit 2 together, make 1, knit 2 together, make 1, knit 2 together, knit 1, make 1, knit 2, make 1, knit 1, knit 2 together, make 2, knit 2 together, knit 1. 4th row—knit 3, purl to the end. 5th row—slip 1, knit 1, make 1, knit 2 together, make 1, knit 2 together, make 1, knit 2 together, knit 1, make 1, knit 3, make 1, knit 1, knit 2 together, make 2, knit 2 together, make 2, knit 2 together. 6th row—knit 2, purl 1, knit 2, purl to the end. 7th row—slip 1, knit 1, make 1, knit 1, make 1, knit 2 together, make 1, knit 2 together, make 1, knit 2 together, knit 1, slip 1, knit 2 together, pass the slipped stitch over, make 1, knit 2 together, knit 7. 8th row—cast off 6, purl 14. Repeat from the first row.

PRACTICAL RECIPES

FOR

MAKING USEFUL AND ORNAMENTAL ARTICLES.

CROCHET.

Baby's Long Crochet Boots.—Cardinal and white single Berlin wool, 1 oz. of each. Fine bone crochet needle. Commence at the heel, with white wool, with 22 chain, miss the first of the chain stitches and work 21 double crochet; 1 chain to turn and work 21 double crochet again, taking up the small loop at the back of the stitches, as the work is to set in ribs. Work 16 rows of double crochet. At the end of the sixteenth row work 10 chain for the instep, join across to the opposite side of the work, and now proceed with the toe in rounds. 1st round—double crochet in every stitch, making 21 double crochet on the work already done, and 10 double crochet on the chain stitches; 31 double crochet in all. 2nd round—18 consecutive double crochet, work 1 double crochet on next *two* double crochet of preceding round, 9 double crochet, 1 double crochet on next *two* double crochet of preceding round. 3rd round—plain. 4th round—18 consecutive double crochet, 1 double crochet on next two of last round, 7 double crochet, 1 double crochet on next two of preceding round. 5th round—plain. 6th round—18 consecutive double crochet, 1 double crochet on next two of last round, 5 double crochet, 1 double crochet on next two of last round. Now continue double crochet, working every fifth stitch 1 double crochet on *two* of the last round, until the toe is reduced to 10 stitches, break off the wool, and with a wool needle draw the wool through the ten stitches, and sew them up close and round. For the Instep—with cardinal wool: work 10 double crochet on the instep chain, and continue working 10 double crochet backwards and forwards for 10 rows, at the end of each row catching up the side stitch of the foot part. Break off when 10 rows are done, and re-commence with the cardinal wool at the heel, working double crochet on each rib of the foot part, 10 double crochet along that side, 10 double crochet on the instep stitches, and 10 double crochet on the opposite side of the foot. Crochet 10 rows of ribbing backwards and forwards, without either increase or decrease. 11th row— increase 1 at the beginning and 1 at the end of the row; then 3 plain rows. 15th row—increase 1 at the beginning and 1 at the end of the row; then 4 plain rows. 20th row—increase 1 at the beginning and 1 at the end of the row; and now work 8 plain rows, and the boot will be sufficiently long. Sew it up the leg, making the raised ribs meet each other. For the Trimming—1st row—with cardinal wool: 1 double crochet in the centre of the instep in the fourth depressed rib, 5 treble on the fifth raised rib of the instep (to make these treble, instead of working in the usual way draw the wool through all three loops of each stitch at once), 1 double crochet in the next depressed rib, 5 treble in next depressed rib, and so on, working 8 groups of five trebles up the leg, then work the same, making 9 groups of trebles, 1 double crochet between each group, round the top of the leg. 2nd row— with white wool: 1 single crochet on the double crochet of last row, 1 more single crochet, 1 double crochet on the second stitch of trebles of last row, * wool over the needle, insert the hook in the next stitch of last row, and draw the wool through, repeat from * four times, draw the wool through all the stitches on the needle together, 1 double crochet on the second stitch of next group of trebles of last row, and repeat. The groups of raised stitches are always to come between the trebles of previous row. 3rd row— with white wool: same as the first row, working the 5 treble stitches in the stitch which draws together the five raised stitches of last row. The trimming down the front is now complete, but work the last two rows again round the top of the leg, once with cardinal wool and once with white, and the boot is finished. Of course any two shades of wool can be employed, or one colour even, if preferred, while the trimming down the front and along top of boot can be varied according to the maker's fancy; or a ribbon, run in and tied in a bow at the side, adds a pretty finish.

Baby's Boots with Fancy Worked Sock.—1 oz. of white, 1 oz. of maroon Cocoon wool or Eider yarn. Bone crochet needle No. 12. With maroon wool commence at the toe with 10 chain, turn, insert the hook in the third chain from the needle and work 8 double crochet; turn, and now work into the back loops so as to form ribs. 2nd row—1 double crochet in the first stitch, 2 in the next, 1 in the next, 1 in the next, 3 in the next, 1 in the next, 1 in the next, 2 in the next, and 1 at the end. 3rd row—plain double crochet. 4th row—1 double crochet in the first stitch, 2 in the next, 4 worked consecutively, 3 in the next, 4 consecutive, 2 in the next, and 1 at the end. 5th row—plain. 6th row—8 consecutive double crochet, 3 double crochet in the next, 8 double crochet. 7th row—plain. 8th row—9 double crochet, 3 double crochet in the next, 9 double crochet. 9th row—plain. 10th row—10 double crochet, 3 double crochet in the next, 10 double crochet. 11th row—plain. 12th row—11 double crochet, 3 double crochet in the next, 11 double crochet. 13th row—plain. This completes the instep. 14th row—12 double crochet, turn, insert the hook in the second stitch, and work back 11 double crochet. 16th row—11 double crochet, turn, insert the hook in the second stitch and work back 10 double crochet. Now work backwards and forwards on these 10 double crochet for 14 rows. Fasten off. Commence again in the middle of the instep, leaving 1 stitch from the side just done, and work 12 double crochet, turn, and work 12 double crochet again. 3rd row—insert the hook in the second stitch and work 11 double crochet, turn, and work 11 double crochet again. 5th row—insert the hook in the second stitch and work 10 double crochet, turn, and work 10 double crochet again. Now work backwards and forwards on these 10 double crochet for 11 rows. Fasten off, and sew the two side pieces together. The join forms the back of the heel. For the sock, with white wool, commence on the raised rib over the join at the heel, and work 16 double crochet on one side, of which the sixteenth is to come in the centre stitch of the instep, and 14 double crochet on the other side, making 30 double crochet in all; join. Next round—insert the hook in just the same place as the first double crochet of last round, draw up a rather long loop and work, as a double crochet stitch, * 1 double crochet on the next double crochet of previous round, taking up both top threads, and a long double crochet in the same place as the next double crochet of previous row is worked into, repeat from *. The next, and all succeeding rounds, are to be worked with 1 double crochet on the long double crochet stitch, and 1 long double crochet over the stitch of plain double crochet alternately. Continue until 16 rounds are done. For the edge— 1 double crochet, * 5 chain, 1 double crochet in the fourth chain from the needle, miss 1 double crochet stitch of last round and work 1 double crochet in the next, repeat from *. For the sole— with maroon wool, work 8 chain, turn, insert the hook in the third chain stitch from the needle and work 6 double crochet, turn, and, taking up the two top threads, work 7 double crochet, turn, and work 7 double crochet, turn and work 7 double crochet again, turn, and in this row work 2 double crochet in the centre stitch, making 8 double crochet in all; turn, and work 8 double crochet backwards and forwards for 16 rows; turn, miss the first stitch, and work 7 double crochet, turn, miss the first stitch, and work 6 double crochet; turn, miss the first stitch and work 5 double crochet; turn, miss the first stitch and work 4 double crochet. Fasten off with a long end, by which sew the sole to the boot, beginning at the toe end.

Baby's Hood and Shawl Combined.—2 oz. of white, 1 oz. of blue Shetland wool. Bone crochet needle No. 8. 2½ yards of 2-inch wide blue ribbon. Commence with the white wool by making a loop, in which work 12 treble; join round. 2nd round—6 treble between each group of 3 treble of last round. 3rd round—6 treble in the middle of each group of 6 treble of last round, to form the four corners, and 2 treble between each group of 6 treble to make the four sides. Continue working round and round, increasing at the four corners by doing 6 treble in the middle of each group of 6 treble of last round, and working 2 treble in each space along the sides, until 16 rounds are completed. Then work along *two* sides, and when you have done 6 treble at the end of the second side, turn, slip along the first 2 of the treble stitches, do 2 chain, and work 5 treble in the centre of the 6 treble; work back along the two sides, turn again, and repeat until you have done 25 of these straight rows. Then, using blue wool, work 3 rows all the way round, still increasing at the sides and in the middle of the shawl, but *not* on the hood. Then work 5 rounds with white wool, and then 4 rounds with blue; and for the last round, which is to form an edge, also with blue, work 6 treble in one space, and 1 double crochet in the next space, alternately. Cut the ribbon in half, and divide 1 piece in half again. The longest piece is to be run through the line of 6 trebles to tie round the neck; the two shorter pieces are to be run in the middle row of the five rows of white crochet, commencing where the ribbon is run round for the neck (to which ribbon the ends are to be sewn), and tied in a bow on the top of the hood.

Baby-Boy's Hat. Turban Shaped.—3 oz. of white single Berlin wool, and bone crochet needle No. 10. Commence with 3 chain, join round, and work 6 double crochet in the circle. Run a cotton in to mark the beginning of each round. 2nd round—2 double crochet in every stitch; always taking up 2 threads of wool, the one at the top and the other at the back of the stitches of the preceding round. 3rd round—2 double crochet in the first stitch, 1 double crochet in the next stitch, and repeat. 4th round—the same. 5th round—1 double crochet in each of the first two stitches, and 2 double crochet in the third stitch, and repeat. 6th round—2 double crochet in the first stitch, and 1 double crochet in each of the three next stitches, and repeat. 7th round—2 double crochet in every fifth stitch. 8th round—2 double crochet in every seventh stitch. And now continue the double crochet, always working into the top and back threads of the stitches of the last round, and increasing at intervals, as often as necessary to make the work lie flat, until you have a circle measuring nine inches in diameter. Then work four rounds of double crochet without increasing. In the next round, work for the border in looped crochet, which is done as follows:—Twist the wool once round a mesh two inches wide, and work a double crochet stitch. Make a loop in every other stitch all round, and in the next round a loop in every stitch. Repeat these 2 rounds until you have done 12 rounds of the looped crochet. But very little increase will be necessary in this border, not more than 2 stitches at intervals in the third, fifth, seventh, and ninth rounds. The hat should measure about twenty inches round the head, but if too large can be drawn in with a ribbon at the back part, and will stretch the size required, if too small. Put in a cap, and strings to tie under the chin.

Baby's Jacket.—3 oz. of white, ½ oz. of blue Andalusian wool or Penelope yarn. Bone crochet needle No. 10. Commence with white wool with 90 chain for the neck, turn, miss 5 chain, 2 treble in the next 2 stitches, then 1 chain and 2 treble 27 times, and 1 chain and 1 treble at the end of the row. This jacket is worked in "sets," and a "set" is 1 treble, 1 chain, 1 treble, all worked into the same hole; an "increase" is 1 treble, 1 chain, 1 treble, 1 chain, 1 treble, all worked into the same hole. Make 3 chain to turn at the end of every row; where there is no "increase" at the beginning of a row the 3 chain and 1 treble form the first "set." 2nd row—increase, 5 sets, increase, 6 sets, increase, 1 set, increase, 6 sets, increase, 5 sets, increase. 3rd row—and every alternate row—to be worked in sets all along, no increase whatever. 4th row—7 sets, increase, increase, 17 sets, increase, increase, 7 sets. 6th row—increase, 7 sets, increase, increase, 9 sets, increase, 9 sets, increase, increase, 7 sets, increase. 8th row—9 sets, increase, 2 sets, increase, 20 sets, increase, 2 sets, increase, 9 sets. 10th row—increase, 9 sets, increase, 2 sets, increase, 9 sets, increase, 2 sets, increase, 9 sets, increase, 2 sets, increase, 9 sets, increase. 12th row—11 sets, increase, 4 sets, increase, 24 sets, increase, 4 sets, increase, 11 sets. 14th row—11 sets, 10 chain, miss 10 sets, which go to form the armhole, 20 sets, 10 chain, miss 10 sets for the other armhole, 11 sets. 15th row—sets all along, and work 3 sets under the 10 chain. 16th row—increase, 22 sets, increase, increase, 22 sets, increase. 17th row—and every alternate row—sets all along. 18th row—sets all along. 20th row—14 sets, increase, 24 sets, increase, 14 sets. 22nd row—sets all along. 24th row—15 sets, increase, 10 sets, increase, 2 sets, increase, 10 sets, increase, 15 sets. 26th row—sets all along. 28th row—16 sets, increase, 28 sets, increase, 16 sets, 30th row—sets all along. For the sleeves—commence under the armhole, and work 18 sets round, join, and continue working round in sets for 6 rounds, then miss 1 set underneath the arm in each of the succeeding 4 rounds, which will reduce the width to 14 sets; when you have done 12 rounds, fasten off. For the border round the jacket and sleeves—with blue wool, work 3 rounds in sets the same as the jacket, increasing at the corners. 4th round—1 double crochet in 1 set, and 5 treble in the next set alternately. Run a blue ribbon through the row of holes at the neck to tie, and also above the blue bordering round the sleeves.

Baby's Little Petticoat with Body.—3 oz. of grey, 2 oz. of blue single Berlin wool. Bone crochet needle No 10. Commence with the blue wool with 139 chain, 1 treble in the fourth chain from the needle, * 1 chain, miss 1, 2 treble, in 2 consecutive chain, repeat from * to the end of the row and break off. Turn the work. 2nd row—with grey wool, commencing where the first row ended; 1 treble on the treble at the beginning, 1 treble under the first chain stitch of previous row, * 1 chain, 2 treble under the next chain of previous row, repeat from * to the end of the row and break off. Turn the work. 3rd row—with blue wool, commencing where the second row ended: 1 double crochet on the first treble, and 1 double crochet under the first chain of previous row, * 6 chain, 1 double crochet in the first stitch of the chain, 1 double crochet under the next 1 chain of previous row, repeat from * to the end of the row and break off. These three rows complete the band for the neck and shoulders. 1st row—for the body—with grey wool, commencing at the side where the foundation chain began, 2 treble on the 2 treble, * 1 chain 2 treble under the 1 chain missed in the foundation, repeat from *. Under the tenth, thirteenth, sixteenth, thirtieth, thirty-third, and thirty-sixth chains missed in the foundation you are to make an "increase," that is, work an extra 1 chain 2 treble in those places. 2nd row—3 chain to turn, 1 treble between the 2 treble, 1 chain 2 treble, as before, nine times, which brings you to the chain before the first increase, 4 chain 2 treble under the chain beyond the third increase, continue working 1 chain 2 treble till you come to the chain before the next increase, 4 chain 2 treble under the chain beyond the sixth increase, then 1 chain 2 treble to the end of the row. 3rd row—3 chain to turn, 1 treble between the 2 treble, 1 chain, 2 treble as before all along the row, putting two groups of 2 treble under the 4 chain. The next 8 rows are a continuation of 1 chain, 2 treble, worked plain, and without any increase or decrease whatever. 12th row—for the waistband, with blue wool, commence where the grey wool was broken off and work the same. 13th row—the same with grey wool. 14th row—the same with blue wool. 15th row—for the skirt, with grey wool, commence where the blue wool was broken off, 2 treble between the 2 first treble, * 1 chain, 2 treble, 1 chain, 2 treble, then an "increase," repeat from * to the end of the row. 16th, 17th, and 18th rows—all a continuation of the same stitch without any increase or decrease. 19th row—1 chain to turn, 1 treble between the two trebles, 1 chain, 2 treble, increase, * 1 chain, 2 treble, 1 chain, 2 treble, increase, repeat from *. 20th, 21st, and 22nd rows— plain, no increase; join round at the end of the 22nd row, and henceforth continue working in rounds. Still using grey wool, work 5 rounds, making 5 increases at regular intervals in every alternate round, one of these increasings to be at the back. Then two rounds with blue wool, no increase, 2 rounds with grey wool, in the first of which make 5 increases, 3 rounds with blue, no increase, 2 rounds with grey wool, in the first of which make 5 increases, 3 rounds with blue, no increase. For scalloped border, still using blue wool—* 1 double crochet under the 1 chain of previous round, 2 chain, 3 treble under the next chain of previous round, 2 chain, repeat from *, and fasten off at the end of the round. Work an edging round the armholes, the same as described in the third row, and this completes the frock. Run a narrow blue ribbon in the second row and the thirteenth row to tie at the neck and waist.

Child's Vest in Treble Crochet.—This will be found a strong, serviceable vest, and is quickly made. If required about 12 inches long, procure 2½ oz. of white merino wool—a smaller size can be made by using 3 balls of Cocoon wool. Bone crochet needle No. 12. Commence with 62 chain, turn, 1 treble in the third stitch from the needle, and treble all along, making 60 treble in all. 2nd row—2 chain to turn, and work 60 treble again. 3rd row—2 chain to turn, work 60 treble again, and this completes the half of one shoulder. 4th row—2 chain to turn, and work 50 treble stitches. Repeat this row till 15 of these short rows are done, and at the end of the fifteenth row make 12 chain, turn, and again work 60 treble up and down for 3 rows. This completes the front of the vest. Re-commence, and work a similar piece for the back. Then sew up the shoulder straps, and sew the sides together, leaving sufficient space for an armhole. For the little edge round the neck and armholes, work 1 double crochet in one ridge of the treble, work 7 treble in the next ridge, and repeat. Run a ribbon in to confine the neck and to tie with a bow in front.

Child's Petticoat with Bodice.—This petticoat will take 6 oz. of white and 1 oz. of pale blue Penelope fingering. Fine bone crochet needle. Commence with white wool for the waist with 171 chain, turn, miss the first of the chain stitches, * 3 consecutive double crochet, 3 double crochet in the next stitch of the chain, 3 consecutive double crochet, miss the next 2 chain stitches, and repeat from *. Turn the work at the end of the row, and for the remainder of the petticoat take up the small loop at the back of the stitches, as the work is to set in ribs. 2nd row—miss the first double crochet stitch, work * 3 consecutive double crochet on the next three double crochet, 3 double crochet in the centre stitch of the three double crochet of last row, 3 consecutive double crochet, miss the 2 next double crochet stitches, and repeat from *. Work 5 more rows the same as the last. 8th row—miss the first double crochet stitch, work * 1 double crochet in each of the two next stitches, 2 double crochet in the next, 3 double crochet in the centre stitch of the 3 double crochet of last row, 2 double crochet in the next, 1 double crochet in each of the two next stitches, miss the two next double crochet stitches, and repeat from *. 9th row—miss the first double crochet stitch, work * 4 consecutive double crochet, 3 double crochet in the centre stitch of the three double crochet of last row, 4 consecutive double crochet, miss the two next double crochet stitches, and repeat from *. Work 9 more rows the same as the last. 19th row—miss the first double crochet stitch, work * 1 double crochet in each of the three next stitches, 2 double crochet in the next, 3 double crochet in the centre stitch of the three double crochet of last row, 2 double crochet in the next, 1 double crochet in each of the three next stitches, miss the two next double crochet stitches, and repeat from *. 20th row—miss the first double crochet stitch, work * 5 consecutive double crochet, 3 double crochet in the centre stitch of the three double crochet of last row, 5 consecutive double crochet, miss the two next double crochet stitches, and repeat from *. Work 4 more rows the same as the last, then join on the blue wool and work 6 rows the same with blue; then 4 rows with white, and 7 rows with blue. Last row—with blue wool; miss the first double crochet stitch, work * 5 consecutive double crochet, 5 double crochet in the centre stitch of the three double crochet of last row, 5 consecutive double crochet, miss the two last double crochet stitches, and repeat from *. For the band —work into the commencing chain, with white wool, 1 double crochet on the first stitch, 1 treble on the next stitch, 1 long treble in the same stitch as the three double crochet of the first row are worked into, 1 treble on the next stitch, 1 double crochet on the next stitch, 1 double crochet under the two missed chain stitches, and repeat. Work 2 rows of plain double crochet. 4th row—1 double crochet, * 1 chain, miss 1 double crochet of last row, 1 double crochet in the next, and repeat from *. 5th row—plain double crochet. Sew the petticoat up the back, joining the raised ribs together neatly, and leaving sufficient space for the placket hole. For the Body—white wool; begin with 110 chain, work 22 rows alternately treble and double crochet. Then work on 27 stitches for 9 rows, leave this piece and work the same on the next 54 stitches, leave this and work 9 rows on the remaining 27 stitches. Now work a row of double crochet all along with 5 chain at each division of the armholes. For neck—work a row of treble and a row of double crochet alternately for 8 rows, decreasing twice on each shoulder in each row to get a nice shape. Finish round the neck, the armholes, and bottom of the skirt, with a little edging thus: 1 double crochet on double crochet of last row, * 2 chain, 3 treble on the double crochet just done, miss two double crochet of last row, 1 double crochet on the next, and repeat from *. Sew the skirt on to the body.

Child's Hood.—This becoming hood will take 3 oz. of single Berlin wool, white or any colour preferred. It is worked in the Scotch fashion with no ridge, inserting the hook so as to take up both the top threads of the previous row. Bone crochet needle No. 10. Commence with the crown by working 4 chain, join round, and work 7 double crochet in the circle. 2nd round —2 double crochet on each double crochet of last round. 3rd round—2 double crochet on the first stitch, 1 double crochet on the next, and repeat. 4th round—the same. 5th round—1 double crochet on each of the first two stitches, 2 double crochet on the next, and repeat. Continue increasing where necessary, and the work after the 6th round should be just a little drawn in, that is, not so perfectly as the crown of a Tam o' Shanter. When the crown measures eight inches across, break off the wool and re-commence about 27 stitches farther on, the missed stitches will form the bottom of the crown. Work round with a slight increase at the top, and again break off at the same place as before. Continue thus working in rows for the front part of the hood till it is as large as is required. For the frill—1 treble on the outside row of the double crochet, 1 chain, 1 treble on the next row, 1 chain, 1 treble on the next row, 1 chain, 1 treble on the next row, 1 chain, 1 treble on the next row, all straight along, 1 chain, turn and work the same back, and so on, up and down, 5 trebles in a line with 1 chain between each treble round the entire front of the hood. Work the same, but only 4 stitches wide round the centre of the hood. Having done this, work 1 double crochet under loop of one chain, 4 chain, 1 double crochet under next 1 chain, and so on all over the frill, which, when finished, tack down in its place. For the curtain—hold the hood the right side towards you, and work a row of double crochet loosely and just a little full, break off at the end of the row. Work 3 more rows of double crochet the same way as the hood is worked. Then a row of double long treble, the wool turned three times round the needle, increase 1 double long treble in every eighth stitch. Then 4 rows of double crochet, and another row of double long treble, and finish with a row of edging : 1 double crochet on one long treble, * 4 chain, 2 treble in the first of the chain, miss three long treble, 1 double crochet on the next, and repeat from *. Make a chain and tassels to tie round the front, and the same on the back of the curtain, make a nice ribbon bow on the top of the hood.

Child's Jacket in Ribbed Russian Crochet.—6 oz. of Cocoon wool. Bone crochet needle No. 12. Begin for the centre of the back with 71 chain, turn, and work 70 double crochet. Do 4 more rows of 70 double crochet in a row, working into the back threads of the stitches of preceding row. The whole of the jacket is worked in ridged crochet. At the end of the fifth, seventh, ninth, and eleventh rows, work 2 double crochet on the last stitch to heighten for the neck; at the end of the 13th row work 3, at end of the 15th row work 2, at end of the 17th row work 3, at end of the 19th row work 2, at end of the 21st row work 3, at end of the 23rd row work 2, and there are 84 double crochet in this row. Now at end of 25th row leave 2 unworked, at end of the 27th row leave 3 unworked, at end of the 29th row leave 2 unworked, and so on; reduce in the same proportion as you before increased till you reduce to 64 double crochet; turn, work 30 double crochet to reach to the armhole, turn, work back; turn, work 25 double crochet, work back, turn, work 30 double crochet to armhole, turn, work back, turn, work 20 double crochet, turn, work back; turn, work 30 double crochet, do 34 chain, turn, work back, and now make two other little gusset rows at the bottom, and increase at the shoulder end to match the decreasings on the shoulder already done, and when 84 stitches are attained decrease for the shaping of the neck, and finish with six rows of 70 double crochet in a row. Re-commence upon the commencing chain and work similarly for the other half of the jacket. For sleeves—begin with 41 chain, and work six rows of plain double crochet, then increase a stitch at the end of every alternate row till 50 double crochet are attained, decrease same way, do 6 plain rows, fasten off, and sew up. Sew up the shoulders and sew the sleeves in. Trim round the jacket and sleeves, and work a collar in the stitch described for the trimming of the baby's long crochet boot or in point Muscovite stitch.

Child's Frock.—This pretty frock is suitable for a child of two or three years; it measures 21 inches in length, but can be made longer if desired, by working additional rows on the flounce. Materials required—5 oz. of cardinal, 2 oz. of black and white mottled Scotch yarn. Crochet needle No. 9. Commence for the body at the back, lengthways, with cardinal wool, with 53 chain, turn, miss the first 3 chain stitches, 1 treble in the next, and work 50 treble stitches. 2nd row—3 chain to turn, and work treble on every stitch of preceding row, inserting the hook at the back of the stitches, so as to make the work sit in ribs. Do 9 rows of treble, and at the end of the 9th row make 12 chain to lengthen for the shoulder, turn, 1 treble in the fourth from the needle, and work 3 rows of treble the whole length of 59 stitches, next row, 30 treble only, and at the end make 32 chain for the armhole and other side of shoulder, turn into the fourth from the needle, and work 3 rows of trebles the whole length of 59 stitches again. 17th row Work 50 treble stitches, and work upon these 50 treble backwards and forwards for 16 rows. At the end of the 33rd row, make 12 chain to lengthen for the shoulder, and work three rows of treble the whole length of 59 stitches, then a row of 30 treble only, at the end of which make 32 chain for the armhole and other side of the shoulder, and work 3 more rows of treble the whole length, then 9 rows of 50 treble in each row. This completes the body. Sew up the shoulders, and sew up about three inches from the bottom, leaving the rest open. Now for the neck band, with black and white mottled wool—work 5 rows of treble, breaking off at the end of every row, and working into the top loops of previous row. 1st row—work 3 treble stitches upon each rib of the ribbed crochet, and 1 treble on each treble along the top of the shoulder. 2nd row, and 3 following rows—work 1 treble on each treble stitch of previous row successively, but on each shoulder make three decreasings, one exactly above the join and others a few stitches away on each side; this will be effected by inserting the hook in two treble stitches of previous row, and working both into one. 6th row, with cardinal wool—1 double crochet on the first treble stitch, * miss 2 treble, 5 treble on the next, miss 2 treble, 1 double crochet on the next; repeat from *. For the sash band, with black and white mottled wool—do a round of double crochet, working 3 stitches on every rib of the body part, then work 5 rounds of plain treble stitches, working into the top loops of previous round. For the flounce, with cardinal wool—1st round—double crochet all round, working 2 double crochet stitches into every stitch of the treble. 2nd round—3 consecutive double crochet, 3 double crochet together in the next, 3 consecutive double crochet, miss 2 double crochet of previous round, and repeat. Work the same as this for 11 rounds. Then do 1 round with the mottled wool, 1 round with cardinal, and finish with 2 rounds with mottled. For the sleeve, with crimson wool, worked lengthways—30 chain, turn. 1st row—1 treble in the third from the needle, 11 consecutive treble, 15 double crochet. 2nd row—treble all along and 2 treble in the stitch at the end of the row. 3rd, 4th, and 5th rows—treble, each time increasing one stitch at the same end, therewith to produce a slope for the shoulder. 6th row, and 3 following rows—decrease 1 treble in each row at the same end as the increasings were made. 10th row—15 double crochet and 12 treble. Sew up the sleeve, and, for the cuff, work 3 rounds of treble stitches with the mottled wool, and 1 round of edging, same as that round the neck, with cardinal wool. Sew the sleeves in. Sew three or four buttons down the back of the frock. Run in a ribbon to tie round the neck, and make a nice wide ribbon bow to place at the back on the sash-band.

Child's Muff and Necktie. Point Muscovite.

—2 oz. of dark brown, 2 oz. of crimson, 1 oz. of cherry-coloured double Berlin wool. Large bone crochet needle. For the muff—commence with a chain of 38 stitches with brown wool, join round; 1 double crochet in the first stitch, * insert the hook in the next stitch, draw the wool through, do 3 chain stitches, and then draw the wool through the last of the chain and the stitch that has remained on the needle; 1 double crochet in the next stitch; repeat from * and join round at the end of the row. 2nd round—insert the hook in the front and back loops of the first double crochet of preceding round, draw the wool through, and do 3 chain stitches, then draw the wool through the last of the chain and through the stitch that has remained on the needle, 1 double crochet in the next stitch, and repeat. Continue in the same way, always working a point, that is 3 chain stitches, over a double crochet stitch, and a double crochet over a point. Do 7 rounds with the brown wool, 5 rounds with the crimson, 5 with cherry colour, 5 more with crimson, and 7 with brown, when the muff will be finished. Line it with crimson flannel, placing a sheet or two of wadding between the crochet and the lining, and ornament with two bows of ribbon. For the necktie—make a chain of 24 stitches with brown wool, join round, and work as directed for the muff, doing 7 rounds with brown wool, and then 5 rounds of crimson and cherry colour alternately, until you have 5 stripes of the former, finish with 7 rounds of brown. Draw in the ends and add tassels. Point Muscovite is also a nice pattern for working stripes or squares for an antimacassar, for the tops of babies' boots, and the borders of children's jackets.

Lady's Petticoat, worked in Treble Crochet.—This petticoat will be found much more comfortable and better fitting to the figure than those made by the usual method of commencing at the bottom. It is to be worked in rows as far as the end of the placket hole, and when the placket hole is completed and joined, the stitch is continued in rounds. The petticoat will take about 1¼ lb. of the best Scotch fingering, Peacock fingering, or Penelope yarn. Commence for the waist with a chain as long as required, the number of stitches to be divisible by nine; 99 chain gives a fair medium size. Make 2 more chain to turn 1 treble into the third chain from the needle, and treble all along to the end. Break off at the end of this and every row. Commence again at the right-hand side, working the first treble over the chain stitch that turned in the previous row, and do treble all along working into 2 threads of the treble stitches of previous row. 3rd row—all plain treble. These 3 rows form the waistband, and you now commence working the pattern, the scallops of which get wider and wider down the petticoat. 4th row—4 consecutive treble over the first 4 treble, 3 treble in the next stitch, * 8 consecutive treble, 3 treble in the next stitch, repeat from *, and there will be 4 treble to finish with at the end of the row. 5th row—miss 1 treble at the beginning of the row, * work 3 consecutive treble over the next 3 treble, 2 treble in the next stitch, 3 treble in the centre stitch of the 3 treble of previous row, 2 treble in the next stitch, 3 consecutive treble, miss 2 treble of previous row, and repeat from *; there will be 3 treble to work at the end of the row, and miss the last stitch. 6th row—miss the first treble at the beginning of the row, * 5 consecutive treble over the next 5 treble, 3 treble in the centre stitch of the 3 treble of previous row, 5 consecutive treble, miss 2 treble of previous row, and repeat from *; miss 1 treble at the end of the row. 7th row—the same as the last row. 8th row—miss the first treble at the beginning of the row, * 4 consecutive treble over the next 4 treble, 2 treble in the next stitch, 3 treble in the centre stitch of the 3 treble of previous row, 2 treble in the next stitch, 4 consecutive treble, miss 2 treble of previous row, and repeat from *; miss 1 treble at the end of the row. 9th row—miss the first treble at the beginning of the row, * 6 consecutive treble over the next 6 treble, 3 treble in the centre stitch of the 3 treble of previous row, 6 consecutive treble, miss 2 treble of previous row, and repeat from *; miss 1 treble at the end of the row. 10th and 11th rows—the same as the last row. 12th row—miss the first treble at the beginning of the row, * 5 consecutive treble over the next 5 treble, 2 treble in the next stitch, 3 treble in the centre stitch of the 3 treble of previous row, 2 treble in the next stitch, 5 consecutive treble, miss 2 treble of previous row, and repeat from *; miss 1 treble at the end of the row. 13th row—miss the first treble at the beginning of the row, * 7 consecutive treble over the next 7 treble, 3 treble in the centre stitch of the 3 treble of previous row, 7 consecutive treble, miss 2 treble of previous row, and repeat from *; miss 1 treble at the end of the row. 14th and 15th rows—the same as the last row. 16th row—miss the first treble at the beginning of the row, * 6 consecutive treble over the next 6 treble, 2 treble in the next stitch, 3 treble in the centre stitch of the 3 treble of previous row, 2 treble in the next stitch, 6 consecutive treble, miss 2 treble of previous row, and repeat from *; miss 1 treble at the end of the row. 17th row—miss the first treble at the beginning of the row, * 8 consecutive treble over the next 8 treble, 3 treble in the centre stitch of the 3 treble of previous row, 8 consecutive treble, miss 2 treble of previous row, and repeat from *; miss 1 treble at the end of the row. 18th, 19th, and 20th rows—the same as the last row. 21st row—miss the first treble at the beginning of the row, * 7 consecutive treble over the next 7 treble, 2 treble in the next stitch, 3 treble in the centre stitch of the 3 treble of previous row, 2 treble in the next stitch, 7 consecutive treble, miss 2 treble of previous row, and repeat from *; miss 1 treble at the end of the row. 22nd row—miss the first treble at the beginning of the row, * 9 consecutive treble over the next 9 treble, 3 treble in the centre stitch of the 3 treble of previous row, 9 consecutive treble, miss 2 treble of previous row, and repeat from * ; miss 1 treble at the end of the row. 23rd, 24th, 25th, 26th rows—the same as the last row. 27th row—miss the first treble at the beginning of the row, * 8 consecutive treble over the next 8 treble, 2 treble in the next stitch, 3 treble in the centre stitch of the 3 treble of previous row, 2 treble in the next stitch, 8 consecutive treble, miss 2 treble of previous row, and repeat from * ; miss 1 treble at the end of the row. 28th row—miss the first treble at the beginning of the row, * 10 consecutive treble over the next 10 treble, 3 treble in the centre stitch of the 3 treble of previous row, 10 consecutive treble, miss 2 treble of previous row, and repeat from * ; miss 1 treble at the end of the row. Now join the end of the row to the commencement, for this finishes the placket hole, and continue the petticoat in rounds without any more breaking off. Work 5 more rounds the same as the last round. 34th round—* 9 consecutive treble over the next 9 treble, 2 treble in the next stitch, 3 treble in the centre stitch of the 3 treble of previous round, 2 treble in the next stitch, 9 consecutive treble, miss 2 treble of previous round, and repeat from * ; join. 35th round—* 11 consecutive treble over the next 11 treble, 3 treble in the centre stitch of the 3 treble of previous round, 11 consecutive treble, miss 2 treble of previous round, and repeat from * ; join. Work 8 more rounds the same as the last round. 44th round—* 10 consecutive treble over the next 10 treble, 2 treble in the next stitch, 3 treble in the centre stitch of the 3 treble of previous round, 2 treble in the next stitch, 10 consecutive treble, miss 2 treble of previous round, and repeat from * ; join. 45th round—* 12 consecutive treble over the next 12 treble, 3 treble in the centre stitch of the 3 treble of previous round, 12 consecutive treble, miss 2 treble of previous round, and repeat from * ; join. Work 11 more rounds the same as the last round. 57th round—* 11 consecutive treble over the next 11 treble ; 2 treble in the next stitch, 3 treble in the centre stitch of the 3 treble of previous round, 2 treble in the next stitch, 11 consecutive treble, miss 2 treble of previous round, and repeat from * ; join. 58th round—* 13 consecutive treble over the next 13 treble ; 3 treble in the centre stitch of the 3 treble of previous round, 13 consecutive treble, miss 2 treble of previous round, and repeat from * join. Work about 12 more rounds the same as the last round, and the petticoat will be long enough. For an edge round the bottom, work 1 double crochet in the second treble of the 13 treble of previous round, * 2 chain, 2 treble in the double crochet stitch you have just done, miss 1 treble of previous round, 1 double crochet in the next treble, and repeat from *. Strengthen the placket hole with a row of double crochet, and the petticoat will be finished.

Bedroom Slippers.—3 oz. of crimson double Berlin wool, a small bone crochet hook, and a pair of cork soles. Make a chain of 12 stitches, and in these work 11 plain double crochet. 2nd row—double crochet, taking up the horizontal loop at the back of every stitch, and increase by working 3 stitches into the centre stitch of preceding row. 3rd row—the same, without increasing. Repeat these 2 rows until you have 11 raised ridges from the toe, which will complete the instep. For the side—crochet 13 stitches, and work backwards and forwards until you have a length sufficient to reach to the back of the sole, when break off, and work a similar piece for the other side. Join together at the heel. Work 4 rows of looped crochet round the top; that is, double crochet, twisting the wool once round a mesh one inch wide before inserting the hook to work the stitch. Then 1 row of plain double crochet. Line the slipper with flannel, and sew to the sole, having first bound the edge of the soles with ribbon. Finish off with a ribbon rosette in front.

Shoulder Cape in Dutch Crochet.—Single Berlin wool of the colour preferred, and No. 9 bone crochet needle. Commence for the neck with a chain of 76 stitches. 1st row—1 double crochet in the fourth from the hook, 1 chain, miss 1, 1 double crochet all along. 2nd row—2 chain to turn, * wool over the needle, and raise a loop under the 1 chain, wool over the needle, and raise another loop in the same place, wool over the needle, and raise a third loop (all the loops to be as long and as loose as possible), draw the wool through all these loops, and then through the 2 stitches on the needle, 1 chain; repeat from *; there should be 37 clumps in the row. 3rd row—3 chain to turn, 1 double crochet above the first clump of loops, taking up both the top threads of wool, 1 chain, 1 double crochet, again in the same clump; * 1 chain, 1 double crochet above the next clump; repeat from *; increase six more times in this row by working an additional 1 chain 1 double crochet above the seventh, thirteenth, nineteenth, twenty-fifth, thirty-first, and thirty-seventh clumps of preceding row. 4th row—2 chain to turn, and work in clumps all along, the same as the second row, but now there should be 44 clumps. 5th row—3 chain to turn, 1 double crochet above the first clump of loops, and 1 chain 1 double crochet in each clump all along, making an increase above each increase of the third row. 6th row—2 chain to turn, and work in clumps the entire length of the row, 51 clumps in all. Repeat these 2 rows, always increasing seven times in the double crochet row, until the cape is the required size, when knot a fringe of wool in round the bottom. Work a row of 1 chain 1 double crochet round the neck, and run a crochet chain through the small holes to tie in front with a tassel of the fringed wool at each end.

Warm Shoulder Cape. Double Point Neige.

—Crimson double Berlin wool, and No. 4 bone crochet needle. Commence with 53 chain for the neck. 1st row—1 single in the fourth from the needle, raise 5 loops as for tricot in the next 5 stitches, pull through all the loops together, including the stitch on the needle, 5 chain, 1 single in the fourth from the needle, * raise a loop in the thread which lies under the chain, another in the lower back thread of the last stitch of the point, another in the same chain the last point was worked into, one in the next chain, and another in the next chain; there will be six stitches on the needle, pull through all, 5 chain, 1 single in the fourth from the needle, and repeat from *; at the end of the row work 3 single down the point to join to the foundation, and fasten off. There should be 23 points in the row. Mark the sixth, twelfth, and eighteenth points with a bit of white wool to save counting, as increasings are to be made above these. 2nd row—commence on the right-hand side with a single below the picot, 6 chain, 1 single in the fourth from the needle, raise 2 loops in the remaining 2 chain, and 3 more loops at the back of the picot, draw through all, 5 chain, 1 single in the fourth from the needle, and work along as described for the first row, but take up the fourth and fifth loops now always at the back of the picots of the previous row. You will work 2 points above the first point of former row, 2 again above the sixth, the twelfth, the eighteenth, and the last, to form increasings, and 1 point above each of the other points; fasten off with 3 single stitches as in the first row. The cape is continued in the same way throughout, increasing 5 points in every row. When deep enough it is complete without the addition of any fringe or bordering, but work a row of double crochet to strengthen the neck, and finish off with a cord and tassels.

Shoulder Cape. Feathery Pattern.—3 oz. of black Shetland wool and ½ lb. of Pearsall's shawl silk; or the cape may be worked entirely with Shetland wool, but the silk gives a rich appearance. Crochet needle No. 8. Commence from the neck with 56 chain. Work 3 treble in the sixth chain from the hook, * miss 1 chain, 3 treble in the next, and repeat from * to the end of the row; there should be 26 groups of 3 treble. Take a thread of white cotton and tie on to the foundation chain in the middle of the piece of work, tie another thread on at each quarter, to mark for the increasings. 2nd row—1 chain to turn, 3 treble between the 2 last treble of previous row, then 3 treble between every group of 3 treble of previous row till you have done 6 groups and come to the first white cotton tie, and above that work an extra group of 3 treble to give an increase for the shoulder, work on, doing 3 treble between every group of 3 treble till you have done 7 more groups and come to the next cotton tie which is the middle of the back, make another increase of 3 treble there, proceed with 7 more groups and you come to the next cotton tie, where increase 3 treble again, then 6 more groups of 3 treble will finish the row. 3rd row—1 chain to turn, 3 treble between the 2 last treble of previous row, then 3 treble between every group of 3 treble of previous row, all along the row, no increase. 4th row—1 chain to turn, 3 treble between the 2 last treble of previous row, then 3 treble in every space till you come to one space before the increase made in the second row at the cotton tie, increase here, and increase again in the space on the other side of the cotton tie, no increase at the back, but the same increase as above on the other shoulder. 5th row—same as the third row. 6th row—1 chain to turn, 3 treble between the 2 last treble of preceding row, then groups of 3 treble as far as directly above the white cotton tie, make an increase here, continue working 3 treble in every space till you come to the tie in the middle of the back, where increase again, and make another increase directly above the tie on the other shoulder. Now work the rows in the following order. Third row. Fourth row. Third row. Sixth row. Third row. Fourth row. Third row. Sixth row. Third row. Fourth row. Third row twice. Sixth row. Third row twice. Fourth row. Third row three times. Sixth row. Third row three times. Fourth row. Third row three times. This will be about sufficient for the length of the cape, but if required longer repeat the last 8 rows. For the Feathered Flakes — with new shawl silk — commencing on the first row of the cape, and working loosely. Insert the hook so as to take up the second treble stitch at the beginning of the row, draw the wool through and work a double crochet stitch, then * 18 chain very loosely, and a double crochet in the middle treble of the next group of 3 treble, repeat from * to the end of the row. Work 18 chain to turn, and a double crochet in the middle treble of the first group of treble in the second row of the cape, and continue in this manner, always working 18 chain and 1 double crochet in the centre treble of the groups till the cape is entirely covered with chain work, which will very much resemble feathery flakes. Strengthen the neck with a row of plain double crochet and sew on three or four buttons and loops.

Three-Cornered Shawl.—¼ lb. of grey, ½ oz. of black, ¼ oz. of two shades of blue single Berlin wool, or the same of Penelope yarn. Crochet needle No. 8. With grey wool, commence for the neck with a chain of 70 stitches. 1st row—wool over the needle and insert the hook in the sixth from the needle, draw the wool through so as to work the half of a treble stitch, wool over the needle and make another half treble, wool over the needle and make a third, draw the wool through the 3 half-treble, and then through the 2 stitches on the needle,* 1 chain, miss 1, 3 half-treble in the next chain; repeat from *; there should be 32 bunches of half-treble in the row, and at the end work 1 chain, 1 treble, and fasten off. 2nd row—beginning on the right-hand side, 1 treble in the loop at the corner, 1 chain, 3 half-treble in the same place, then work 1 chain and 3 half-treble under each chain of preceding row, increasing in the centre by working 2 bunches under the same chain, and at the end of the row work 1 chain, 1 treble as at the beginning; fasten off. Continue working the same as the second row, always increasing a bunch in the middle of the row, until the shawl is nearly large enough; then work 2 rows with black wool, 2 rows with darkest blue, 2 rows with lightest blue, 2 more rows with darkest, 2 rows with black, and 2 rows with grey. Fringe the shawl with grey wool, cutting the wool into lengths of six inches, and with the crochet needle knot four pieces of the wool under each chain stitch. Work a row of 1 chain, 1 double crochet up each front and round the neck. Run a crochet chain through the small holes round the neck to tie in front, having a tassel of the fringed wool at each end.

Half-Square Shawl. Scallop Shell Pattern.—5 balls

of Cocoon wool, black, or any colour that is preferred. Crochet needle No. 10. Commence for the top of the shawl with a chain as long as required; 244 chain makes a nice size for a shoulder shawl. 1st row—4 long treble (made by putting the wool twice round the needle) in the fourth chain from the hook, 3 long treble in the next chain, * miss 3 chain, 1 double crochet in the next, miss 3 chain, 4 long treble in the next, and 3 long treble in the next; repeat from * to the end of the row, which gives 27 shells of treble. 2nd row—turn, slip along the first 3 treble stitches, and work a double crochet on the fourth treble, * 7 long treble on the double crochet stitch of previous row (inserting the hook right in the double crochet stitch, so as to have 2 threads of wool on each side of it), 1 double crochet on the centre treble of the next group of 7 treble; repeat from *; at the end of the row on the last group of 7 treble, work a single crochet instead of a double crochet. 3rd row—same as the second row. 4th row—same as the second row until the end, and there work 9 long treble upon the single crochet stitch at the end of the second row, and catch the last of these 9 treble into the middle treble at the end of the first row. 5th row—turn, slip along the first 5 treble stitches, work a double crochet on the sixth treble, and then work, as before, all along the row, and at the end work 9 long treble upon the single crochet stitch at the end of the third row, and catch the last of these 9 treble into the double crochet stitch at the top of the group of treble in the first row. Repeat from the second row seven times, in each repeat slanting off and working down the 9 long treble into the 2 preceding rows, making in all 8 groups of the 9 treble on each side of the shawl; when this is done, slant off to a point more rapidly by working every row like the second row was worked, till you finish off at last with only one shell. Fringe round all three sides of the shawl, knotting 2 threads of wool into every stitch of the crochet.

Crossover Shawl.—4 oz. of dove-colour, and ½ oz. each of three shades of blue Andalusian wool, a long bone tricot needle No. 9, and a crochet needle the same size. Commence with grey wool, with 240 chain, pick up 239 stitches on the needle, and work 1 row of plain tricot; this is the entire size round the bottom of the shawl above the border. Continue working in plain tricot, but pick up 2 stitches together at the beginning of every row, 3 stitches together in the exact centre of the row, and 2 stitches together at the end of the row, till the shawl is reduced to about 9 stitches in the centre, so forming a triangular-shaped piece of work. Now, along the top of the crossover, work, with grey wool, a row of double crochet. For border along two sides of the crossover work: 1st row—with darkest blue wool, plain double crochet, 1 stitch in every stitch of the foundation chain. The second row and 6 following rows are worked in point neige stitch (described page 126). 2nd row—with palest blue. 3rd row—with medium blue. 4th row—with grey. 5th row—with darkest blue. 6th row—with grey. 7th row—medium blue. 8th row—palest blue. 9th row—darkest blue, plain double crochet, 2 stitches on every stitch of point neige. 10th row—grey, wool over the needle, and insert the hook in the first stitch of last row, and draw the wool through, wool over the needle, insert the hook in the next stitch, and draw the wool through, wool over the needle, insert the hook in the next stitch, and draw the wool through; 6 loops are on the needle, draw the wool through all, * 1 chain, wool over the needle, insert the hook in the same stitch as last loop is worked into, and draw the wool through, wool over the needle, insert the hook in the next stitch, and draw the wool through, wool over the needle, insert the hook in the next stitch, and draw the wool through, draw the wool through the 6 loops on the needle, then draw through 2 stitches on the needle, and repeat from *. 11th row—grey, plain double crochet all along, turn at the end of the row, and work double crochet back, taking up the threads at the *back* of the stitches of the eleventh row. 13th row—same as tenth row. 14th row—same as eleventh row. Now, along the ends of this border, and along the entire top of the shawl, work with grey a row of plain double crochet; then a row thus : 1 double crochet on the first stitch, * 3 chain, 1 treble in the same place the double crochet is worked into, miss 1, 1 double crochet in the next, and repeat from *. Cut some grey wool into strands, and fringe by knotting two threads in every stitch of the border, and the crossover is finished.

Square Shawl. Cobweb Pattern.—Merino or Shetland
wool. Medium-sized bone crochet needle. Begin with 6 chain, join round, and in the centre work 6 treble, 3 chain four times, and join round. 2nd round—1 double crochet in the middle of the 6 treble stitches, 3 treble, 3 chain, 3 treble, 3 chain, 3 treble, all to be worked under the 3 chain of preceding round ; repeat. 3rd round—1 double crochet over the double crochet of last round, 3 treble, 3 chain, 3 treble, under the 3 chain, a double crochet in the corner on the middle stitch of 3 treble, 3 treble, 3 chain, 3 treble, under the next three chain of last round ; repeat. 4th round —1 double crochet over the double crochet of last round, 3 treble, 3 chain, 3 treble, under the 3 chain, 1 double crochet, 3 chain, 1 double crochet, over the double crochet in the corner, 3 treble, 3 chain, 3 treble, under the next 3 chain ; repeat. 5th round— 1 double crochet, over the double crochet of last round, 3 treble, 3 chain, 3 treble, under the 3 chain, 1 double crochet on the last of the 3 treble, 3 treble, 3 chain, 3 treble, 3 chain, 3 treble, all to be worked in the small loop at the corner, 1 double crochet on the first of the 3 treble, 3 treble, 3 chain, 3 treble, under the 3 chain of last round ; repeat. The working of the third, fourth, and fifth rounds is to be repeated for the whole size of the shawl ; the increasing at the corner produces an extra web which gradually inclines to the side, thereby keeping the shawl square and without any fulness. The border is to consist of 3 pattern rounds worked with a different coloured wool to the ground of the shawl.

Square Shawl. Crazy Pattern.—Shetland wool or fine Eider yarn. Crochet needle No. 10. Commence with 4 chain. Join. 1st round—1 double crochet, 2 chain, and 3 treble, in the circle; repeat three times, and then join by drawing the wool through the first double crochet stitch. This shawl is not worked round in the usual way, but the work is to be *turned* at the completion of every round. 2nd round—make 3 chain and turn, and under the first 2 chain of last round, work * 1 double crochet, 2 chain, 3 treble, twice in the same place, and repeat from * under each 2 chain of previous round, and join by drawing the wool through the first double crochet stitch. 3rd round—3 chain and turn, and work * 1 double crochet, 2 chain, 3 treble, under the first 2 chain of last round, and 1 double crochet, 2 chain, 3 treble twice, under the next 2 chain of last round, and repeat from *. 4th round—3 chain and turn, and under the first 2 chain of last round work 1 double crochet, 2 chain, 3 treble, and the same under the next 2 chain; then for the corner, work the same twice under the next 2 chain of last round, and repeat. Continue every round the same, always increasing at the four corners and working straight along the four sides. For the border, work 3 or 4 rounds with a different coloured wool to that used for the ground of the shawl.

Square Shawl. Open Chain Net-Work.—Shetland wool, and bone crochet needle No. 10. Commence with chain for the length required. 1st row—1 double crochet in the twelfth chain stitch from the needle, * 7 chain, miss 6 of the foundation chain, 1 double crochet in the seventh, and repeat from *. Turn at the end of this and every row. 2nd row—7 chain, 1 double crochet on the double crochet stitch of last row, and repeat. 3rd row—7 chain, 1 double crochet in the centre chain stitch of the 7 chain in the first row, working over the loop of 7 chain in the second row; repeat. 4th row—7 chain to turn, 1 double crochet on the first double crochet of previous row, * 7 chain, 1 double crochet on the next double crochet of previous row, repeat from *; and at the end of the row work 3 chain, 1 double crochet in the chain stitch that turned. 5th row—7 chain, 1 double crochet in the centre chain stitch of the 7 chain in the third row, working over the loop of 7 chain in last row; repeat; at the end of the row, the double crochet stitch comes in the fourth chain stitch that turns. 6th row—7 chain, 1 double crochet on the double crochet stitch of last row, and repeat. Repeat from the third row for the length required. For the border—first of all to get the two sides and the finishing-off row perfectly straight, work 1 double crochet, 7 chain, alternately, all round the shawl. 1st round—1 treble in every stitch all round the shawl, increasing at the corners. 2nd round—1 treble on the first treble of last round, * 1 chain, 1 treble on the next treble, 1 chain, 1 long treble in the same place, 2 chain, another long treble in the same place, 1 chain, 1 treble in the same place, 1 chain, 1 treble on the next treble, miss 3 treble of last row, and in the next work 2 half-treble, thus—wool over the needle, insert the hook in the stitch and draw the wool through, wool over the needle and draw through 2 stitches on the needle, wool over the needle, insert the hook again in the same place and draw the wool through, wool over the needle and draw through 2 stitches on the needle, wool over the needle and draw through the 3 stitches on the needle, miss 3 treble of last row, 1 treble on the next treble ; and repeat from *. 3rd round—1 treble under the 1 chain between the treble and first long treble of last round, 1 chain, 1 treble under the 2 chain, 1 chain, 1 long treble in the same place, 2 chain, another long treble in the same place, 1 chain, 1 treble in the same place, 1 chain, 1 treble under the next 1 chain of last round, 1 chain, 2 half-treble stitches between the half-trebles of last round, 1 chain, and repeat. 4th round—1 treble under the first 1 chain of last round, 1 chain, 1 treble under the chain between the treble and first long treble of last round, 1 chain, 1 treble under the 2 chain, 1 chain, 1 long treble in the same place, 2 chain, another long treble in the same place, 1 chain, 1 treble in the same place, 1 chain, 1 treble under the next 1 chain of last round, 1 chain, 1 treble under the next 1 chain, 1 chain, 2 half-treble between the half-trebles of last round, 1 chain, and repeat. 5th round—the same as the fourth round, working an additional 1 chain, 1 treble on each side the scallop. 6th round— 1 treble under the first 1 chain of last round, * 5 chain, 1 single crochet picot into the first of the chain, 1 treble under the next one chain of last round, repeat from *, working 4 treble stitches with a picot between each under the 2 chain at the head of the scallop, and working the half-trebles as before.

Shawl or Wrap. Tufted Pattern.—White Peacock fingering wool. Crochet needle No. 6. Commence with chain sufficient for the width of the shawl. 1st row—1 double crochet in the first chain from the hook, 1 double crochet in the next, * wool over the needle, and insert the hook in the next chain, and draw the wool through, so as to work the half of a treble stitch, wool over the needle, and make another half-treble, wool over the needle, and make a third half-treble, draw the wool through the 3 half-treble and through the other stitch that is on the needle, 2 double crochet in 2 consecutive chain, repeat from * to the end of the row; turn. 2nd row—2 double crochet above the 2 double crochet of previous row, * 3 half-treble above the 3 half-treble, and 2 double crochet above the next 2 double crochet, repeat from *. Every succeeding row is worked the same as the second row. The shawl is to be finished off with fringe.

Scarf. Point de Chantilly.—Double Berlin wool of the colour preferred, and rather large bone tricot needle. Commence with 24 chain. Insert the hook in the second chain from the needle, raise a loop, and work a chain stitch in it, then raise another loop in the next stitch, and work a chain in that, and so on to the end of the row, keeping all the chain stitches on the needle. To work back, draw the wool through the last stitch, and then through 2 stitches together, until all are worked off. 2nd row—1 chain, insert the hook in the first perpendicular loop, and also through the chain stitch belonging to it, raise a loop, and work a chain stitch in it, * insert the hook in the next perpendicular loop and through the chain stitch belonging to it, raise a loop, and work a chain stitch in that; repeat from *, keeping all the chain stitches on the needle, and work them off the same as before. Every succeeding row is the same as the second row. The scarf should measure from one and a half yards long. Fringe the ends.

Scarf or Muffler. Scotch Diaper Pattern.—White double Berlin wool, and medium-sized bone tricot needle. Commence with 24 chain. Raise a row of loops in the chain, keeping them all on the needle, and to work back, draw the wool through the first stitch, and then through 1 stitch at a time until all are off. 2nd row,—raise another row of loops, taking up the perpendicular stitches below the rib at the back of the work—this produces a raised rib to the front. Work back as in the first row. Continue working as the second row until the scarf is large enough. Finish off the ends with a fringe.

Scarf. Crossed Treble Stitch.—4 oz. of white and 1 oz. of pale blue Peacock wool, and a bone crochet needle No. 8. With white wool, work 39 chain. 1st row—1 treble in the fourth chain from the needle, * miss the next stitch, 1 treble in the next, pass the hook in front of the treble just done, insert it in the missed chain stitch and work a treble loosely across the other, repeat from * to the end of the row, making in all 18 groups of treble stitches ; break off the wool at the end of this and every row. 2nd row— re-commencing on the right-hand side, 1 treble in the first space of previous row, pass the hook in front, insert it at the top of the first treble of last row and work a treble loosely across the first treble, * then a treble in the next space of previous row and another treble across that into the space to the right where a treble is already worked into, repeat from * to the end of the row, and there, for want of another space, work a treble on the last treble of last row and cross it as the others are crossed. Every succeeding row is the same as the second row, always making 18 crossed stitches in the row, as loosely and evenly as possible. Continue with the white wool for 36 rows, then work 3 rows with blue, 3 rows with white, 3 rows with blue, and again 3 rows with white for the end. Re-commence upon the foundation chain and work the other side of the scarf in the same manner. Fasten all the ends of wool in securely. Edge all round the scarf with white, 1 double crochet into a space of the scarf, * 4 chain, 1 single crochet at the top of the double crochet just done, 1 double crochet in the next space, and repeat from *. Fringe the ends by knotting 4 strands of wool into the loops of 4 chain.

Fascinator.—This is intended to be worn folded cornerways, the corners to come on the top of the head to the front, the ends tie under the chin or pass round the neck. Procure 2 oz. of white Shetland wool and a No. 10 bone crochet needle. Make a chain of 100 stitches, and work 3 treble into every third stitch. 2nd row—3 chain to turn, 3 treble in every space. Every succeeding row is the same as this row. Continue till 52 rows are done, or till your work forms a perfect square; then turn with 3 chain and work 3 groups of 3 treble stitches forwards and backwards for 36 rows, and break off wool. Begin again at the opposite corner in the chain stitch at the turning of the row, and work 3 groups of 3 treble stitches, and complete another end of 36 rows to correspond. The border is worked all round the square and ends. 1st round—4 treble into one space, 1 treble into the next space, and repeat; put 6 treble to ease the corners. 2nd round—4 treble in between the second and third trebles of last round, 1 treble on the previous 1 treble, and repeat; put 8 treble to ease the corners. 3rd round—8 treble in between the second and third treble of last round, 1 chain, 1 treble on the previous 1 treble, 1 chain, and repeat; put 10 treble to ease the corners. Now make little daisy tufts by winding the wool 12 times round a black lead pencil and sew tightly with a needle and cotton, cut and trim to shape, and sew one tuft on the point of every scallop round the square, not round the ends.

Lady's Capôte.—1 lb. of best Penelope fingering, pale blue or cherry brown; crochet needle No. 7. This capôte is to be worked loosely. Commence at the neck with 51 chain. Work 8 long treble stitches (wool twice round the needle) in the fourth chain from the needle, miss 3, 1 double crochet in the next, miss 3, 9 long treble in the next, and repeat, making in all 7 shells of 9 trebles in a shell, the trebles should be about an inch and a quarter high. 2nd row—slip along to the centre 1 of the 9 long treble, there work a double crochet stitch, * work 9 long treble on the double crochet of last row and 1 double crochet on the centre stitch of next group of treble, and repeat from *, making 6 shells of 9 treble in a shell. 3rd row—again 7 shells. 4th row—6 shells. 5th row—7 shells. 6th row—6 shells. 7th row—5 shells. 8th row—6 shells. 9th row—5 shells. 10th row—4 shells. 11th row—3 shells. 12th row—4 shells. 13th row—3 shells. 14th row—2 shells. 15th row—1 shell; and fasten off. For cape—holding the right side of the first row towards you, re-commence upon the foundation chain, working 7 shells of 9 long trebles opposite the long trebles of the first row, and 1 double crochet opposite the double crochet of the first row. 2nd row—5 chain to turn, work 9 long treble on the first long treble of last row, * 1 double crochet on the centre stitch of the group of 9 long treble, 9 long treble on the double crochet stitch, and repeat from *, making 8 shells of 9 treble in a shell. 3rd row—5 chain to turn, and work as described for the second row, making 9 shells in the row. Proceed thus, increasing 1 shell in every row till you have done 18 rows and have 24 shells in the row. For border—continue the pattern of shells up the side of the cape, round the hood, and along the other side of the cape. Then finish off with a chain-stitch fringing, thus— 1 double crochet in first stitch of the cape, * 20 chain, 1 double crochet in the next, and repeat from * all round the cape and hood. Run a ribbon round the front of the hood with bow at top; run another ribbon round the neck to tie.

Tam O'Shanter.—3 oz. of single Berlin wool, any colour that may be preferred, and medium-sized crochet needle. Commence with 3 chain, unite, and work 6 double crochet in the circle. Run a cotton in to mark the beginning of each round. The Scotch way of working these caps is to insert the needle so as to take up the 2 upper threads of wool, leaving no ridge; but if you prefer a ridge, work the double crochet in the top and back loops. 2nd round—2 double crochet in every stitch. 3rd round —2 double crochet in the first stitch, 1 double crochet in the next stitch, and repeat. 4th round—the same. 5th round—1 double crochet in each of the first 2 stitches, and 2 double crochet in the third stitch, and repeat. 6th round—2 double crochet in the first stitch, and afterwards in every seventh stitch. 7th round —2 double crochet in every tenth stitch. Continue the double crochet, increasing at intervals in each round as often as required to make the work lie flat, until you have a piece measuring 11 inches in diameter. Then work 4 rounds of plain double crochet without increasing. In the next 2 rounds decrease by missing every seventh stitch; afterwards, and until the cap is the size required for the head, decrease about six times in each round. For the band, work 6 rounds in plain double crochet, finishing off with 3 single stitches. A tuft of wool is to be added in the centre of the crown, to make which wind a good quantity of wool over a piece of card about three inches wide, tie it strongly together, sew it on, and cut and pull it into the shape of a round ball. The cap should be lined with silk the colour of the wool with which it is worked.

Tam O'Shanter. Worked in Tufted Tricot.—This Tam O'Shanter consists of ten sections of tufted tricot with ten lines of open-worked tricot between, through which a narrow ribbon is run. Our model is worked in pale blue, but a pretty cardinal can be used if preferred, and will look equally well. Procure 3 oz. of single Berlin wool, a tricot needle No. 8, 2 yards of ¼-inch wide corded ribbon to match the wool, and a silk pompon for the centre of the crown. Commence with 30 chain, pick up 24 stitches (25 in all on the needle), leave 5 chain, and work back, wool over the needle and draw through 1 stitch, * 4 chain, wool over the needle and draw through the last of the chain and 1 stitch, wool over the needle and draw through the stitch so formed and the next stitch of tricot, and repeat from * to the end of the row. There should be 12 tufts of tricot with 2 plain stitches between each tuft. 2nd row—pick up 22 stitches, and work back, wool over the needle and draw through 1 stitch, * 4 chain, wool over the needle and draw through the last of the chain and 1 stitch, wool over the needle and draw through the stitch so formed and the next stitch of tricot, and repeat from * to the end of the row, and there should be 11 tufts of tricot. Continue working in this way, picking up 2 stitches less in each row till you have worked off all the stitches, when you should be able to count 12 tufts every way. 13th row—pick up the stitches all along right to the end of the commencing chain, and having 30 stitches in all on the needle, work straight back as in ordinary tricot. 14th row—pick up 27 stitches, and pick up the last 2 together as 1, and having 29 stitches on the needle, work back in ordinary tricot. 15th row—pick up 25 stitches, inserting the hook in the small loop at the *back* of the stitches of last row, pick up the last three together as 1, and having 27 stitches on the needle, work back as usual, by picking up at the back of the stitches, this will be an open-work row. 16th row—pick up 23 stitches in the usual manner, pick up the last three together as 1, and having 25 stitches on the needle, draw back as ordinary tricot. 17th row—pick up 21 stitches, then two together as 1, and having 23 stitches on the needle, work back in the usual way. This completes one section of the cap. Work nine more sections, ten sections in all forming the crown of the cap, join it round. For the underpart—work 1 round of double crochet round the extreme edge of the tricot rather tightly. Then work 8 rounds of double crochet, inserting the hook into both upper loops of the double crochet of last round, and decreasing all the time just sufficiently to make the work lie flat, which will be about one stitch in eight. The two outside rounds of tufted tricot should turn over and show upon this underpart. For the band—into the last round of double crochet work in this manner : wool over the needle as if about to make a treble stitch, insert the hook, taking up both upper loops of double crochet stitch of previous round and draw the wool through, wool over the needle and draw through the three stitches on the needle, and repeat, join at the end of the round. And now work a round of single crochet, thus : insert the hook, taking up both upper loops of stitch of previous round and draw the wool through and through the stitch on the needle, insert the hook in the same manner in the next stitch of previous round and complete the stitch in the same way, and repeat. This makes a row which looks like a row of chain stitches on the front of the work. Repeat these two rounds three more times. Run the narrow ribbon in the open sections of the crown, and place the pompon in the centre, and the cap is finished.

Smoking or Travelling Cap.—1½ oz. of Navy blue, 1 oz. of amber single Berlin wool. Bone crochet needle No. 11. With Navy blue wool, work 7 chain and join round. 1st round—3 chain to stand for a treble, work 16 treble in the circle. 2nd round—inserting the hook into the two top threads of previous round, work 32 treble. 3rd round—1 treble on the first stitch of last round, 2 treble on the next, and so on alternately, making 49 treble in the round. 4th round—1 treble on each of the first 2 stitches of last round, 2 treble on the next, and repeat, making 66 treble. 5th round—1 treble on each of the first 3 stitches of last round, 2 treble on the next, and continue, making 83 treble. 6th round—work 1 treble on each of the first 2 stitches of last round, but stop before drawing the second treble stitch through the last time and take the amber wool and finish the stitch with amber, work the first part of a treble stitch with amber on the next stitch of previous round and finish it with blue, then * 2 blue treble on the next stitch of last round and 1 on the next, but finish the last stitch with amber, and work the first part of a treble with amber on the next stitch of last round and finish it with blue, and repeat from * to the end of the round; this method of procedure makes the stitch of each colour clear and distinct, work *over* the wool that is not in use and so pass it from stitch to stitch invisibly; there are to be 28 amber treble stitches in the round and 3 blue between. 7th round—no increase, work 1 blue treble over the centre stitch of the three blue treble of last round, then 3 amber treble, and repeat. 8th round—all amber, work 6 consecutive treble, 2 treble on next stitch, and repeat, making 127 treble in the round. 9th round—with blue wool, 1 double crochet on each stitch of last round, which, working a double crochet on the chain that stands for a treble, makes 128 double crochet in the round, and this number is to be adhered to for the remainder of the cap. You now work for the band. 10th round—also with blue, double crochet into the *lower* thread at the *back* of the stitches of last round. Then 4 rounds of blue double crochet taking up both front threads of the stitches of last rounds. 15th round—work 3 double crochet with blue, 1 double crochet with amber, changing the wools in the manner described in the sixth round. 16th round—1 blue double crochet on the centre stitch of the 3 blue double crochet of last round, then 3 amber double crochet, and repeat. Work 5 rounds of plain double crochet with amber wool. 22nd round—1 blue double crochet to come exactly over the 1 blue double crochet in the sixteenth round, 3 amber double crochet, and repeat. 23rd round—1 amber double crochet over the centre stitch of the 3 amber double crochet of last round, 3 blue double crochet, and repeat. Now work 6 rounds of plain double crochet with blue wool. Strengthen the edge with a round worked into the lower thread at the *back* of the stitches of last round, and the cap is finished.

Sofa Blanket. Excelsior Stripe.—Black and amber single Berlin wool, crimson Wick wool. Medium-sized bone tricot needle. For the groundwork of the pattern make a chain of 12 stitches with the black wool, raise loops along the chain, 12 loops in all, and work backwards and forwards in plain tricot until the stripe is long enough. The foundation of the sofa blanket is entirely of black stripes, which are to be bordered and joined with amber. The Wick wool is to be twisted in and out through the stripes in imitation of a cable, crossing over and under the 6 middle stitches at intervals of 2 rows between each twist. Having made a number of stripes, work a row of double crochet with the amber wool round each, and join them with a kind of raised plait, thus—keep the amber wool under the stripes, and work, very loosely, 1 single crochet in the first double crochet on the left-hand stripe, then 1 single crochet in the corresponding stitch on the right-hand stripe, and so on alternately. When the stripes are all joined a row is to be worked with amber wool all round the blanket, as follows: 1 double crochet, * 3 chain, 1 double crochet in the lower part of the double crochet just done, miss 1 stitch, 1 double crochet in the next; repeat from *. The top and bottom of the sofa blankets are fringed, the fringe being tied on the black stripes underneath the amber edge. Three knots of black wool, four strands of wool in each knot, and two single knots of Wick wool, are to be tied on every black stripe. Or work the Grecian key or some other pattern, in cross-stitch, with red wool, on the black tricot stripes.

Sofa Blanket. Honeycomb Lattice Pattern.—This is worked in rows backwards and forwards, four rows with ruby and eight rows with olive green double Berlin. Bone crochet needle No. 8. Commence with chain the length required. Do the whole of the work taking up two threads, and turn at the end of every row. 1st row—plain double crochet. 2nd row—insert the hook in the same stitch of the commencing chain that the third double crochet of last row is worked into, draw up from the back a long loop loosely, wool over the needle and draw through the long loop, wool over the needle and draw through the 2 stitches on the needle, this stands for the first stitch. * work 3 double crochet on 3 consecutive stitches of last row, insert the hook in the same chain stitch the last long loop is worked into and draw up a long loop loosely, insert the hook in the fourth chain stitch from the last long loop and draw up another long loop, wool over the needle and draw through the 2 long loops, wool over the needle, and draw through the 2 stitches on the needle; repeat from *; and the row must *end* with the 1 long loop that is worked after the 3 double crochet. 3rd row—plain double crochet. 4th row—2 double crochet, * insert the hook in the top part of the long loop to the right of the needle (that is, in the centre of the little stitch that looks like a ring) and draw up a long loop, insert the hook in the top part of the long loop to the left of the needle and draw up another long loop, wool over the needle and draw through the two long loops, wool over the needle and draw through the two stitches on the needle, 3 double crochet on three consecutive double crochet of last row, and repeat from * ; and the row must end with 2 double crochet stitches as it began. These four rows constitute the pattern.

Couvrepied. Pine Pattern.—To be worked in stripes with double Berlin, two or more colours. Tricot needle No. 6. For a stripe make a chain of 14 stitches. 1st row—wool over the needle and insert the hook in the third chain from the needle, draw the wool through so as to work the half of a treble stitch, wool over the needle and make another half-treble, wool over the needle and make a third half-treble, draw the wool through the 3 half-treble, raise a loop in the next chain, 3 half-trebles again in the next, a loop in the next, and so on to the end of the row, keeping all the stitches on the needle. The loops should be raised loosely. To work back, draw the wool through one loop first, through that again, and then through one at a time till all the stitches are off. 2nd row—1 chain to begin with, raise a loop over the pine of last row, taking up the perpendicular thread only, * then 3 half-treble over the loop of last row, taking up the loop with a top thread of the chain that lies under it, and a loop in the perpendicular stitch of the next pine; repeat from *, and at the end of the row raise one extra loop to keep the pattern straight. Work back as for the first row. 3rd row—1 chain to begin with, * 3 half-treble over the loop of last row, taking up the loop with the top thread of the chain that lies under it, then a loop over the pine, taking up the perpendicular thread only; repeat from *, and work back as for the first row. There will be 6 pines in the first row, 5 in the second, 6 again in the third, and so on alternately to keep the pattern straight. Repeat the second and third rows for the length required, and make as many stripes as are necessary for the width of the couvrepied. Join the stripes together with a row of plain double crochet, and finish off the top and bottom of the couvrepied with a fringe of four strands of wool knotted into each pine.

Cradle Quilt. Angola Pattern.—Procure white, and five shades of blue, double Berlin. Crochet needle No. 7. Commence with darkest shade of blue, and make a chain the length required, turn, and work 1 double crochet in the second chain from the needle, * insert hook in the next chain, draw the wool through and work 6 chain stitches, wool over the needle and draw through two stitches on the needle, 1 double crochet in next stitch of the foundation, and repeat from * to end of row, where break off the wool. 2nd row—with next shade of blue, re-commencing on the right-hand side, 1 double crochet on double crochet stitch of last row, taking up both front threads, * 1 double crochet under the loop of chain stitches, insert hook in next double crochet of last row, draw the wool through and work 6 chain stitches, wool over the needle and draw through two stitches on the needle, and repeat from * ; there will be 2 double crochet to work at the end of the row as at the beginning, and break off the wool. 3rd row—with next shade of blue, 1 double crochet on first stitch of last row, loop of chain on next, double crochet under chain loop of last row, and continue. Proceed in this manner for the width of the quilt, one row of each shade, or two rows of each shade, as preferred, three rows of white to come next the palest shade of blue, and then shade blue again gradually back to the darkest. This makes a lovely furry-looking quilt. It may be fringed all round, or ornamented with a border of daisy balls as described for edging the berceaunette cover.

Berceaunette Cover. Squares of Tricot and Crochet.—Pink and white double Berlin wool. Tricot needle No. 6. Crochet needle No. 8. Commence with pink wool, work 15 chain, in which pick up 14 tricot stitches and draw back ; work plain tricot forwards and backwards till you have made a perfect square. Then, still with pink wool, and holding the tricot the wrong side towards you, work double crochet all round the square, doing three double crochet at the turning of the corners. 2nd round—with white wool, hold the tricot the right side towards you, and inserting the hook to take up the back thread of the stitches of last round, work round in treble, doing three or five treble to ease at the corners. 3rd round—with pink wool, 2 double crochet on two consecutive stitches of last round, working into both top loops, insert the hook in the pink where next treble stitch is worked into, draw up the wool loosely and work a double crochet, and repeat, and fasten off at end of the round. Work the tricot part of the next square with white wool, border it with a round of pink, white, and pink again, like the square already done. On the white tricot square, work a rosebud spray, with shaded filoselles. On the pink tricot square, work five lines of coral stitch, all with pink filoselle. Join the squares together by a pink row of double crochet. For border round the cover: hold the work the wrong side towards you, and taking up the 1 top thread, work with pink wool a round of double crochet. 2nd round—with white wool, hold the work the right side towards you, insert the hook to take up the back thread of the stitches of last round, 1 double crochet, 6 chain, miss 2, and repeat. 3rd round—with white, 1 double crochet under loop of 6 chain, 6 chain, and repeat. Make a number of daisy balls of pink and white wool mixed, and sew one upon every alternate loop of chain stitches, and one at every corner of the quilt squares.

Bassinette Cover. Point Neige.—To be worked with double Berlin wool of two colours, four or five shades of each colour, and in rows alternating from dark to light and to dark again. Crochet needle No. 6. With the darkest wool make a chain the length required. 1st row—raise 5 loops in 5 successive stitches of the chain, pull through all the loops and the stitch on the needle together, 1 chain, * raise a loop in the thread that lies under the chain, another in the lower thread at the back of the last stitch of the group, another in the same chain the last group was worked into, one in the next chain, and another in the next chain, there will be 6 stitches on the needle, pull through all, 1 chain; repeat from *, and fasten off at the end of the row. 2nd row—with the next lightest shade of wool, beginning on the right-hand side; 1 single in the first stitch of previous row, 2 chain, raise a loop in the first chain, another in the single stitch, another in the top thread of the group of stitches in previous row, another in the hole formed by the 1 chain, and another in the top thread of the next group of stitches, there will now be 6 stitches on the needle, pull through all, 1 chain, * raise a loop in the thread that lies under the chain, another in the lower thread at the back of the last stitch of the group, another in the same stitch the last group was worked into, another in the hole formed by the 1 chain, and another in the top thread of the next group of stitches, pull through all, 1 chain; and repeat from *. Be careful to keep the same number of points in every row. The work throughout is the same as described for the second row. Supposing you have five shades, each of two different colours, there will be 9 rows to be worked in a colour, and 45 rows should make the bassinette cover sufficiently wide. Or, to make a smaller one, have four shades, and work 7 rows in a colour, 35 rows in all. Knot a fringe in all round. This pattern is also very suitable for a sofa blanket or carriage rug. For the latter, use No. 2 crochet needle, and Wick wool of two good contrasting colours, and work 1 row of each colour alternately.

Square for Quilt in Raised Diamonds.—Strutts' 3-thread knitting cotton No. 8. Steel crochet needle, Penelope No. 2.

Commence with 8 chain, join round, and work 3 double crochet in the first stitch, 2 double crochet in the next stitch, and repeat; there should be 20 double crochet in all. 2nd round—3 double crochet in the centre stitch in each corner, and 4 double crochet along each side of the square, working into the top loops only. 3rd round—3 double crochet in the centre stitch in each corner, and 6 double crochet along each side of the square. 4th round—3 double crochet in the centre stitch in the corner, 4 double crochet, 5 chain, 4 double crochet, and repeat. The 5 chain form a raised tuft, and no double crochet are to be missed. 5th round—3 double crochet in the centre stitch in each corner, and 10 double crochet along each side of the square. 6th round—3 double crochet in the centre stitch in the corner, 4 double crochet, 5 chain, 4 double crochet, 5 chain, 4 double crochet, and repeat. 7th round—3 double crochet in the centre stitch in each corner, and 14 double crochet along each side of the square. The raised diamond is increased thus until there are 5 tufts of 5 chain along each side of the square, and afterwards decreased until only 1 tuft is left. A plain round follows after each round of tufts, and 2 plain rounds after the last tuft. 23rd round—1 treble in the centre stitch at the corner, 1 chain, 1 treble in the same place, 1 chain, 1 treble again in the same place, 1 chain, miss 1, 1 treble along the side of the square, and repeat. 24th round—same as the 23rd round. 25th round—3 double crochet in the centre stitch in each corner, and plain double crochet along the sides of the square. 26th round—3 double crochet in the centre stitch at the corner, 4 double crochet, 5 chain (to form tufts) along the side of the square, and repeat. 27th round—same as the 25th round. 28th round—same as the 26th round. 29th round—same as the 25th round. 30th round—same as the 23rd round. This completes the square.

Border and Fringe for Quilt.—This may be worked on the quilt itself after the squares are joined together, or may be crocheted separately, beginning with a chain the length required. 1st row—plain double crochet. 2nd row—double crochet with a tuft of 5 chain at intervals of every 4 stitches. 3rd row—plain double crochet. 4th row—double crochet with a tuft of 5 chain at intervals of every 4 stitches; these tufts to come between those done in the second row. 5th row—plain double crochet. 6th row—5 long treble into every fifth stitch of previous row. For the fringe cut a skein of cotton into lengths of 7 inches, and knot 2 pieces into every stitch of the long treble.

Square for Quilt.—With a border of tufts, and a tufted diamond in the centre. Strutts' 3-thread knitting cotton No. 6. Steel crochet needle, Penelope, No. 2. Commence with 51 chain, and work the first 3 rows forwards and backwards in plain double crochet, 51 stitches in each row, and inserting the hook in the back thread of the stitches of previous row, so as to make the work set in ridges. 4th row—5 double crochet, * 5 treble into the next stitch and catch the last of the treble stitches into the first to bind them together in a tuft, 3 double crochet, and repeat from *, ending the row with 5 double crochet as it began. 5th row—double crochet, and 1 treble stitch worked at the back of each tuft. 6th row—3 double crochet, tuft, 7 double crochet, tuft, 3 double crochet, tuft, 7 double crochet, tuft, 3 double crochet, tuft, 7 double crochet, tuft, 3 double crochet, tuft, 3 double crochet, tuft, 7 double crochet, tuft, 3 double crochet. 7th row—same as the fifth row. 8th row.—13 double crochet, tuft, 11 double crochet, tuft, 11 double crochet, tuft, 13 double crochet. 9th row—same as the fifth row. 10th row—3 double crochet, tuft, 43 double crochet, tuft, 3 double crochet. 11th row—same as the fifth row. 12th row—5 double crochet, tuft, 39 double crochet, tuft, 5 double crochet. 13th row—same as the fifth row. 14th row—3 double crochet, tuft, 3 double crochet, tuft, 13 double crochet, tuft, 3 double crochet, tuft, 3 double crochet, tuft, 13 double crochet, tuft, 3 double crochet, tuft, 3 double crochet. 15th row—same as the fifth row. 16th row—5 double crochet, tuft, 13 double crochet, tuft, 3 double crochet, tuft, 3 double crochet, tuft, 3 double crochet, tuft, 13 double crochet, tuft, 5 double crochet. 17th row—same as the fifth row. 18th row—3 double crochet, tuft, 13 double crochet, tuft, 3 double crochet, tuft, 7 double crochet, tuft, 3 double crochet, tuft, 13 double crochet, tuft, 3 double crochet. 19th row—same as the fifth row. 20th row—15 double crochet, tuft, 3 double crochet, tuft, 11 double crochet, tuft, 3 double crochet, tuft, 15 double crochet. 21st row—same as the fifth row. 22nd row—3 double crochet, tuft, 9 double crochet, tuft, 3 double crochet, tuft, 15 double crochet, tuft, 3 double crochet, tuft, 9 double crochet, tuft, 3 double crochet. 23rd row—same as the fifth row. 24th row—5 double crochet, tuft, 9 double crochet, tuft, 9 double crochet, tuft, 9 double crochet, tuft, 9 double crochet, tuft, 5 double crochet. 25th row—same as the fifth row. 26th row—3 double crochet, tuft, 3 double crochet, tuft, 5 double crochet, tuft, 9 double crochet, tuft, 3 double crochet, tuft, 9 double crochet, tuft, 5 double crochet, tuft, 3 double crochet, tuft, 3 double crochet. 27th row —same as the fifth row. Now work the same as directed for the 24th row, and continue thence backwards, ending with 3 rows of plain double crochet, which completes the square. Without breaking off the cotton, proceed to work round all four sides of the square, do a treble stitch at the corner, 5 chain, another treble in the same place, 2 chain, miss 2 stitches of the square, 1 treble in the next, and repeat the 2 chain, 1 treble, with increase in turning the corners. 2nd round—double crochet in every stitch of last round, working 3 double crochet in the stitch at the corners. When a sufficient number of squares are worked, sew them together.

Tufted Border for Quilt.—To be worked with the same-sized cotton and needle as used for the squares. Commence with 22 chain; turn, work 21 double crochet in the row. 2nd row—insert the hook always into the back threads, so that the work may set in ridges, 4 double crochet, 1 tuft, 16 double crochet. 3rd row—16 double crochet, insert hook into the first row, and work 1 treble at the back of the tuft, 4 double crochet, 3 chain. 4th row—2 double crochet in 2 stitches of the chain, 2 double crochet on 2 first double crochet of last row, tuft, 3 double crochet, tuft, 14 double crochet. 5th row—14 double crochet, 1 treble, 3 double crochet, 1 treble, 4 double crochet, 3 chain. 6th row—2 double crochet in 2 stitches of the chain, 2 double crochet on 2 first double crochet of last row, tuft, 3 double crochet, tuft, 3 double crochet, tuft, 12 double crochet. 7th row—12 double crochet, 1 treble, 3 double crochet, 1 treble, 3 double crochet, 1 treble, 4 double crochet, 3 chain. 8th row—2 double crochet in 2 stitches of the chain, 2 double crochet on 2 first double crochet of last row, tuft, 3 double crochet, tuft, 3 double crochet, tuft, 3 double crochet, tuft, 10 double crochet. 9th row—10 double crochet, 1 treble, 3 double crochet, 1 treble, 3 double crochet, 1 treble, 3 double crochet, 1 treble, 4 double crochet. 10th row—6 double crochet, tuft, 3 double crochet, tuft, 3 double crochet, tuft, 12 double crochet. 11th row—12 double crochet, 1 treble, 3 double crochet, 1 treble, 3 double crochet, 1 treble, 4 double crochet, leave 2 stitches unworked. 12th row—6 double crochet, tuft, 3 double crochet, tuft, 14 double crochet. 13th row—14 double crochet, 1 treble, 3 double crochet, 1 treble, 4 double crochet, leave 2 stitches unworked. 14th row—6 double crochet, tuft, 16 double crochet. 15th row—16 double crochet, 1 treble, 4 double crochet, leave 2 stitches unworked. 16th row—21 double crochet. 17th row—3 chain, 1 treble on the third double crochet of last row, * 1 chain, miss 1, 1 treble on the next, and repeat from * eight times; break off the cotton, draw the end in neatly. Re-commence on the right-hand side working for the first row 21 double crochet, and continue the scallops for the length required. For the edging round the scallops, work 1 double crochet under the treble stitch at the end of the open row, 1 chain, 1 single on the last stitch of the double crochet row, 6 chain, 1 single in the third from the needle, 3 chain, single into the second from the needle; 1 single on the point, 9 chain, 1 single in the fifth, 6 chain, single in the fifth, 5 chain, single in the fourth, single into the next chain from this bunch of picots; 3 chain, single on next point, 11 chain, single in the fifth, 6 chain, single in the fifth, 5 chain, single in the fourth, single into the next chain from this bunch of picots; 3 chain, single on the next point, 9 chain, single in the fifth, 6 chain, single in the fifth, 5 chain, single in the fourth, single into the next chain from this bunch of picots; 3 chain, and single on the opposite side of the point, this being the centre point of the scallop, 9 chain, single in the sixth, 6 chain, single in the fifth, 6 chain, single in the fifth, single into the next chain from this bunch of picots; 5 chain, single on next point, another picot the same, and single on next point, 4 chain, single in the third; 4 chain, single in the third, 2 chain, single on end of the close work of the scallops, 1 chain, and repeat round each scallop in the same way. For heading along the top: 1st row—1 treble, 1 chain, alternately, working all treble stitches into a depressed row of the ridges; break off cotton at end of each row. 2nd row—double crochet on every stitch of last row. 3rd row—1 double crochet, * 5 chain, miss three, 1 double crochet on the next, and repeat from *. 4th row—1 double crochet in the centre stitch of 5 chain, 3 chain, and repeat. 5th row—double crochet on every stitch of last row. 6th row—1 treble, 1 chain, alternately, missing a stitch of previous row between each treble stitch.

Shell for Quilt.—Strutts' 3-thread knitting cotton No. 6. Steel crochet needle, Penelope, No. 2. Commence with 3 chain, turn; 3 double crochet in the second chain from the needle, 1 double crochet in the last chain, turn. The double crochet throughout the shell is to be worked into the back of the stitches so as to form ridges. 2nd row—1 double crochet in the first double crochet of previous row, 1 double crochet in the next, 3 double crochet in the next, 1 double crochet in the next, and 1 double crochet on the chain at the end, turn. 3rd row—3 double crochet in 3 consecutive stitches, 3 double crochet in the centre stitch, 3 double crochet in the next 3 consecutive stitches, turn. Continue as the third row, always working 3 double crochet to increase in the centre stitch, and by this means 1 more double crochet will come on each side in every row. Work until there are

10 ridges done; that is, 21 rows.   22nd row—3 chain, miss the first double crochet of previous row, 2 treble in the next stitch, miss 2 and work 3 treble six times, miss 2, 5 treble in the centre stitch of the shell, miss 2 and work 3 treble six times, miss 2, 2 treble in the next stitch, and 1 treble in the last stitch, turn.   23rd row—23 double crochet along the side, 3 double crochet on the centre stitch of the 5 treble, 23 double crochet along the other side. This completes the shell, but if you wish it to be larger, repeat the 22nd and 23rd rows. The shells are to be joined, so that the open rows come uppermost. Half-shells must be made to fit in round the outside of the quilt.

Border and Fringe for Quilt.—To be worked with the same sized cotton as used for the shells. Commence with 24 chain, turn; * miss 12 stitches, 6 double crochet into the next 6 stitches, turn; 6 double crochet, 12 chain, turn; 6 double crochet, turn; 6 double crochet, 12 chain, turn; 6 double crochet, then 1 chain, 1 treble on the fifth chain of the commencement, 1 chain, miss 1, 1 treble, 1 chain, miss 1, 1 treble, turn; and above the 3 treble and the 3 chain stitches work 6 double crochet, turn; and continue until there are 5 little rows of double crochet done, then 1 chain and 1 treble three times on the first block of double crochet, 12 chain, turn; and repeat from *. When a sufficient length of this heading is done, a cross is to be worked upon each block of double crochet with a sewing needle and double cotton. For fringe, cut some cotton into lengths of 7 inches, and knot 4 pieces into every loop of 12 chain.

Antimacassar. Raised Crosses of Chain.—Olive green double Berlin wool, and a skein of bright crimson filoselle. Tricot needle No. 8. Commence with 20 chain, raise loops all along, making 20 stitches in all, and work back as in ordinary tricot.   2nd row—pick up all the loops in the usual manner, and in working back, draw through 6 stitches, work 12 chain, draw through 2 stitches, 12 chain, draw through 4 stitches, 12 chain, draw through 2 stitches, 12 chain, draw through 6 stitches.   3rd and 4th rows—plain tricot, keeping the loops of chain in front of the work.   5th row—raise 4 stitches, * pull the second loop of chain up and insert the hook through it and in the next stitch of tricot, draw the wool through both, raise 2 stitches, pull the first loop of chain across over the second; insert the hook through it and in the next stitch of tricot, and draw the wool through both, raise 2 stitches, repeat from * and raise 5 stitches at the end of the row; coming back, draw through 3 stitches, work 12 chain, draw through 2 stitches, 12 chain, draw through 4 stitches, 12 chain, draw through 2 stitches, 12 chain, draw through 4 stitches, 12 chain, draw through 2 stitches, 12 chain, draw through 3 stitches. 6th and 7th rows—plain tricot, keeping the loops of chain in front of the work. 8th row—raise 1 stitch, * pull the second loop of chain up and insert the hook through it and in the next stitch of tricot, and draw the wool through both, raise 2 stitches, pull the first loop of chain across over the second, insert the hook through it and in the next stitch of tricot, and draw the wool through both, raise 2 stitches, repeat from *; coming back, draw through 6 stitches, work 12 chain, draw through 2 stitches, 12 chain, draw through 4 stitches, 12 chain, draw through 2 stitches, 12 chain, draw through 6 stitches. 9th and 10th rows—plain tricot, keeping the loops of chain in front of the work. Repeat from the fifth row for the length required. Four stripes will be sufficient for an antimacassar, join them together by a row of double crochet. With a needle and filoselle work a large double cross or star upon the plain tricot between the raised crosses of chain. Fringe the antimacassar at the top and bottom.

Antimacassar. Tricot Vandyke.—Procure single Berlin wool, in two good contrasting colours, say red and white, the same quantity of each, and a bone tricot needle, No. 10. For the first wide stripe, make 14 chain with red wool, and 6 chain with white wool, all in a piece. 1st row—pick up 6 white tricot stitches, then 14 red stitches, and draw back in the usual way, through each stitch with its own colour, but pass the white wool across the red wool where the colours are to change. 2nd row to the 9th row—pick up 1 white tricot stitch more in each row and 1 red stitch less, and in the 9th row there should be 14 white and 6 red stitches. 10th row—13 white stitches and 7 red. 11th row to the 17th row—pick up 1 white stitch less in each row, and 1 red stitch more, and in the 17th row there should be 6 white stitches and 14 red stitches. Repeat from the second row till you have a stripe as long as required. For the second wide stripe, make 6 chain with white wool and 14 chain with red wool, all in a piece. 1st row—pick up 14 red tricot stitches, then 6 white stitches, and work back, drawing through each stitch with its own colour. 2nd row to the 9th row—pick up 1 red stitch less in each row and 1 white stitch more, and in the 9th row there should be 6 red and 14 white stitches. 10th row—7 red stitches and 13 white. 11th row to the 17th row—pick up 1 red stitch more and 1 white stitch less in each row, and in the 17th row there should be 14 red stitches and 6 white stitches. Repeat from the 2nd row till you have a stripe the same length as the first stripe. For the narrow stripe, commence with red wool with 6 chain, and work 3 rows of plain tricot. 4th row—pick up 6 stitches, and in working back draw through 3 stitches (one at a time), then do 3 chain, and draw through the remaining 3 stitches. 5th row—pick up 6 stitches, keeping the 3 chain stitches to the front, and in working back draw through 2 stitches, 3 chain, draw through 2 stitches, 3 chain, draw through the remaining 2 stitches. 6th row—the same as the 4th row. 7th row to the 11th row—plain tricot. Repeat from the fourth row for the same number of rows as worked for the wide stripes. With a wool needle, work a small star between each raised spot of chain stitches in the narrow stripes. Sew the stripes together stitch by stitch, a narrow stripe (alternately one red and one white) goes between each wide one. Fringe the ends.

Antimacassar. Domino Pattern.—Double Berlin wool of two colours, four or five shades of each colour, crochet needle No. 6. With the darkest wool make a chain the length required. 1st row—plain double crochet; turn the work. 2nd row—1 double crochet worked into the one *top* thread of double crochet stitch of last row, wool over the needle, insert the hook in the *back* thread of the next double crochet stitch of last row, and draw the wool through, draw the wool through the last stitch on the needle, wool over the needle, insert the hook again in the same place, and draw the wool through, draw the wool through the last stitch on the needle, draw the wool through 4 stitches on the needle (this forms the "domino"), then through the 2 stitches on the needle, and repeat a double crochet stitch and a domino stitch alternately, ending the row with a double crochet as it began.

3rd row—with next lightest shade of wool, plain double crochet, taking up the one top thread of the stitches of last row; turn the work. 4th row—work same as second row. Continue thus, doing 2 rows with each shade, till the antimacassar is sufficiently wide. Finish with a row of plain double crochet. Work an edge up each side of the antimacassar, 1 double crochet, 2 chain, 3 treble on the double crochet just done, miss 1 stitch of the antimacassar, 1 double crochet on the next, and repeat. Fringe at top and bottom.

Antimacassar. Princesse Stripe.—Required 6 shades of olive green, 6 shades of crimson, double Berlin wool, crochet needle No. 7. With the darkest shade of green make a chain loosely the length required, any number divisible by nine and four over, and work a row of plain double crochet. Break off the wool at the end of the row, and re-commence on the right-hand side, and henceforward work into the 1 top thread of stitches of preceding row. Do another row of double crochet with the darkest green wool, then a row with each of the next 4 intermediate shades. 7th row—with lightest green, work 3 double crochet, * insert the hook in the next stitch, and draw the wool through, insert the hook in the stitch immediately underneath that (that is, in the same place where the fourth double crochet of last row is worked into), and draw the wool through loosely, insert the hook in the stitch underneath that, and draw the wool through, insert the hook in the stitch below that, and draw the wool through, insert the hook in the next stitch underneath, and draw the wool through, insert the hook in the stitch below that, and draw the wool through, and now you have six loops on the needle, raised in a straight line one under the other, and each one longer than the other, so that they stand level with the row you are working upon, wool over the needle, and draw through the six loops, wool over the needle, and draw through 2 stitches on the needle, work 8 consecutive double crochet, and repeat from * ; there will be 9 double crochet to work at the end of the row. 8th row—with same shade of wool, work 4 double crochet, insert the hook in the next stitch, and draw the wool through, and proceed with the raising of 6 loops all in a line, one under the other, same as you did in the last row; these will lie just to the left of the raised stitches of last row, and as they are one row higher at the top, they will also be one row higher from the beginning of the work; do 8 double crochet, a set of 6 raised stitches, and repeat. 9th row—with next darkest shade begin with 5 double crochet, then a set of 6 raised stitches, 8 consecutive double crochet, and repeat, and there will be 7 double crochet to work at the end of the row. 10th row—with next darkest shade begin with 6 double crochet, work a set of 6 raised stitches, 8 double crochet, and repeat, and there will be 6 double crochet to work at the end of the row. 11th row—with next darkest shade begin with 7 double crochet, work a set of 6 raised stitches, 8 double crochet, and repeat, and there will be 5 double crochet to work at the end of the row. 12th row—with next darkest shade, 8 double crochet, then a set of 6 raised stitches, 8 double crochet, and repeat, and there will be 4 double crochet to work at the end of the row. 13th row—with darkest shade of wool, 9 double crochet, then a set of 6 raised stitches, 8 double crochet, and repeat, and there will be 3 double crochet to work at the end of the row. 14th row—with darkest shade of wool, plain double crochet. This is one stripe. Now work the next stripe with shades of crimson in the same way. Three stripes of green and two stripes of crimson will make a good-sized antimacassar. Fringe each row, top and bottom, with its own colour.

Antimacassar. Narcissus Square.—Double Berlin wool. Yellow, grey, black, white, and two shades of green. Crochet needle No. 8. Commence, with the yellow wool, with 7 chain, join round, and work 16 double crochet in the circle. 2nd round—with white wool, 1 double crochet over any of the double crochet stitches, taking up the top loop only, 6 treble in the next double crochet, 1 double crochet in the next, 6 treble in the next, and so on all round, making 8 tufts of 6 treble. 3rd round—with grey wool, 1 single crochet in every stitch. 4th round—with lightest shade of green wool, 1 single crochet at the back of any stitch of the white double crochet, * 6 chain, turn, miss 1, 5 double crochet along the 5 chain, 1 single crochet at the back of the next white double crochet; repeat from *, making 8 leaves round the white centre. 5th round—with darker shade of green wool, * 1 double crochet over the single crochet stitch of last round, 5 double crochet up the side of the leaf, 3 double crochet at the top, and 5 double crochet down the other side of the leaf; repeat from *. 6th round—with black wool, 1 single crochet in every stitch all round the leaves. 7th round—with black wool, 3 double crochet in the 3 stitches at the top of any leaf, 5 chain, * 3 double crochet on the next leaf, 5 chain; repeat from *. 8th round—with black wool, * 11 double crochet, commencing over the 3 double crochet on a leaf, and working over the 3 double crochet on the next leaf, then 7 treble in the next 5 chain stitches, putting 3 treble in the centre chain stitch; repeat from *; the treble stitches form the corners. 9th round—with yellow wool, 1 double crochet in the middle one of the 3 treble at the corner, * 5 chain, 1 single in the first chain, 5 chain, 1 single in the first chain, 5 chain, 1 single in the first chain, 1 single in the double crochet stitch to keep the picot firm, 6 consecutive double crochet, and repeat from *. The squares may be sewn together by the picots, or united to each other by a single crochet in the course of working.

Antimacassar. Sea Anemone Square.—Single Berlin wool, amber, mauve, black, and white. Crochet needle No. 10. Commence with the black wool with 3 chain, join round, and work 1 treble 3 chain, four times in the circle. 2nd round—with white wool, 1 double crochet under any 3 chain, * 14 chain, 1 treble in the fourth from the needle, 2 chain, miss 2, 1 treble, 2 chain, miss 1, 1 treble, 2 chain, miss 2, 1 double crochet; 1 chain to cross the arm, and work round again, doing 3 double crochet in each space with 6 double crochet in the point; join the arm with a single crochet, 1 chain, 1 double crochet on the black treble stitch; repeat from * until you have done 8 arms. Each alternate time of repeating, the last-named double crochet will be worked under the 3 chain instead of on a treble. 3rd round—with black wool, 1 treble at the back of the first of the 6 double crochet stitches of ast round, 2 chain, 1 treble in the centre of the 6 double crochet stitches, 2 chain, 1 treble at the back of the last of the 6 double crochet stitches of last round, 8 chain; repeat from *. Each alternate time of repeating, make 3 chain instead of 8 chain. 4th round—with black wool, 11 treble under the 8 chain which form the corners of the square, 3 treble under every other space. 5th round—with black wool, work a double crochet on every treble stitch, with 3 double crochet on the centre stitch at each corner. 6th round—with black wool, 1 treble over the middle double crochet stitch along the side, 1 chain, miss 1, 1 treble all round; and at each corner work 5 treble stitches consecutively, with 1 chain between each stitch. 7th round—with amber wool, 1 double crochet over the middle treble stitch along the side, * 5 chain, 1 double crochet into the fourth from the needle, 2 chain, miss 1 space, 1 double crochet into the next space, 5 chain, 1 double crochet into the fourth from the needle, 2 chain, miss 1 space, 1 double crochet on the next treble; repeat from * all round the square, increasing 1 picot at each corner. For the raised part of the anemone, with mauve wool—1 double crochet on the second double crochet of a white arm; 5 chain, 1 double crochet in every stitch all round the arm, and when getting to the second double crochet from the end, go over to the next arm, and work the same. For the centre of the anemone, with amber wool —double crochet all round the black centre, putting 3 double crochet between each white stitch, 24 double crochet in all, join round; then work 1 double crochet, 5 chain twenty-four times on the 24 double crochet. This completes the anemone. Six anemones will be sufficient for a small antimacassar; unite them with amber wool, working 1 double crochet, 2 chain, from picot to picot.

Antimacassar. Venetian Lattice Stripe with White Narcissus Flower.—Single Berlin wool, blue, white, grey, and a very small quantity of amber. Crochet needle No. 12. Commence, with the blue wool, with 25 chain, work 1 double crochet in the third chain from the needle and double crochet all along the row, 23 stitches in all. Work 4 more rows of plain double crochet in each row, doing 1 chain to turn and 23 double crochet. 6th row—1 chain to turn, 2 double crochet, 2 long treble in the fifth double crochet of the second row (finish off the 2 long treble in one, and then end by working the 2 loops left on the needle as a double crochet stitch), 4 double crochet, 2 long treble in the sixth double crochet of the second row, 2 long treble in the twelfth double crochet of the second row, 4 double crochet, 2 long treble in the thirteenth double crochet of the second row, 2 long treble in the eighteenth double crochet of the second row,

4 double crochet, 2 long treble in the nineteenth double crochet of the second row, 3 double crochet; 3 rows of plain double crochet. 10th row—1 chain to turn, 4 double crochet, 2 long treble over the first of the long treble in the sixth row, 2 long treble over the next long treble (in this way the lattice diamonds are formed), 4 double crochet, 2 long treble over the third long treble in the sixth row, 2 long treble over the next, 4 double crochet, 2 long treble over the fifth long treble in the sixth row, 2 long treble over the next, 5 double crochet; 3 rows of plain double crochet; repeat from the sixth row. When working the 26th row leave a space of plain double crochet in the middle of the row, working only 4 long treble at the beginning and 4 at the end; in 30th row, work only 2 long treble at the beginning and 2 at the end; and in the 34th row, 4 long treble at the beginning and 4 at the end; this is to make space for placing the Narcissus flower. Afterwards repeat from the sixth row for the length required, and when the stripe is complete, take the grey wool and work all round it a row of double crochet, making alternately 1 long and 1 short stitch. With white wool, work a stripe of plain tricot, 17 stitches in each row, and the same length as the lattice stripe, and on this work diamonds with grey wool, sewing the grey wool over the tricot, like doing chain stitch backwards. Commence the diamond with a point, and widen it to within 4 stitches of the sides of the stripe; put a tiny grey dot, 4 chain joined in a circle, and worked round with double crochet, in the centre of each diamond. Border this white stripe with grey wool as directed above for bordering the blue stripe, to which it is to be joined with a row of grey double crochet. For the Narcissus flower: work 7 chain, 1 double crochet in the chain stitch next the needle, 4 treble, 6 treble in the top stitch, 4 treble and 1 double crochet down the other side, and a single crochet to fasten off; secure the ends in firmly. Make six of these white leaves and arrange them together, and for the petal in the centre of the flower take the amber wool, work 4 chain, join in a circle, and work 2 rounds of double crochet. Sew the flower down nicely on the plain crochet part of the blue stripe. It will require three blue stripes and two white stripes for the antimacassar. For a border all round, work with grey wool. 1st row—1 double crochet, 6 chain, miss 4 double crochet of the foundation, and repeat. 2nd row—1 double crochet over the

double crochet of previous row, 7 chain, and repeat. 3rd row—work 1 double crochet, 4 chain, 2 double crochet, 4 chain, 1 double crochet, 4 chain, 2 double crochet under every 7 chain of previous row.

Kettle Holder.—Amber and black double Berlin wool. Crochet needle No. 8. Make a chain of 5 stitches with the amber wool, join round, work 12 double crochet in the circle, join again, and do 1 double crochet on each stitch, taking up the top thread only; fasten off. With black wool, work 2 treble into each stitch of double crochet, and join round. Work now into the front and back loops of former round, * 2 treble in the first stitch (making 3 chain to stand for the first treble), 1 treble in the next, 2 treble in the next, 1 treble in the next, 2 treble in the next, 5 treble in the next, which is to be a corner, and repeat from *. Next round—* 8 double crochet in 8 consecutive stitches, 1 treble in the next, 1 treble in the next, 5 treble in the centre one of the 5 treble of last round; repeat from *, and fasten off. Next round with amber—1 treble in every stitch along the sides, and 5 treble in the corner stitch. Next round—1 double crochet in every stitch along the sides, and 3 double crochet in the corner stitch, and fasten off. Last round—the same with black. Work a small spray of 5 stitches with yellow filoselle over the five treble stitches at each corner of the second black round. Line the holder with flannel. A number of these squares joined together are very pretty for an antimacassar.

Tea Cosy.—Make several strips of crochet tricotee in pretty contrasting colours, commencing them from two to three inches wide, and gradually decreasing to form a point at the top; the length must depend upon the size you wish the cosy to be. It is best to cut out a paper pattern, and measure the length, width, and number of stripes by it. Join them by putting the needle first into a loop on the right, then on the left, and drawing the wool through, thus forming a raised chain stitch. Work a pretty fancy pattern in cross stitch on each strip. Line the cosy with flannel, and edge it with a cord, put a tassel of variegated wool on the top. Egg cosies can be made in the same way.

PRACTICAL RECIPES.—CROCHET.

Queen Anne Mat.—1 oz. of grey, 1 oz. of cherry colour double Berlin wool; 1 ball of silver tinsel. Crochet needle No. 8. Work rather closely. Commence, with the grey wool, with 6 chain, join, and work 12 treble in the circle. 2nd round—2 treble on every treble stitch of previous round, working always into the top thread of the trebles. 3rd round—2 treble again on every treble of last round, 48 treble in all. 4th round—2 treble on the first treble of previous round, 1 treble on the next, 1 treble on the next, and repeat, making 64 treble in all. 5th round—1 treble on the first treble of previous round, 1 chain, 1 treble on the next, 1 chain, miss 1, 1 treble on the next, and repeat, making 48 treble in all. 6th round—with cherry colour; 1 treble upon every treble of last round, with 1 chain between each treble. 7th round—1 double crochet on the first treble of previous round, * 5 chain, 1 single in the second of the chain, miss 2 stitches of previous round, 1 double crochet in the next, repeat from *. For the frill: 1st round—with grey wool; work into the top front loops of the trebles of fourth round, 2 treble on the first stitch, 2 treble on the next, 3 treble on the next, and repeat; there will be 147 treble in all. 2nd round—with cherry colour; 2 treble into every treble stitch of previous round. 3rd round—with silver tinsel; 15 consecutive double crochet, catch into the first double crochet, * 10 double crochet, catch into the fourteenth double crochet from the needle, 11 double crochet, catch into the fourteenth double crochet from the needle, and repeat from *.

La Belle Mat.—Single Berlin wool, scarlet, green, purple, amber, black, white. Crochet needle No. 10. Commence with white wool with 6 chain, join round, and work 12 treble in the circle. 2nd round—black; 1 treble between every treble of last round with 1 chain between each treble. 3rd round—amber; 2 treble under the 1 chain of previous round, 1 chain, and repeat. 4th round—scarlet; 3 treble under the 1 chain of last round, 1 chain, and repeat. 5th round—white; 3 treble under the 1 chain of last round, 3 chain, and repeat. 6th round—white; 1 long treble between each treble of previous round, and 5 long treble in each hole of 3 chain, and all these long treble are to have 1 chain between them. 7th round—purple; 1 long treble in the hole over the centre treble of the 3 white treble in the fifth round, 1 chain,

* 2 long treble in the next hole, with 1 chain after each treble, repeat from * five times, then after 1 chain work 1 long treble in the next hole. Break off purple, join on green, and work the same, doing the first long treble of the green in the same hole with the 1 purple long treble; then join on scarlet, and work the same; join on amber, and work the same. And then repeat from purple until the round is completed, making three puffs of each colour. 8th round—white; 1 double crochet under the chain stitch of previous round, 1 chain, and repeat. 9th round—black; holding the mat the right side towards you, insert the hook in the double crochet stitch that is worked between the joins of colour in the seventh round, and also in between the 2 amber treble in the third round, and work a double crochet stitch (this confines the puffed edge and brings it in the form of a shell), 4 chain, and repeat.

For a larger sized mat, use double Berlin wool, coral, ruby, and myrtle green. Crochet needle No. 8. Commence and work the 1st round with coral wool, the second round with green, the next 4 rounds with ruby. Commence the 7th round and work * 1 shell with ruby, the next with coral, and the next with green, and repeat from * until you have worked 12 shells round the mat. Work the 8th and 9th rounds with green wool.

Water Lily Mat. Required 1 oz. each of two shades of green, 1 oz. of white, and ½ oz. of pale yellow single Berlin wool, ½ oz. of lemon-coloured double Berlin, a piece of green window blind cord, and a little fine bonnet wire. Crochet needle No. 12. For the centre of the mat with the lighter shade of green wool, work 5 chain, join round, and crochet round and round in double crochet over the blind cord for 7 rounds, then do 2 rounds with the darkest green, and fasten off. Now for the leaves which are to go round this centre piece; with light shade of green commence with 13 chain, work 11 consecutive double crochet, 3 double crochet in the stitch at the end, and 11 double crochet along the opposite side, join round, and fasten off; round this, work 3 rounds of plain double crochet with dark green wool, putting 3 double crochet in the centre stitch at top and bottom to round the ends nicely, and working a piece of bonnet wire under the stitches of the last round, and fasten off. Make 10 of these green leaves. Then make 11 light-coloured leaves in the same manner, using the pale yellow wool for the first round and doing the 3 outer rounds with white. Sew the green leaves by the fastening off end upon the outer edge of the centre piece. Sew the white leaves a little nearer in towards the centre, about three rounds from the outer edge, these will lap a little over each other. Cut the lemon-coloured wool into bits about two inches in length, and sew them four or five bits in a bunch upon the foundation, just within the line of white leaves to cover the sewing thereof, and to stand up in a fringe like the stamens of a lily. The space in centre of the mat should be just large enough to contain a tumbler or a small pretty vase for flowers.

A Little Blue Tidy.—Procure 1 oz. of palest blue single Berlin, a crochet needle No. 12, and eight inches of perforated silver cardboard; join this round, and on it, with a rug needle and wool, work a pattern up and down in cross-stitches, and edge each side of the cardboard with a line of button-hole stitches. On one side of this, work for the bottom of the tidy, doing a round of treble stitches, one stitch in each stitch of the button-holing, join round. Work 3 more rounds of treble, the same number of stitches in each round. 5th round - a treble stitch upon every 2 treble of last round. 6th round- the same. 7th round the same, and this should join into a round closely; with the rug needle run the wool into the top threads of the stitches and sew up. For edging at top of the tidy, work 3 treble in three consecutive stitches of the button-holing, 3 chain, single crochet in the first of the chain, miss one of the button-hole stitches, and repeat. Work 2 pieces of chain to attach on either side for a handle, tie in a bow at the top with tasseled ends. Make also bows of chain and tassels to place at the sides where the handle is sewn on, and at the bottom of the tidy.

Toilet Glass Cloth.—Evans' crochet cotton No. 16. Steel crochet needle, Penelope, No. 3. Commence with 16 chain, join round. 1st round—1 long treble in every chain stitch, with 2 chain between every long treble. 2nd round—3 double crochet under every space of 2 chain of previous round. 3rd round— 4 double long treble (cotton three times round the needle) in 4 consecutive double crochet of last round, 6 chain, and repeat. 4th round—11 double crochet under the 6 chain, 1 double crochet on the second long treble, and repeat. This completes one circle. Join the circles together in process of working, and afterwards (to fill in the space between) make small crosses, 7 chain, join to circle, and work back with 7 double crochet, and repeat three times. Finish the glass cloth with a thick fringe. Pretty toilet mats can be made with seven circles, one being in the centre, and six circles surrounding it.

Bread Tray Cloth.—Evans' crochet cotton No. 10. Steel crochet needle, Penelope, No. 3. Commence with a sufficient number of chain, divisible by 36 and 5 over, for the width of the cloth; turn, insert the hook in the third chain from the needle. Whatever the number of chain to be worked, the same number of stitches are to be missed in the preceding row, and the end of each row is to correspond with the beginning. 1st row—2 treble, * 6 chain, 2 treble, 2 chain, 5 treble, 4 chain, 5 treble, 2 chain, 2 treble, 6 chain, 2 treble, repeat from *, and break off at the end of this and every row, commencing again on the right-hand side. 2nd row—3 treble, * 5 chain, 2 treble, 2 chain, 6 treble, 2 chain, 6 treble, 2 chain, 2 treble, 5 chain, 4 treble, repeat from *. 3rd row—4 treble, * 4 chain, 4 treble, 2 chain, 4 treble, 2 chain, 4 treble, 2 chain, 4 treble, 4 chain, 6 treble, repeat from *. 4th row—5 treble, * 3 chain, 6 treble, 2 chain, 2 treble, 2 chain, 2 treble, 2 chain, 6 treble, 3 chain, 8 treble, repeat from *. 5th row—6 treble, * 4 chain, 6 treble, 2 chain, 2 treble, 2 chain, 6 treble, 4 chain, 10 treble, repeat from *. 6th row—7 treble, * 5 chain, 2 treble, 2 chain, 6 treble, 2 chain, 2 treble, 5 chain, 12 treble, repeat from *. 7th row—same as the fifth row, and work reversely hence to the first row, which will complete one pattern. Repeat from the first row for the length required for the cloth. Finish off with fringe.

Cheese Cloth.—Evans' crochet cotton No. 10. Steel crochet needle, Penelope, No. 3. Commence with 8 chain, join round, and work 12 double crochet in the circle, join. 2nd round—6 chain, 1 treble on the first of the double crochet stitches, 3 chain and 1 treble ten times, 3 chain, join to the third chain at the commencement of the round. 3rd round—1 treble on the treble of previous round, 1 chain, 6 treble on the middle chain of the 3 of previous round, and catch the last of the 6 treble into the first, 1 chain, and repeat. 4th round—2 double crochet on every treble stitch, 2 double crochet on every bunch, and 1 double crochet in every chain stitch of last round, making 72 double crochet in all. 5th round—bunches of treble worked as directed for the third round, making 18 bunches in all. 6th round—plain double crochet. 7th round—1 double crochet, 5 chain, miss 3 double crochet, and repeat. 8th round—1 double crochet in the middle chain of the 5 of previous round, 5 chain, and repeat. 9th round—1 double crochet in the middle chain of the 5 of last round, 6 chain and repeat. 10th round—plain double crochet. The last seven rounds are to be repeated, working according to the increased size of the cloth, till large enough. Finish the cloth with a deep thick fringe.

Purse.—Blue and gold purse silk. Crochet needle, Penelope, No. 3. With blue silk make a chain about eight inches long, and work 1 double crochet in the third from the needle, 1 chain, miss 1, 1 double crochet all along. Every row is to be worked in the same way, the double crochet under the chain stitch of previous row. Turn, and work another row with blue. Then 3 rows with gold, and 5 rows with blue, until five inches are done. Sew the beginning and the end of the work together, leaving about two and a half inches in the middle for the opening of the purse, round which work a row of 1 double crochet, 1 chain. Sew the ends up, and crochet a scalloped edging along the sides and ends, 1 double crochet, 1 treble, 1 long treble, 1 treble, 1 double crochet, all into 1 stitch, miss 3 stitches, and repeat. Slip on two gilt purse rings, and affix a tassel of gold and blue silk at each corner.

Watchguards.—These may be made in crochet with purse silk, using a fine steel needle. Commence with a chain of 8 stitches, join, and work double crochet round and round, taking up top loops until the guard is of sufficient length. Affix a snap to fasten the ends together. If beads are used, they must be threaded on the silk before commencing the chain, and one bead must be worked in with each stitch of double crochet. A coiled-looking chain is made by working from the inside, so that the wrong side of the crochet comes outside. A flat guard is worked as follows:—Begin with 2 chain, turn, and work 3 double crochet in the first stitch, * slip a bead close to the hook, 1 chain, turn, 3 double crochet into the middle one of the 3 double crochet of last row, working into the back loop, repeat from *, and continue for the length required. Attach a swivel at one end, and a pendant at the other, with bar to fasten into the button-hole.

Edging for Underlinen.—Evans' crochet cotton No. 20. Steel crochet needle, Penelope No. 4. Commence with 11 chain, 1 treble in the fourth chain from the needle, 2 consecutive treble in the next 2 chain, 5 chain, 1 treble in the last stitch of the commencement, 3 chain, 1 treble in the same place; 2 chain, turn the work, 6 treble under the 3 chain, 3 chain, 1 double crochet under the 5 chain, 3 chain, 1 treble on the first treble stitch, 2 chain, 1 treble on the chain stitch that turned at the end of the row; * 3 chain, turn, 2 treble under the 2 chain of previous row, 1 treble on the treble stitch, 5 chain, 1 treble on the first of the 6 treble of last row, 3 chain, 1 treble in the same place; 2 chain, turn, 6 treble under the 3 chain, 3 chain, 1 double crochet under the 5 chain, 3 chain, 1 treble on the first treble stitch, 2 chain, 1 treble on the chain stitch that turned at the end of the row; repeat from * for the length required.

Narrow Lace Edging.—Evans' crochet cotton No. 24. Steel crochet needle, Penelope, No. 4. Make 9 chain, join round, and work 12 double crochet in the circle, 9 chain again, 1 double crochet in the same place as the last double crochet was worked into, do 6 double crochet in this loop, making the right side of the stitches come the same side of the work as the previous 12 double crochet, 6 chain, turn the needle to the right and insert the hook in between the sixth and seventh double crochet stitches and draw the cotton through the stitch on the needle, work 12 double crochet under the loop of 6 chain, and 6 double crochet into the loop where 6 double crochet are already worked, 9 chain, 1 double crochet in same place as last double crochet was worked into, 6 double crochet in this loop, 6 chain, turn the needle to the right, insert the hook in the lower row of double crochet at the junction of the upper loop and draw the cotton through the stitch on the needle, work 6 double crochet in this loop, 6 chain, turn the needle to the right, insert the hook in between the sixth and seventh double crochet and draw the cotton through the stitch on the needle, work 3 double crochet, 5 chain, alternately, till you have three loops of 5 chain and 12 double crochet stitches. For the top of the scallop, do 6 double crochet in each of the two loops to the left, and the first scallop is complete; continue for the length required.

Lace Edging.—Evans' crochet cotton No. 20. Steel crochet needle, Penelope, No. 4. Commence with 10 chain; 1 treble in the fourth chain from the needle, 3 consecutive treble in the next 3 chain, 3 chain, miss 1 of the foundation, 1 treble in the next, 3 chain, 1 treble in the next, 3 chain, 1 treble in the next, 2 chain, turn the work, 4 treble under the first 3 chain, 1 chain, 4 treble under the next 3 chain, 1 chain, 4 treble under the next 3 chain, 3 chain, 1 treble on the chain stitch that turned at the end of the row, * 3 chain, turn, 3 treble under the 3 chain of previous row, 3 chain, 1 treble between the second and third of the first group of 4 treble, 3 chain, 1 treble between the third and fourth of the same group of treble, 3 chain, 1 treble under the 1 chain, 2 chain, turn, 4 treble under the first 3 chain, 1 chain, 4 treble under the next 3 chain, 1 chain, 4 treble under the next 3 chain, 3 chain, 1 treble on the chain stitch that turned at the end of the row; repeat from * for the length required.

Border.—Evans' crochet cotton No. 24. Steel crochet needle, Penelope, No. 4. Begin with 30 chain; work 1 treble in sixth stitch from the needle, 2 chain, another treble in the same place, 1 chain, miss 1, 1 double crochet in the next, 1 chain, miss 1, 8 consecutive treble, 5 chain, 8 more consecutive treble, 1 chain, miss 1, 1 double crochet in the next, 1 chain, miss 1, 1 treble at the end, 2 chain, another treble in the same place, turn with 5 chain. 2nd row—1 treble under the 2 chain, 2 chain, another treble in the same place, 2 chain, 4 treble on first 4 treble of last row, 5 chain, 1 double crochet under 5 chain of last row, 5 chain, 4 treble on last 4 treble stitches, 2 chain, 1 treble under 2 chain, 2 chain, another treble in the same place, turn with 5 chain. 3rd row—1 treble under the 2 chain, 2 chain, another treble in the same place, 1 chain, 1 double crochet under 2 chain, 1 chain, 2 treble on first 2 treble stitches, 4 chain, 1 double crochet on centre stitch of 5 chain, 5 chain, 1 double crochet on centre stitch of next 5 chain, 4 chain, 2 treble on last 2 treble stitches, 1 chain, 1 double crochet under 2 chain, 1 chain, 1 treble under 2 chain, 2 chain, another treble in the same place, turn with 5 chain. 4th row—worked same as second row. 5th row—worked same as first row. And repeat for the length required. To head top, work a row of 3 treble under every turning of chain stitches, 3 chain between each group of treble. For scallop at bottom: 1st row—2 long treble, 3 chain, 2 long treble, worked into each turning of chain stitches. 2nd row—7 treble stitches under first loop of 3 chain with 1 chain worked between each treble stitch, 1 chain, 1 double crochet under next loop of 3 chain, 1 chain, and repeat. 3rd row—1 double crochet under each chain stitch of last row with 5 chain worked between each stitch of double crochet, and repeat.

Border.—Evans' crochet cotton No. 24. Steel crochet needle, Penelope, No. 4. Commence with 26 chain; work 1 treble in the sixth from the needle, 2 chain, another treble in the same place, 2 chain, miss 2, 2 treble in the next, 2 chain, 2 more treble in the same place, 5 chain, miss 5, 1 treble in the next, 3 chain, another treble in the same place, 5 chain, miss 5, 2 treble in the next, 2 chain, 2 more treble in the same place, 2 chain, miss 2, 1 treble in the next, 2 chain, another treble in the same place, turn with 5 chain. 2nd row—1 treble under the 2 chain, 2 chain, another treble in the same place, 1 chain, 1 double crochet under 2 chain, 1 chain, 2 treble under next 2 chain, 2 chain, 2 more treble in the same place, 4 chain, 1 treble under loop of 3 chain, 1 chain and 1 treble alternately 6 times in the same place, 4 chain, 2 treble under 2 chain, 2 chain, 2 more treble in the same place, 1 chain, 1 double crochet under next 2 chain, 1 chain, 1 treble under 2 chain, 2 chain, another treble in the same place, turn with 5 chain. 3rd row—1 treble under 2 chain, 2 chain, another treble in the same place, 2 chain, 2 treble under next 2 chain, 2 chain, 2 more treble in the same place, 2 chain and 1 treble alternately 6 times in the centre spaces, 2 chain, 2 treble under 2 chain, 2 chain, 2 more treble in the same place, 2 chain, 1 treble under next 2 chain, 2 chain, another treble in the same place, turn with 5 chain. 4th row—1 treble under the 2 chain, 2 chain, another treble in the same place, 1 chain, 1 double crochet under 2 chain, 1 chain, 2 treble under next 2 chain, 2 chain, 2 more treble in the same place, 1 double crochet under next 2 chain, 3 treble under each of the next 2 chain and a double crochet between, worked on the 4 centre treble stitches, 1 double crochet under 2 chain, 2 treble under 2 chain, 2 chain, 2 more treble in the same place, 1 chain, 1 double crochet under 2 chain, 1 chain, 1 treble under 2 chain, 2 chain, another treble in the same place, turn with 5 chain. 5th row— same as the first row, the 1 treble, 3 chain, 1 treble, to be worked on the centre treble stitch of previous row. Continue for the length required, and when sufficient is done edge the top and bottom as directed for the border described above.

Border.—Evans' crochet cotton No. 18. Steel crochet needle, Penelope, No. 4. Begin with 38 chain ; 1 treble in the eighth from the needle, 5 chain, miss 5, * 1 treble, 6 chain, 1 single crochet on top of the treble just done, repeat from * till you have 3 piques of chain and 4 treble stitches worked in the same place (this in future will be called "a leaf"), 5 chain, miss 5, 1 treble in the next, 2 chain, another treble in the same place, 5 chain, miss 5, a leaf, 5 chain, miss 5, 1 treble in the next, 2 chain, another treble in the same place. 2nd row—9 chain to turn, a leaf under 2 chain of last row, 5 chain, 1 treble in centre leaf of last row, 2 chain, another treble in the same place, 5 chain, a leaf under 2 chain, 5 chain, 1 treble in centre pique of next leaf, 2 chain, another treble in the same place, 5 chain, 1 treble on treble of last row, 2 chain, 1 treble on third chain that turned. 3rd row—5 chain to turn, 1 treble on treble of last row, 5 chain, a leaf under two chain, 5 chain, 1 treble in centre pique of leaf of last row, 2 chain, another treble in the same place, 5 chain, a leaf under 2 chain, 5 chain, 1 treble on centre pique of leaf, 2 chain, another treble in the same place, 3 chain, 17 treble under loop of 9 chain. 4th row—turn with 3 chain, 1 treble on third treble of last row, * 2 chain, miss 1, 1 treble on the next, repeat from * till 8 treble stitches are done, 3 chain, and finish row same as the second row. 5th row—same as the third row till you have worked 2 treble stitches on the last leaf, then 7 chain, 2 treble under each 2 chain round the scallop, with 2 chain over each treble stitch of last row, 4 chain, join to end of the commencing chain (afterwards join into previous scallop), 4 chain, turn. 6th row—1 double crochet on first treble stitch of last row, * 3 chain, a leaf under first 2 chain, 3 chain, 1 double crochet under next 2 chain, repeat from * 3 times, working the last double crochet under loop of 7 chain, and finish row same as the second row.

MISCELLANEOUS ARTICLES.

Tufted Fringe for Mats.—Get skeins of single Berlin wool of different shades of any colour, dark and light, green is preferable; lay it in strands of ten; thread a rug needle with some of the wool, tie it to the ends of the strands, beginning on the left-hand side, and with the wool in the needle tie the stranded wool tightly twice round about an inch distant from the first tie, sewing it in a firm knot. Proceed in this way until you have tied it at regular intervals all along. Then break off the wool with which you have been sewing, and cut the strands in the centre of every space between the ties. This leaves a series of little tufts on the wool you have been sewing with, and the fringe is complete. Sew it round a foundation, in loops of any length preferred, mixing the shades so as to produce a good effect.

Ball Penwiper.—Get some black broadcloth, and cut eighteen circles the size you wish the penwiper to be. Overcast the edge of each circle with long stitches of sewing silk, and upon each stitch thread eight beads of any colour, not gold or silver, because these tarnish. When the circles are trimmed, fold each into half, and then into half again, and sew them all strongly together at the points, so as to form a ball with the beaded edges outside.

Braces.—Work a stripe about fourteen stitches wide in plain crochet tricotee with single Berlin wool, for the length required; then with a contrasting colour make little stars in cross stitch up the centre. Line with silk, and add buckles. Or stronger braces may be made of a pretty Berlin wool stripe worked on canvas.

Gentleman's Housewife.—Procure three-quarters of a yard of crimson or navy blue ribbon, about four inches wide; line it with another ribbon or a piece of brown holland, and at one end turn it up so as to form a pocket three inches deep; at the other end let there be a mattress-pincushion, two inches deep, and the width of the ribbon. On this pincushion place a couple of pieces of flannel, overcast at the edges, to hold the needles, with small loops underneath on the surface of the pincushion, through which to pass a bodkin, scissors, and penknife. Next, cut a piece of silk or holland the same width as the ribbon, and about fifteen or sixteen inches long, which lay flat upon the housewife, and run on, in four divisions, to hold skeins of cotton or thread, darning cotton or wool, and a skein or so of black sewing silk. In drawing these threads into place, let the looped ends be next the pincushion, so that the cut ones may be stored away tidily in the pocket, where, also, a few shirt and other buttons may be placed. Put a double string in the centre of the pocket at the edge, and roll up the housewife from the cushion end.

Soft Ball for Children.—Cut two circular pieces of cardboard about six inches in diameter, and cut a hole the size of a sixpence in the centre of each circle; place the two pieces together, and sew them evenly over round and round with wool (any odd pieces will do) until all the cardboard is covered, and the hole filled up close. Then cut the wool round the outer edge, and slip a string between the two pieces of cardboard, tying it firmly so as to keep the wool together. Tear the card away, and pull the ball into shape. The small balls, used for making ball fringe, are made on the same principle.

Children's Reins.—Cut out a loose-fitting body in American cloth, bind each part with scarlet braid, and sew it neatly together; trim the front with a narrower scarlet braid and white buttons; put scarlet rosettes and little bells on the shoulders, and buttons and loops up the back. Have a band of tape round the waist, under the American cloth, to give additional strength, and fasten the ends of the reins upon this at each side, with a rosette over the join. Wide scarlet braid is used for the reins.

Sunday School Banners.—Have a set of letters of the required size cut out in cardboard; lay those that are wanted for the motto upon a piece of material, the colour of which must contrast with the background of the banner, and trace all round the outline with a black-lead pencil. Work over the pencil line in button-hole stitch with Berlin wool of a third colour; then cut the shape of the letter round outside the button-hole stitches. The background may be of red Turkey twill, with letters of blue twill or oatmeal cloth, button-holed with yellow; or a cream-coloured ground with red letters, button-holed with blue. The letters must then be arranged on the background, and sewn on with cotton. The lower edge of the banner may be bordered with fringe, and a tassel placed at each corner. Banners of this description will not hurt if exposed in a shower of rain.

Antimacassars.—Very handsome antimacassars can be made of common huckaback towelling, with a large flower or spray worked in crewels in the centre, and a small one at each corner, and all the ground ornamented with gold-coloured knitting silk. A long needle is required, and the gold silk is darned in and out of the raised pattern of the huckaback, taking up the two perpendicular threads, in straight lines from right to left, and reversely, so as to cover the whole surface excepting that occupied by the flowers; thus, the design stands out in colour and bold relief, and the groundwork at a distance looks like gold. A coarse Torchon lace is afterwards sewn round.

Similar antimacassars are made with an outline design in place of the crewel work. Any good design will answer the purpose, and the outline only should be worked, using two shades of blue or brown silk, and enclosing the design all round in a straight line, so as to form a terminating point for the darned background.

Another pretty style, and very durable, is a ground of pale blue Roman satin, on which is worked Briggs' transfer design of yellow iris and swallows, or kingfisher and bulrushes, with filoselles shaded according to the shade numbers supplied with the transfer.

A most lovely antimacassar can be made upon a ground of coarse linen, eighteen threads being drawn out lengthways about two inches from each side, and again at an interval of about eighteen threads, then leave a space of about two and a half inches, and draw other threads as before; the drawing is to terminate two inches from the top and two inches from the bottom, and not to be continued the entire length of the linen. Thread a needle with crimson double Berlin wool the length of the whole antimacassar, and darn along the centre of the drawn threads, twisting three threads over three, so that the threads form a series of crosses. Then work feather stitch with any dark-coloured double Berlin wool upon the plain threads between the open work. That done, get some coloured satin, a trifle narrower than the wide strip of plain linen, work a scroll or any pretty border design with filoselle in cross stitch over canvas, upon it. Each piece of satin should be a different colour, and worked with a different pattern; outline round the edge of the pattern with gold thread caught down with fine gold silk. Draw the canvas away thread by thread. Place the satin upon the linen, lay three gold threads along each edge, and sew over securely to the foundation. There may be four or five stripes of satin, according to the width of the antimacassar. The coloured wools and the straight lines of gold thread are to extend the whole length of the antimacassar, and a fringe is to be formed by unravelling the linen to within about a dozen threads of the open work.

The white glass and tea cloths woven with red or blue check are utilised for antimacassars. Work over the check with wool or ingrain cotton of the same colour, in coral stitch, feather stitch, or any other pretty fancy stitch, and finish with a flower or a star worked in cross stitch in the centre of each square, or appliqué a bud or a flower from cretonne. Or a flower may be worked at the intersection of each square. Border with lace. These are very effective, and quickly made.

Very pretty light antimacassars can be made of a cross of wide satin ribbon, in each angle of which is sewn a square of Guipure d'art. Border the whole with Guipure lace.

Another variety is formed of six squares of Guipure, set into bands of linen, the linen threads being drawn and worked.

Other antimacassars are made of alternate strips of ribbon and lace insertion, each about four inches wide, the ribbon crewel worked in a tiny pattern of flowers and leaves; these are trimmed with lace all round and bows at the corners.

Or have nine six-inch squares of satin, divided by lace insertion and bordered with lace to match, work a spray of leaves and flowers in each square, or get some of the crewel flowers that are now sold ready worked, and appliqué on.

Japanese squares can be made up very prettily for antimacassars by laying them between bands of ribbon velvet, edging each square with gold braid; make a border of the same, and add a ball fringe at top and bottom.

German linen, both white and ecru, is much used for antimacassars; it is woven in stripes and in various diamond patterns, is ready fringed, and is intended to be worked with a suitable design in cross stitch with either ingrain cotton or washing silks.

Very handsome antimacassars are made of serge on which a good design, such as bulrushes, water-lilies, etc., is worked at the lower part of one end, or, if preferred, a bold sunflower or passion-flower may occupy the whole centre; the serge should be herring-boned top and bottom, and fringed with wool of a shade to match.

Most useful antimacassars can be made of strips of raised wool crochet alternated with strips of plain tricot, the latter embroidered in some pretty running pattern. The newest style is to place strips of Berlin wool canvas, nine inches wide, between the crochet strips, having previously worked a pattern upon the canvas with filoselles in cross stitch, and edged it with double crochet with the same wool as the crochet strips are worked.

Cosy-shaped antimacassars are very nice for easy chairs, as there is no danger of their falling off or getting out of place. Cut a paper pattern the size and shape required, and work accordingly, either in wool crochet, or crochet alternated with strips of tricot or Berlin canvas; or the shape can be cut out in Roman satin, velvet, serge, or other material, and embroidered.

A novel antimacassar, fitting to the chair, is made of two pieces of claret woollen serge about half-a-yard deep, and cut like a trefoil rising in the centre, the lower part is embroidered with crewel wools in a design of primroses on one side and marguerites on the other; the antimacassar is edged all round with silk cord, and the lower part is bordered with lace.

Chair Covers.—There is a certain kind of German canvas woven in large diamonds of grey ecru colour shaded with white that is very effective for chair coverings. It must be cut to the shape of the chair, and a properly woven and fringed bordering sewn round. A set design of a star or cross is worked with wool or ingrain cotton upon the open threads in the centre of each diamond. These covers are quickly made, and are very durable.

Small squares are much used for the seats of chairs, and are pinned on cornerways; very pretty squares can be made of Java canvas bordered with coarse furniture lace, having a monogram in the centre, and a border and corners worked in cross stitch with ingrain cotton or washing silks.

Squares made in Oriental work are much admired, and present a very rich and elegant appearance.

Cushions.—These are now made a larger size than formerly, and form conspicuous objects on which to lavish the most elaborate embroidery. A sunflower has a fine effect worked in subdued shades of yellow and green filoselle on a foundation of dark green or olive brown plush.

Or a branch of crimson passion flower as if twined carelessly in a half-circle, and thrown on a square of cream-coloured satin.

Poppies, too, and wild roses, designed either as wreaths or sprays, look remarkably well; the effect is very natural and pretty if the spray appears as if coming out of a simulated slit which is worked across the lower left-hand corner of the cushion.

A lovely cushion design is a squirrel, crewel worked in natural colours, as if sitting on a bough of oak and eating an acorn he has just plucked from an overhanging branch.

A charming and uncommon cushion is of white or dark green satin on which is worked the S.A.N. design of a spider and her web, a spray of shaded green leaves straying up the left side and top of the cushion, and a small spray of briar roses low down on the other side, the web stretching across between, the threads of the web, both the circular ones and those radiating from the centre one, are worked with the best fine gold thread, just carried over the surface and caught down with a necessary stitch here and there, a large spider is worked in two or three shades of brown embroidery silk, a little to one side as if making towards a fly caught on the opposite side of the web. Or a silver web worked on a ground of pale blue satin has a pretty effect.

Berlin wool work upon canvas is handsome for a cushion, and is very durable; a set geometrical pattern looks well, or a small allover pattern, and the wool must be nicely shaded; finish off with a cord all round and tassels at the corners.

Carriage Rugs.—A good useful carriage rug can be made of brown Holland bound with dark blue or red braid, and worked entirely in either one or the other colour, with a large monogram in the centre, and a spray of flowers at each corner. Or Holland with chintz flowers arranged all round and appliquéd on.

Another pretty arrangement is to work a design of flowers and leaves on a broad band of dark blue or red material, and stitch this to a Holland or sheeting carriage cloth, adding long spiky stitches on each side of the band; these stitches are very effective, and very quickly done.

An elegant carriage rug can be made of sage green serge with a border of shaded dark and light green leaves worked in wool crewels about three inches from the edge; this should be lined throughout with a deep maroon merino, which, when thrown back, looks exceedingly pretty.

D'oyleys.—D'oyleys may be either round or square, of close or open material. Very pretty d'oyleys are made of squares of fringed linen with a border of drawn threads, and a small spray of flowers in crewel work in the centre; or the whole of the d'oyley may be of drawn threadwork, drawing the threads at intervals one way of the material, and working over those that remain with a needle and thread, so as to form a pattern.

Other d'oyleys are of linen or fine twill fringed and worked in outline embroidery, in designs such as nursery stories or figures from the comic operas, or with pretty Watteau figures cut out from sateen and appliquéd in the centre.

Exceedingly pretty d'oyleys are made of white or very pale coloured silk, cut circular shape, with an edging of Valenciennes lace, the lace only just fulled in sufficiently to lie flat; they can be plain, but if a flower, bird, or small picture is painted on each, the effect is quite lovely. Chinese white should be mixed with the first coat of paint to prevent the colour from running. Many pretty designs and little figures suitable for the purpose may be found in illustrated books and papers, cartoons from "Punch" being very amusing. The patent silk ornaments are well adapted for this style of d'oyley, and can be transferred to the material so as to give exactly the appearance of hand painting.

Satin jean is very much used for etching, and when well done etched d'oyleys are very effective. Use Bond's marking ink and a fine-pointed steel pen, and be careful to work the right way of the jean to avoid spluttering.

D'oyleys of scarlet cloth, embroidered with white floss silk, and edged with white silk fringe, are much admired.

Very pretty light d'oyleys can be made of Brussels net, on which a pattern is worked in gold and pale blue embroidery silk, in ordinary darning stitch, and the edge button-holed in scallops.

D'oyleys of a pale blue or pink ground look well with a few stalks of grain crossing each other, embroidered in gold washing silk; or the same ground with bunches of cherries, raspberries, and other fruit, embroidered in natural colours.

L

Guipure d'art is much used for d'oyleys, and looks well over a coloured lining.

Crochet d'oyleys are very pretty and durable.

Mantel Borders.—These should be from six inches to eighteen inches in depth. A very elegant one can be made of black or crimson satin sheeting worked with a conventional scroll pattern in shades of gold-coloured crewel silks, and edged with a cord and handsome fringe.

Another pretty style is a light blue ground with pomegranates worked in arrasene; or a ruby velvet ground with white arrasene lilies.

A lovely mantel border can be made of old-gold satin, on which is worked a design of wheat ears and shaded cornflowers and leaves.

Briggs' designs of single dahlia, of large poppy, and of wild rose, are effective worked on black satin with filoselles.

Embossed velvet is used for mantel borders, and looks exceedingly well, having the pattern outlined with gold thread, or the new gold or silver tinsel wool, and fringed with a mixture of chenille and gold thread.

A wool canvas border, nine inches wide and ready fringed worked with washing silk in a good cross-stitch pattern, looks well.

Macrâme mantel borders are in good taste, and are everlasting wear.

Five-o'clock-Tea Cloths.—These should be made of washing materials. Bolton sheeting is very suitable, cut to the required size and fringed out to the depth of three or four inches. It may be worked with a border of running flowers and leaves, with gold knitting silk, and the centre of the cloth powdered over with small single flowers.

A very pretty style is a ground of fine oatmeal cloth, with a design of leaves and large lilies traced on red Turkey twill and appliquéd with red ingrain knitting cotton.

A much-admired cloth has for its foundation a square yard of Bolton sheeting, fringed all round, and worked with crewel wools in the S.A.N. design of water-lilies and bulrushes.

Other favourite cloths are made of fine cream-coloured linen, crewel-worked in a pattern of leaves and white roses.

Or a square of fine linen, with a three-inch-wide band of pale blue washing sateen, then an insertion of lace, another band of blue sateen, and finish off with a lace edging.

German damask is much used for tea cloths. It is manufactured in various sizes, ready fringed, and has a border woven specially to give room for cross-stitch work in cotton, silk, or wool, as preferred.

Nightdress Cases.—These are intended to lie outside the bed or on the pillow; in blue, pink, pale yellow, and old gold, they are most fashionable now; some have a cross-bar design worked all over in chain stitch, and a small flower in each division.

Pretty inexpensive cases can be made of Java canvas, ornamented with a border of cross stitch, worked with coloured ingrain cotton; very strong ones are of satin jean, embroidered with white knitting cotton in Mont Mellick work; others are made of coloured sateen in a design of marguerites in appliqué; these all would be edged with torchon lace.

Another simple style is made of coloured sateen, covered with a piece of fine cotton knitting, worked in a pretty fancy stitch, with a narrow knitted border for edging, and bows of ribbon placed at each corner.

Handsome sachets have the foundation of pale blue, crimson, or old gold satin, made up envelope shape, a large monogram worked with silk in the centre, and a smaller monogram on the other side on the flap, a pretty scroll pattern running below, and trimmed with coloured lace or silk fringe.

A pretty sachet design is an owl perched on a bough of acorns and oak leaves.

Some new nightdress cases are made in the shape of a cracker, and have bands of crewel work placed on either side midway between the ends and the centre.

Others to contain both nightdress and dressing-gown are made of a piece of plush 32 inches long and 27 inches wide, folded in the middle like a portfolio, and embroidered on each side with a long spray of flowers, or the embroidery may be worked on a band of contrasting plush and feather stitched on; the lining is of quilted sateen in two pieces, opening down the centre so as to form two pockets; the sachet is tied with bows of ribbon.

Pincushions.—Cracker pincushions are a novelty, and, as the name denotes, are made in the form of a cracker. For lining, procure a piece of material 6 inches long and 5 inches wide, join it lengthways, tie one end tightly round about an inch from the edge, then fill the bag part with bran and tie again tightly about an inch from the other end, this central part is to stick pins in. The outer covering may be of satin embroidered, or net over satin, and should measure 7 inches long and $5\frac{1}{4}$ inches wide; on either end sew a piece of gold or silver lace, and above this sew two or three rows of tinsel; join the whole lengthways and draw it over the foundation, and tie a piece of tinsel over the place where the lining is already tied, and to this attach a ribbon to hang the cushion up by.

Sunflower pincushions are made on a circle of cardboard $2\frac{1}{2}$ inches in diameter, as foundation, cover this with a piece of black silk, and on the outer edge, on the side the silk is folded over, leaving about an inch space in the centre, pleat two strips of yellow twilled flannel which has previously been cut, one strip 2 inches wide the other $1\frac{1}{2}$ inches wide, so that the edges come one within the other; notch the outer edges of the flannel, and in the centre, place a little padded dark green plush cushion, in imitation of the raised centre of the flower. Sew a 6-inch length of dark green ribbon at the back with a bow at the top by which to suspend the cushion.

Another pincushion is a similar sunflower, but larger, the whole flower measuring 9 inches across from tip to tip, and the edges of the flannel cut more indented, about the depth and width of one's little finger; this is mounted on one of the penny Japanese fans and makes a pretty ornament for a drawing room.

Dahlia pincushions are made in the same way, using ruby or purple flannel, cut in scallops, for the outside, and slate or fawn velvet for the centre.

A new style of pincushion, not at all difficult to make, is of satin or velvet ornamented with a horse's brass face-piece, procurable at any saddler's, the hook which fastens it to the harness being sawn off. Get a piece of baize as long as the brass face-piece measures from end to end, and sufficient to roll round and round till it will lie thick and flat at the back of the ornament; or sew a piece of lining like a bolster strip, and pad it, not too thickly, with bran; cover this roll with a bright piece of satin, and sew the face-piece firmly on so that a piece of satin shows on each side; make a bow of ribbon with long ends, and secure an end to each side of the pincushion to hang it up by.

Other pretty pincushions are shaped in imitation of a shell, a pair of bellows, a butterfly, a guitar, etc.; these are simply made of two pieces of cardboard cut to the required shape, and covered with silk, and sewn neatly together, the pins being stuck in round the edges.

Quilts.—These are very pretty in cretonne work. Cut out from the cretonne, scraps of birds, flowers, or any small subject, and appliqué them with washing silk on to diamond-shaped pieces of pink and blue sateen or twill. Make up the diamonds over papers the same as for patchwork, and then sew them together, a pink and a blue diamond alternately; half-diamonds must be fitted in along the outside of the quilt, and the whole should be bordered with a deep-coloured lace or fringe.

A handsome summer counterpane may be made of fine sheeting, with a border appliqué in a design of pomegranates and leaves in red Turkey twill. A monogram or large device can be arranged for the centre. Finish with a fall of wide ecru lace.

Others are made of Bolton sheeting, with a trellis-work pattern of leaves and flowers embroidered all round, and a monogram in the centre. Six inches round of the Bolton sheeting may be unravelled and knotted in Macramé work for fringe.

A simple and neat quilt is formed of eight-inch squares of white linen, every square having a border of drawn threads and a spray of coloured flowers crewel-worked in the centre.

Very pretty counterpanes are made of oatmeal cloth in six-inch squares of light blue and cream, the border to be all round of one colour with corners of the other, and edged with a deep coarse lace; each square of oatmeal cloth should be embroidered with ingrain cotton with a small spray of leaves, or a little geometrical pattern, cream upon the blue, and blue upon the cream squares.

Or have the ground of red or blue oatmeal cloth, with a large monogram in the centre worked with wool, and a border of jessamine and shaded leaves, making the corners large and handsome, the branches running out as a spray meeting in the centre of each side. Border with coarse wide lace.

An elegant counterpane can be made of white oatmeal cloth, with ivy leaves cut out in red or pink washing twill and arranged as a border to be chain stitched upon the oatmeal cloth, and long spikey stitches worked round each leaf. All the work should be executed with ingrain cotton of a shade to match, and the veining of the leaves, and the stems for connecting the leaves together may be done either in chain stitch or crewel stitch.

Many quilts are made of the new German canvas worked with ingrain cottons in cross stitch. The canvas is full quilt size, woven in a diamond pattern and fringed all round. A design can easily be arranged suitable for working upon the open threads of the material.

A strong, useful quilt may be made with a charity blanket, fringed by knotting in wool of the same colour, and about three inches from the edge, work a bold border in cross stitch, with wool over canvas, taking large double cross stitches.

For a warm winter quilt procure a quantity of pieces of silk or woollen material; either will look well, but not the two mixed. Make up a number of little bags three inches square, and having three sides of the bag sewn, fill the interior with shreds or cuttings of any kind, not too full, before sewing up the fourth side; afterwards join the squares together with due regard to the arrangement of the colours.

A patchwork quilt looks well made entirely of silk and satin patches, arranged in some artistic design, black being plentifully used to throw the colours up well; great care must be taken to have the shapes perfectly symmetrical, as if one side be longer than another the work will not fit in properly when put together. Pieces of cloth make nice bed quilts for the poor, and are handsome if plenty of different colours are put in, besides being very warm.

Handsome counterpanes are made in knitting and crochet, working in sectional pieces which are afterwards joined together, and completing with a border to match; these are very durable, and as the pieces are easy to accomplish and may be taken up at odd times, counterpane knitting is generally a favourite occupation.

Wall Pockets.—Very pretty wall pockets can be made of cheap Japanese fans; procure a piece of stout cardboard which cut to the shape of the lower part of the fan but a little larger at the top and rounded so that when sewn upon the edge of the fan it curves out in the form of a pouch. Cover this cardboard with satin, embroidered according to fancy, and sew it to the fan, the upper part of the fan may be ornamented or not, if so it should be arranged before the front is sewn on; trim with ball fringe, and where the handle meets the fan, add a ribbon bow with a loop to reach to the top of the handle to hang up by.

Another variety of the same kind is to pleat chintz round the lower part of the fan and make a hem a little way from the top wherein to run a piece of elastic to gather it up, this makes a bag pocket.

Handsome wall pockets are made of sateen over a cardboard foundation, and fronted with macrâme work, the edge overlapped with sateen ruching, these are very durable.

LIST OF USEFUL BOOKS ON NEEDLEWORK.

"The Ladies' Work Series." Knitting, Crochet, Netting, Art Needlework, Crewel Embroidery. All by E. M. C. Published by Hatchard's, 187, Piccadilly.

"Lady's Work," and "Sequel to Lady's Work." By Zeta. Hatchard's, 187, Piccadilly.

"Cutting Out." Swan Sonnenschein & Co., Paternoster Square.

"Plain Cutting Out." Griffith & Farran, St. Paul's Churchyard.

"The Standard Needlework Book." Longmans, 39, Paternoster Row.

"Underlinen; How to Cut, Make, and Trim it." Weldon & Co., 7, Southampton Street, Strand.

"Practical Dressmaking." L. Upcott Gill, 170, Strand.

"Cards on Stocking Knitting;" "Winter Comforts, and How to Knit Them;" "Children's Comforts, and How I Knit Them." All by Miss RYDER, H. Hurworth, Richmond, Yorkshire.

"The Stocking Knitter's Manual." By Mrs. CUPPLES. "Book on Knitted Counterpanes;" "The Home Knitter." Johnstone, Hunter & Co., Edinburgh.

"Handbook of Embroidery." By L. HIGGIN. Published by the authority of the Royal School of Art Needlework. "Needlework as Art." By Lady MARIAN ALFORD. Sampson Low, Marston, Searle, & Rivington, 188, Fleet Street.

"The Dictionary of Needlework." By S. F. A. CAULFEILD and BLANCHE C. SAWARD. L. Upcott Gill, 170, Strand.

"The Queen Lace Book." The Queen Office, 346, Strand.

"The Art Designer." A quarterly publication, containing full-sized practical drawings, suitable for all purposes of Art Needlework, and for China and Glass Painting, &c. Office, 4, St. Ann's Square, Manchester.

"Sylvia's Needlework Series." Ward & Lock, Salisbury Square.

"The Silkworm Series." Polonaise Lace, Macramé Lace, Elementary Needlework, Dressmaking Lessons. Myra & Son, 39 and 40, Bedford Street, Covent Garden.

"Fancy Work Series." Macramé, Tatting, Patchwork, Crewel-work, Appliqué, &c. L. Upcott Gill, 170, Strand.

Mrs. LEACH'S "Fancy Work-Basket." Published monthly. R. S. Cartwright, 8, Johnson's Court, Fleet Street.

WELDON'S "Practical Needlework Series." Knitting, Crocheting, Patchwork, Macramé Lace, &c. Issued monthly; each number complete in itself. Weldon & Co., 7, Southampton Street, Strand.

LIST OF WORK SOCIETIES.

Further particulars can be obtained by writing to the Manager of each Society, enclosing a stamped and addressed envelope for reply.

The Royal School of Art Needlework, Exhibition Road, South Kensington, is under the presidentship of H.R.H. the Princess Christian. Applicants must be gentlewomen by birth and education, must reside in London, and undertake to devote seven hours daily to work at the school; no work is given out. For the preliminary course of instruction, consisting of nine lessons of five hours each, through which every applicant is required to pass, a charge is made of £5, and, if satisfactorily completed, a certificate is given, which renders the worker eligible for employment whenever the school needs her services. The exhibition of work at the school is open daily from 10 to 5 o'clock.

The Decorative Needlework Society, 45, Baker Street, W., is under the patronage of H.R.H. the Princess Christian, and is established by ladies who have till recently held leading positions in the Royal School of Art Needlework, for the production, at moderate cost, of the highest classes of decorative needlework. Special attention is paid to the faithful restoration of antique embroidery. Lady workers are employed, who, on first joining, go through a course of instruction, and are then eligible to become members when a vacancy occurs. The work is all done at the rooms. Private lessons are given to amateurs either at their own residences, or at the rooms of the Society. For particulars, address to the Secretary, Miss Haworth.

The Ladies' Work Society, 31, Sloane Street, S.W., is under the presidentship of H.R.H. the Princess Louise, and has been founded to provide employment for gentlewomen whose circumstances render it necessary that they should employ their leisure time remuneratively. The objects of the Society are—first, to benefit the workers; secondly, to raise the standard of needlework. That these objects should be attained the Committee find it necessary to accept such work only as they consider good, both in design and execution. A commission of 2½d. in the shilling is charged on all work sold, and each working member is allowed to have twelve articles for sale at a time. There is a greater demand for plain and useful work than for fancy articles, unless the latter are artistically and tastefully executed. Manager, Miss Wetton.

The Society for Promoting Female Welfare, 47, Weymouth Street, Harley Street, W.—This Society, under the patronage of H.R.H. the Duchess of Connaught, interests itself in all kinds of charities, industrial, educational, benevolent, and missionary, which are designed to promote the welfare of women, and undertakes to furnish every information to subscribers and the public as to the working, the terms of admission, existing vacancies, etc., in the institutions associated with it. A depôt is kept for the sale of ladies' work, and an annual bazaar is held in the Royal Albert Hall for disposal of work sent in from the Work Societies in union with the office. Secretary, Miss Hutchinson.

The Working Ladies' Guild, 113, Gloucester Road, Queen's Gate, S.W., is a very extensive Society, organised by a number of influential ladies and gentlemen to give practical aid and sympathy to gentlewomen requiring assistance. It has a registry for employment, as well as special departments for artists' work, plain work, art needlework, and knitting. Application must be made through an associate or member to whom the applicant is personally known. Secretary, Miss Mackenzie.

The Ladies' Industrial Society, 11, Lower Porchester Street, Hyde Park, W.—The object of this Society is to afford to gentlewomen the means of disposing of their work. A member may send twelve articles at a time to the Society for disposal. The entrance fee is 5s., and 1d. in the shilling on work sold is charged as commission. Needlework, embroidery, and underlinen, are the most saleable articles. Secretary, Miss Blunt.

The Gentlewomen's Self-help Institute, 15, Baker Street, Portman Square, is an association for the benefit of necessitous ladies only, who must be of gentle birth, and in need of help; two letters of recommendation must be sent in, one from a clergyman. The sale of work is combined with a registry for employment. Secretary, Miss Lupton.

Gentlewomen's Work Society, 56, Regent Street.— Established for the sale of any kind of work. Members must be able to supply the fac-simile of any article sent by them and supposed to be their own. Entrance fee, 5s.; annual subscription, 10s.; and a percentage of 1d. in the shilling on work sold. Three articles, or three sets, are allowed at a time, and may be replaced by others as soon as sold. Secretary, Miss Grey.

Mrs. Elliott Scrivenor in 1884 undertook the management of **The London Institute for the Advancement of Plain Needlework,** at 40, Upper Berkeley Street, Edgware Road, W. She now keeps on the room at 40, Upper Berkeley Street, herself, under the name of **The Institute of Needlework,** and gives lessons in every kind of needlework—plain needlework, knitting, and embroidery—in private or public. Mrs. Elliott Scrivenor holds a first-class certificate from the first tailor cutters in Europe, and gives lessons in modelling dresses on the true tailor principle. Lessons are also given in dressmaking, and in the modelling of under-clothes on the same principle. There is a good opening for ladies to qualify under her, when certificates will be granted for teaching of cutting out, etc. Orders are also received for every kind of needlework, and are executed by the ladies of Mrs. Elliott's Work Society, which is kept up in a less extensive place than formerly. Letters of inquiry must contain three stamps for reply.

The Church Heraldic and Artistic Work Depôt, 15, Dorset Street, Baker Street, W.—The promoters of this depôt do not receive work for sale, but give lessons in, and take orders for, every kind of ecclesiastical and artistic work. Secretary, Miss Constantine.

The Ecclesiastical Art Depôt, 11, Maclise Road, Kensington, W.—This depôt has been opened for the sale of ladies' church and art work, at a yearly subscription of 5s., with a commission of 1d. in the shilling on all work sold. Twelve articles are allowed at once. Lessons are given at the depôt in church and art embroidery. All materials are sold to help in making the depôt self-supporting. Work is also designed and commenced for ladies to finish. Manager, Miss Kirkman.

The Ladies' Work Stall, Soho Bazaar, Oxford Street, W. —This Society is for enabling ladies to dispose of their fancy-work and plain needlework, and all kinds of fancy paintings, and novelties of all descriptions. Entrance fee, 21s. a year, and five per cent. commission on everything sold. Secretary, Mrs. Willoughby.

The Ladies' Crystal Palace Stall.—A limited number of ladies are admitted as members of this Society upon payment of 21s. annually. Eight articles may be exhibited for sale at one time, and replaced as sold; the money produced by the sale of the work will be forwarded once a month, less 1d. in the shilling commission to defray expenses, and strictest confidence is observed with regard to the names and addresses of the members. Hon. Secretary, Miss E. Mercy.

Miss Rendell's Work Depôt, 12, Shawfield Street, King's Road, Chelsea, S.W.—Ladies wishing to become working members must bring a reference. The terms of subscription are 5s. per annum; 2s. 6d. to those who live by their work; and a commission of 2d. in the shilling on all work orders and sales. Honorary members subscribing 7s. 6d. per annum can appoint one working member free. Work is given out to order as far as possible, so as to avoid the uncertainty of keeping a quantity of ladies' own work on sale. In connection with the depôt there is an employment agency through which various engagements can be obtained; entrance fee, 2s. 6d.

The West End School of Needlework and Painting, 25, Wigmore Street, W.—Subscription 10s. 6d. annually; 3d. in the shilling commission charged on all work sold or orders executed. A worker may send six articles at a time, and replace when any are sold. Work is given out according to orders received. The number of workers is limited. Lessons given. Manager, Miss Fordham.

The North-Western Ladies' Needlework and Painting Society, 79, Haverstock Hill, N.W.—Established for the sale of needlework. Orders given to subscribers, and materials supplied at a reduction. Subscription, 21s. per annum, and 1d. in the shilling commission on sales. Manager, Mrs. Barton.

The Co-operative Needlewomen's Society, is an association to benefit the poorer class of workers by securing to them better wages than they could receive by the ordinary system of paid needlework, and at the same time offers an advantage to the purchaser by presenting genuine work at the lowest possible prices. The workers assemble day by day in a room set apart for the purpose. Every kind of plain needlework is undertaken. Manager, Mrs. Alison, 18, Theobald's Road, W.C.

The Royal Charitable Repository, The Parade, Leamington, is the oldest institution for the sale of ladies' work, and aims at helping those whose distressed circumstances lead them to wish for a means of procuring assistance from their own talents and industry. Every annual subscriber of 21s. is entitled to recommend one worker. Any person wishing to become a working member must apply through a subscriber. The number of articles that may be sent for sale is practically unlimited, and the only premium charged is 1d. in the shilling commission on all work sold. Bazaars in connection with this Society are held periodically. Conductress, Miss Dawe.

Gentlewomen's Home-work Association, Surbiton.— Formed in the hope of providing home employment for a limited number of ladies, whose work is sent on sale to different places, and to whom orders are given whenever possible.. Each member pays an annual fee of 1s. 6d., which entitles her to send eight articles at one time, and to replace each as it sells; 2d. in the shilling is charged as commission off the sale price. Numbers are now full. Orders requested, and carefully executed. Address, Miss E. M. Burney, St. Mark's Vicarage, Surbiton.

Gentlewomen's Aid Society, 55, Waterloo Street, Brighton.—A provincial Society intended only for ladies who reside in Brighton or neighbourhood. The number of workers limited, and full at present. Manager, Mrs. O'Kell.

Depôt for the Sale of Work by Ladies of Limited Means, 2, Portland Street, Clifton, Bristol.—This Society is managed by a Committee, and consists of fifty members, each nominated by a subscriber of not less than 10s. 6d. annually, subscriptions being considered due in January. Specimens of work must be sent in before any member can be elected; if approved, members are entitled to send in work and to receive orders for needlework, the Committee reserving to themselves the right to reject unsaleable or badly-made things. All expenses being paid by subscription, no deduction is made from amounts received. The Society undertakes every branch of needlework, besides other employments for ladies, such as poultry and bee keeping, preserve making, etc. Treasurer, Miss Read, 15, West Mall, Clifton.

The Ladies' Work Society, 83, Bold Street, Liverpool, was formed by a committee of ladies for the purpose of enabling ladies in reduced circumstances to dispose of their work quietly and advantageously. Working members must furnish a satisfactory reference and produce a specimen of work. The subscription is 5s. annually, and 1d. in the shilling off prices realised by the sale of the articles sent will be deducted for expenses. Twelve pieces of work may be sent at one time, and replenished as sold. Superintendent, Miss Geyer.

The Ladies' Work Bazaar, 23, Hardman Street, Liverpool. —Opened by Mrs. Kelly, under her own immediate superintendence. Subscription 5s. per annum, and 1d. in the shilling deducted as commission on all work sold. Twelve articles are allowed to be sent, and may be replaced as soon as any of them are sold.

The Ladies' Work Society, 16, King Street, Manchester.
—All subscribers of a guinea annually are entitled to nominate two working members, subject to the approval of the managers. Ladies are admitted as members on receipt of 5s. annually, to be paid in advance after receiving a subscriber's nomination, and 1d. in the shilling is deducted on prices realised by the sale of work. Eight pieces of work may be on sale at a time, and be replenished as sold. Superintendent, Mrs. Hubert Schmidt.

The Ladies' Work Society, 217, Lord Street, Southport.
—Ladies are admitted as members on receipt of 5s. annually, after first obtaining a subscriber's recommendation, and 1d. in the shilling on work sold is deducted for expenses. Twelve articles are permitted to be on sale at a time. Superintendent, Mrs. Ashley.

Yorkshire Depôt for the Sale of Ladies' Work, 9, Oxford Place, Leeds.—This institution is intended for the benefit of ladies in reduced circumstances, and for the disposal of work for charitable purposes. Subscribers of 10s. and upwards are entitled to work for themselves or for charity, or may nominate one working member, such nomination being subject to the approval of the committee; those who work for their own benefit must subscribe 5s. annually, unless nominated by a subscriber; a deduction of 1d. in the shilling is made on account of work sold. Twelve articles are allowed at the depôt at one time. Secretary, Mrs. R. H. Braithwaite.

Miss Clifford's Work Society, Newport, Mon.—The spécialité of this Society is decorative table and bed linen, exquisite German damask, drawn linen, and Mount Mellick, counterpanes, sham sheets, pillow shams, sideboard, tea, and tray cloths, serviettes, etc., imported direct from Germany, and worked by members of the Society in beautiful original designs, completed with border of real Portuguese lace, or commenced for ladies' own working. Other branches of fashionable art needlework are undertaken. The number of workers being limited, and no miscellaneous work received on sale, all orders are executed with careful attention.

Mrs. Brett's Work Depôt, 11, Queen Street, Lytham, Lancashire.—Established for the sale of any kind of work. An entrance fee of 5s., paid in advance, is charged, and a commission of 1d. in the shilling deducted on all work sold. Orders are given to members when possible. Twelve pieces of work may be on sale at a time, to be replenished as sold.

Mrs. Geyselman's Depôt for Ladies' Work, 2, Lower Uncroft, Torquay, with which is incorporated an agency for governesses and ladies who give lessons in Torquay. Subscription 10s. 6d. annually, and 2d. in the shilling commission on all work sold, or orders given for execution. A worker may send six articles at a time to the depôt, which may be replaced when any are sold; low prices are urged to induce a ready sale. All plain work must be hand sewn, well executed, and pretty useful patterns. Orders taken for work of any kind.

Irish Ladies' Work Society, 25, Mellifont Avenue, Kingstown, Co. Dublin.—The object of this Society is to give ladies with insufficient incomes a means of helping themselves. A great variety of plain and fancy work is always on sale at the depôt of the Society—lace, embroidery, crochet, etc. A subscription of 4s. per annum entitles a lady to send work for sale; a commission of 1d. in the shilling is charged on all sales. Orders taken for plain work, knitting, etc.; ladies' own material can be sent. The members of this Society are most thankful to get orders for needlework to earn the help they need. For information, address to the Honorary Secretary, Miss Banks.

www.ingramcontent.com/pod-product-compliance
Lightning Source LLC
Chambersburg PA
CBHW020309170426
43202CB00008B/546